A Passion for Jesus

Daily Devotions

with Calvary Chapel Pastors' Wives

COMPILED BY M. MACIEL

A Passion for Jesus
Daily Devotions with Calvary Chapel Pastors' Wives

Complied by Mark Maciel

Copyright © 2004 by Mark Maciel / Calvary Chapel Downey

Published by Calvary Chapel Publishing (CCP),
a resource ministry of Calvary Chapel Costa Mesa
3800 South Fairview Road
Santa Ana, California 92704

First printing, 2004

All Scripture quotations in this book, unless otherwise indicated, are taken from the New King James Version. Copyright © 1982 by Thomas Nelson, Inc. Used by permission. All rights reserved.

Scripture quotations marked KJV are taken from the King James Version of the Bible.

Scripture quotations marked NLT are taken from the Holy Bible, New Living Translation, copyright © 1996. Used by permission of Tyndale House Publishers, Inc., Wheaton, IL 60189 USA. All rights reserved.

Scripture quotations marked ISV taken from the Holy Bible: International Standard Version®. Copyright © 2003 by The ISV Foundation. Used by permission of Davidson Press, Inc. All Rights Reserved Internationally.

Scripture quotations marked MSG taken from The Message. Copyright © by Eugene H. Peterson 1993, 1994, 1995, 1996, 2000, 2001, 2002. Used by permission of NavPress Publishing Group.

Scripture quotations marked NIV are taken from the Holy Bible, New International Version®. NIV®. Copyright © 1973, 1978, 1984 by International Bible Society. Used by permission of Zondervan. All rights reserved. The "NIV" and "New International Version" trademarks are registered in the United States Patent and Trademark Office by International Bible Society. Use of either trademark requires the permission of International Bible Society.

Scripture quotations marked TLB are taken from The Living Bible, copyright © 1971. Used by permission of Tyndale House Publishers, Inc., Wheaton, IL 60189 USA. All rights reserved.

Scripture quotations marked NASB are taken from the New American Standard Bible®, © Copyright 1960, 1962, 1963, 1968, 1971, 1972, 1973, 1975, 1977, 1995 by The Lockman Foundation. Used by permission. (www.Lockman.org)

Scripture quotations marked RSV and NRSV are taken from the Revised Standard Version of the Bible, © copyright 1952 [2nd edition, 1971] by the Division of Christian Education of the National Council of the Churches of Christ in the United States of America. Used by permission. All rights reserved.

Scriptures quotations marked GNB are from the Good News Bible © 1994 published by the Bible Societies/ HarperCollins Publishers Ltd., UK Good News Bible © American Bible Society 1966, 1971, 1976, 1992. Used with permission.

Library of Congress Control Number: 2003096920

ISBN: 1-931667-76-4

Cover Design: Mike Cox / Alpha Advertising

Printed in the United States of America.

Foreword

Recognizing how essential daily time with the Lord is to every woman's growth and walk, I am pleased to recommend this devotional, which has been gathered from the spiritual insights of many Calvary Chapel pastors' wives. My hope and prayer is that these devotions will encourage and minister to you as you take time each day for the one thing that is needful.

> And she had a sister called Mary, who also sat at Jesus' feet and heard His word. But Martha was distracted with much serving, and she approached Him and said, "Lord, do You not care that my sister has left me to serve alone? Therefore tell her to help me."
> And Jesus answered and said to her, "Martha, Martha, you are worried and troubled about many things. But one thing is needed, and Mary has chosen that good part, which will not be taken away from her."
> *Luke 10:39–42*

Kay Smith
Senior Pastor's Wife
Calvary Chapel Costa Mesa
Santa Ana, California

The Calvary Chapel Movement

In the late '60s, the Lord, by His Spirit, began a movement that was labeled by the press the JESUS PEOPLE. Indeed that is what we were, people totally devoted to Jesus.

Thousands of young people had fallen in love with Jesus. Through the wonderful work of the Holy Spirit, Calvary Chapel became one of the centers where these young people came to get saved, learn the Bible, and worship the Lord. As they learned the Word of God, hundreds of these young people went out to establish Bible studies all over the world, and many of these Bible studies have developed into the largest churches in the United States. The worship music that was introduced by these young people has become the standard for the church today.[1]

This passion for the Lord is what you will read and be strengthened by through the encouraging words of our pastors' wives through the continuous work of the Holy Spirit.

A Virtuous Woman

Her worth—more precious than rubies;
she works diligently for her family,
she opens her arms to the poor and
extends her hands to the needy.
She speaks with wisdom,
faithful instruction is on her tongue.
Her children rise up and call her blessed,
her husband also,
she merits his full confidence.
She is clothed with strength and
dignity; she can laugh
at the days to come.
A woman who fears the LORD
is to be praised.
Give her the reward she has earned.[2]

Pleasing God

⤬

"I do always those things that please him."
John 8:29 KJV

"Live to please the heart of God." The speaker repeated the phrase several times. The third time she said it, I really heard it! For weeks, Chuck's messages had been focused on the events preceding the return of Christ. These sermons caused me to evaluate my life and my walk with the Lord in a fresh way.

Because I was born again, I knew I wouldn't be left behind, but if the Lord were coming for His church *today*, what would I want to be sure I had done? The more I thought about it, the more concerned I became. So I prayed a simple prayer: "Lord, how do You want me to live in these last days?"

I don't know how I expected Him to answer, but these words came clearly into my mind: "Live to please Me." To please means to bring pleasure to; to satisfy; to gratify. That became my goal—to live a life pleasing to God.

During the next few weeks, the Lord used four Scriptures to confirm His answer to me. The first was Revelation 4:11: "Thou art worthy, O Lord, to receive glory and honour and power: for thou hast created all things, and for *thy pleasure* they are and were created" (KJV, emphasis added). What an awesome thought! I was created for His pleasure.

Next, I casually pulled a Scripture out of a Bible promise box. It was John 8:29. Jesus confirmed that it is God's will that we live to please Him when He said, "I do *always* those things that please [the Father]" (KJV, emphasis added). This is our Jesus in whose footsteps we are to walk.

The third confirmation came out of a little antique devotional I happened to be reading one day. It was based on Colossians 3:23: "And whatsoever ye do, do it heartily, as to the Lord, and not to men" (KJV). A short selection from an old hymn accompanied the verse:

Teach me, my God and King,
In all things Thee to see,
And what I do in anything
To do it as for Thee.[3]

Finally, God confirmed His answer to me through Hebrews 11:5: "By faith Enoch was translated that he should not see death; and was not found, because God had translated him: for before his translation he had this testimony, that *he pleased God*" (KJV, emphasis added). Those words, "That he pleased God," struck a responsive chord in my heart.

"Does this please the heart of God?" simplifies my life. It isn't always a choice between right and wrong; it is more often the choice between pleasing self and pleasing my heavenly Father. It should always be our desire to follow the example of Jesus and to "always do those things that please [the Father]."

Kay Smith
Calvary Chapel Costa Mesa
Santa Ana, California

January 2

. . . for you have given me hope. My comfort in my suffering is this:
Your promise preserves my life.
Psalm 119:49–50 NIV

Reflecting on the past two years, I remember staring at my bedroom ceiling, wondering why and how this could have happened to me. Depressed, anxious, and in pain, I daily turned to the God whom I had believed in and served for many years. God surely walked with me on this difficult path and allowed me, along with our wonderful congregation, to be taught the deeper ways of God as His power was displayed among us (John 9:1–3).

Difficulty is sent to reveal what God can do in answer to the faith that prays and works. Are any of you suffering today? Allow me to share four certainties with you:

- ❖ God will make you well—perhaps not on earth, but surely in heaven.
- ❖ God hurts when you hurt—"In all their affliction He was afflicted" (Isaiah 63:9).
- ❖ God knows why you are suffering.
- ❖ God is in control.

Today I am feeling and doing much better. My cancer (lymphoma meningitis) is in remission and I am thanking Jesus for His great grace and mercy!

"When your eyes see me, you will rejoice and God will be honored."[4]

Millie Juarez
Calvary Chapel Montebello
Montebello, California

January 3

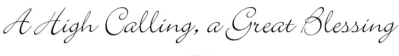

*Train up a child in the way he should go, and when he is old he will
not depart from it.*
Proverbs 22:6

You shall love the LORD your God with all your heart, with all your
soul, and with all your might. And these words which I command you
today shall be in your heart. You shall teach them diligently to your
children, and shall talk of them when you sit in your house, when you
walk by the way, when you lie down, and when you rise up.
Deuteronomy 6:5–7

What a high calling it is that our Father has entrusted His children to us.
He requires us to love the Lord our God and to teach His statutes and His
faithfulness to our children. Their obedience to us begins with our obedience to Him. May we tell of His goodness when we sit in our houses,
when we walk by the way, when we lie down, and when we rise up. He
requires that we spend time with our children! May our children desire
the Father's love because they see His love in us, and may others see in
them the impact of our love for our Father in heaven.

I have no greater joy than to hear that my children walk in truth.
3 John 4

Sheila Walker
Calvary Chapel Living Word
Irvine, California

January 4

Remember Whose You Are

The God of heaven Himself will prosper us; therefore we His servants
will arise and build, but you have no heritage or right or memorial in
Jerusalem.
Nehemiah 2:20

Nehemiah spoke with confidence when he confronted the leaders of the
land. God had called him to rebuild the walls of Jerusalem that had been
destroyed during the Babylonian invasion, and Nehemiah was fired up
and ready to get started! But the opposition was aggressive, clever, and
relentless.

So it is in our day-to-day Christian walk. We have a calling to pursue,
and our heart's desire is that our actions and attitudes bring honor to the
Lord and accomplish His purposes. But we are continually distracted by
the world, tempted in our flesh, and accused by the Enemy of our souls.
Even if we don't get sidetracked, we can become discouraged.

It is then that the Spirit of God reminds us *whose* we are! The God of
heaven Himself is the One who gives us marching orders and empowers
us to do His work.

For we are His workmanship, created in Christ Jesus for good works,
which God prepared beforehand that we should walk in them.
Ephesians 2:10

When we stay focused on Jesus and surrendered to Him, other influences might harass us, but they shall have no heritage, right, or memorial
in our lives.

Betty Ritchie
Crossroads Community Church
Vancouver, Washington

One Nation Under God

There is no truth or mercy or knowledge of God in the land.
Hosea 4:1

Sitting in the dental office one morning waiting for my daughter, I came across an article in one of the more prominent weekly newsmagazines. It was about a twelve-year-old boy and his eighteen-year-old sister who lived in a third-world nation and were sentenced to an unspeakable punishment for a crime they clearly had not committed.

When I shared what I was reading with the dental receptionist, her response was, "How lucky we are to be living in the United States." I countered with, "We are blessed to be living in one nation under God." Silence was her only reply.

This third-world nation is destroying its people because of a lack of the knowledge of God, His Word, and His law. Hosea 4:6 tells us, "My people are destroyed for lack of knowledge." Are we underestimating the blessing of living in a nation whose civil laws were created by a people who did have a knowledge of God, His Word, and His law?

We are truly privileged to live in a country where we can openly seek the knowledge of God! In the book of Acts, Luke gives us this pattern to live by: "[Continue] steadfastly in the apostles' doctrine and fellowship, in the breaking of bread, and in prayers" (Acts 2:42).

Just as Luke admonishes the early church to continue steadfastly in sound doctrine, fellowship, Communion, and prayer, so must we as a nation, return to righteousness by acknowledging His laws. As women of God, let's acknowledge the blessing of living in a nation that was brought forth by the hands and wisdom of godly men and women. Let us thank God and pray for our lawmakers and leaders.

Terry Urciuoli
Calvary Chapel Ontario
Ontario, California

January 6

Big Trouble in My Little World

⤳

"I have told you these things, so that in me you may have peace. In this world you will have trouble. But take heart! I have overcome the world."
John 16:33 NIV

"Where are my keys? I'm going to be late again!" The phone interrupts my ranting with news of my mother-in-law's admittance to the hospital, while my child comes screaming into my arms with blood oozing from a gash. That morning an e-mail informed me the Sunday school director had quit and I would be teaching the two- and three-year-olds every Sunday until Jesus returns.

Because we live in a fallen world, it seems that not a day goes by without some kind of calamity, stress, strife, or conflict. We are often left feeling overwhelmed and exhausted, and we become easily frustrated with our husbands or children. However, it never ceases to amaze me how in a moment of stillness, when I take the time to call upon the name of Jesus, I sense tranquility even in the midst of a troubling situation.

He gives me composure and I can rest in His care. Just humming a worship tune brings harmony; breathing a prayer, "Jesus, help me," calms my racing heart. Opening His Word brings clarity and often a direct answer . . . a reminder to rest . . . a reassurance of His love . . . or a gentle call to repentance. We can have courage because He has overcome and we belong to Him.

You will keep him in perfect peace, whose mind is stayed on You.
Isaiah 26:3

Dee Hensman
Good News Calvary Chapel
Pitt Meadows, BC, Canada

January 7

Never the Wrong Age

Zechariah said to the angel, "How can I know this will happen? I'm an old man now, and my wife is also well along in years."
Luke 1:18 NLT

Age is an obsession with our culture. Although youth is worshiped, no one wants a young doctor or airline pilot. No one wants to be your first employer or patient, because experience counts on the job. However, have you ever considered the fact that Mary, a young virgin, was too youthful to be taken seriously? Yet, God used a faithful teenager to be the mother of His precious Son Jesus.

Elizabeth, at the other end of life, was too old. Even Zechariah, her dear husband, thought she was an impossible choice for motherhood. Yet, this older woman trained John the Baptist, whose job it was to prepare the way of the Lord. "Look, I am sending my messenger before you, and he will prepare your way" (Mark 1:2 NLT).

God wants to use our youth and our old age for His glory. So remember the example of Mary and Elizabeth. Today, you are the perfect age to serve the Lord with great joy.

Arlene Schroer
Calvary Chapel Central Islip
Central Islip, New York

January 8

No Such Word As Can't

I can do all things through Christ who strengthens me.
Philippians 4:13

As Christians we must learn to be content "in" circumstances since we won't always be content "with" circumstances. But how do we do that? What does it mean to do all things "through Christ," by His strength? Before writing that we can do all things through Christ, Paul says,

> Whatever things are true, whatever things are noble, whatever things are just, whatever things are pure, whatever things are lovely, whatever things are of good report, if there is any virtue and if there is anything praiseworthy—*meditate on these things.*
> *Philippians 4:8, emphasis added*

Throughout our lives we may encounter stress, hardship, or ill health. These things often can't be avoided. It is the way we handle these situations that sets us apart. Keeping our eyes on Christ and meditating on the promises of His Word gives us hope and perspective. We Christians must learn to do all things through Christ because He provides for us, strengthens us, and gives us His peace which surpasses all understanding.

Seven years ago my mother was diagnosed with cancer of the esophagus and given a one-in-a-billion chance of survival. Throughout her ordeal, she held on to God's promises and showed she had learned that God's peace and strength would sustain her, no matter what the outcome. Praise God, with the right attitude, she beat the odds and showed all of us what it means to do all things through Christ who strengthens us.

Donna Fisher
Calvary Chapel Albany
Albany, Western Australia

January 9

Floating with Hope

⤏

A man's heart plans his ways, but the LORD directs his steps.
Proverbs 16:9

While visiting family in New Zealand, we went black water rafting in glowworm caves. It was dark and unpredictable, which was exciting for my children and my adventurous husband. On the other hand, I was nervous and completely out of my comfort zone, hoping that the trip would soon end. When I saw daylight in the distance, I stopped shaking and realized I had enjoyed the excursion.

Organizing, planning, making lists, and following routines are methods I use to run my life. I don't appreciate being caught unaware or unprepared. This works for projects around my house, for packing my suitcase, and in my work as a secretary for an elementary school. However, my life's blueprint doesn't seem to work out the way I plan. My life seems more like the underwater caves—rushing water with pools of calm. I don't know what's around the bend. I can't always see what's in front of me, but I can see the light. I'm happy and hopeful floating on the cool water.

Thankfully, God undertakes to interrupt our routines. "His ways are perfect" (see 2 Samuel 22:31). Even though we're unaware of the details of His intentions for our lives, we can know He has them mapped out, and that "all things work together for good for those who love God, to those who are the called according to His purpose" (Romans 8:28). We just need to keep floating.

For I know the thoughts that I think toward you, says the LORD,
thoughts of peace and not of evil, to give you a future and a hope.
Jeremiah 29:11

Dee Hensman
Good News Calvary Chapel
Pitt Meadows, BC, Canada

January 10

My Inadequacies, God's Opportunities

"We have here only five loaves of bread and two fish," they answered.
"Bring them here to me," he said.
Matthew 14:17–18 NIV

How often I find thoughts of my own inadequacies entering my mind. As a former missionary, there were many situations that found me with no idea how to respond. Many times I made laughable cultural errors. Circumstances required responses beyond my depth and abilities.

But beyond my abilities is a good place to be. It is then that I bring what little I think I do have to Jesus. In His hands my five loaves and two fish are more than enough. My inadequacies are God's opportunities to be glorified.

Second Corinthians 3:5 states, "Not that we are competent in ourselves to claim anything for ourselves, but our competence comes from God" (NIV). Place the little you have in the hands of Jesus; it will be enough. Step out beyond your comfort zone and be bold for Christ.

Janet Scalice
Calvary Chapel Big Bear Lake
Big Bear Lake, California

January 11

A Great Way to Start Each Day

Set your hearts on things above.
Colossians 3:1 NIV

Many years ago, our family of four sat around the kitchen table and memorized Colossians chapter 3 during breakfast. I have always loved this passage and have pondered it in my heart many times. This year, however, quoting Colossians 3 became my lifeline. Setting my heart on things above became absolutely essential as I fought against our very formidable adversary, the prince of this world. At times I would ask the Lord to pick me up, hold me in His lap, and let me see things from the vantage point that is mine as a child of God.

Having my life centered upon Christ in God is an anchor for me, as it is for every believer. We are not of this world. We have the power of God in our lives to put our flesh to death every day, to rise above all that the Enemy sends our way, to let the peace of Christ rule in our hearts, and to be thankful.

As I think of all the wonderful things my husband has done for us as a family, my favorite will always be that he gave us this tool against Satan—hearts full of Colossians 3—that we can purpose to set our hearts on things above. Heaven is, after all, our real home.

Lanie Grubbs
Calvary Chapel Christian Fellowship
Alpharetta, Georgia

January 12

A Promise for the Journey

The LORD will guide you continually, and satisfy your soul in drought, and strengthen your bones; you shall be like a watered garden, and like a spring of water, whose waters do not fail.
Isaiah 58:11

Have you ever walked through the valley feeling alone? Have you ever wanted to cry out, "Lord, are You there?" The answers may not come; the silence may be long. In such times you can find rest and comfort in the assurance that Jesus "will never leave you nor forsake you" (Hebrews 13:5).

It is by the Lord's hand and heart that He will "guide us continually"—going before us, preparing the way, lighting the path, then speaking a word behind us, saying "This is the way, walk in it" (Isaiah 30:21). Not only does the Lord "guide us continually," He also gives us promises for the journey of life. The Lord satisfies our souls in the dry times, strengthens us physically, and pours out to us spiritually. Isaiah says that we will "be like a watered garden, and like a spring of water, whose waters do not fail"—this description is a type of the Holy Spirit. In addition to providing guidance, the Lord satisfies us, strengthens us, and fills us with His Holy Spirit—refreshing us and enabling us to make it through the valley as He walks alongside us.

As we walk through times of change and uncertainty, even if there seems to be silence, we can be certain that the Lord is with us and will guide us through every detail of our lives for His glory, as we continue to trust in Him and His promises.

Pat Mitchell
Calvary Chapel Ocean Gateway
Salisbury, Maryland

January 13

Need a Cure from the "Grumpies?"

A merry heart does good, like medicine.
Proverbs 17:22

It is a proven fact that laughter is good for us. Yet, with all the busyness and stress of everyday life, we have forgotten how to laugh. The word *merry* means "to be cheerful; full of mirth and laughter." Take time to be with your family and friends. Enjoy one another's company and take some time for a good ol' healthy dose of laughter. Try it—you'll like it.

A merry heart makes a cheerful countenance.
Proverbs 15:13

Cindy Hagerman
Joshua Springs Calvary Chapel
Yucca Valley, California

January 14

Forgiven

〜⦾〜

*Though your sins be as scarlet, they shall be as white as snow; though
they be red like crimson, they shall be as wool.*
Isaiah 1:18 KJV

Daddy was a missionary in South America for most of his life. His greatest
passion was the salvation of souls. His vital organs were slowly deteriorat-
ing due to the microscopic bug *chagas*, which infiltrated his body on the
mission field. He was dying of heart failure. By his request, the bed next
to him was to be used for patients who were finishing life's journey. There
he led them to Christ as he waited to "cross the river of death to reach the
heavenly shore."

One day, while Daddy lay death-ridden, the empty bed next to him
waited for a dying soul to find salvation through his and Mother's constant demonstration of God's love. I held Daddy's hand and waited, when
suddenly he opened his eyes. A tear ran down his cheek as he said to me,
"I am forgiven." "Daddy, of course you are," I interrupted. "You know
that! You have dedicated your whole life to that very message—that Jesus
died on the cross for our sins . . . that through His blood anyone, no matter what they have done, can be forgiven by repenting, turning from their
sins, and confessing Him as LORD!"

"Sherry, Sherry, listen to me," he insisted, gripping my arm, "I am
really forgiven . . . my sins are gone . . . all of them!" I then sensed the
presence and holiness of God in our midst. My heart filled with joy as I
realized that Daddy had received a deeper spiritual revelation than he had
ever known of the cleansing power of the blood of the spotless Lamb of
God who takes away the sin of the world.

Behold! The Lamb of God who takes away the sin of the world!
John 1:29

Sharon Faith Ries
Calvary Chapel Golden Springs
Diamond Bar, California

Are You Trusting God Today?

Trust in the LORD with all your heart, and lean not on your own understanding; in all your ways acknowledge Him, and He shall direct your paths.

Proverbs 3:5–6

This Scripture has carried me and continues to carry me through the many trials that come my way. I hold on to these powerful and encouraging words, and the Lord has been faithful to see me through.

Trust in the LORD with all your heart . . .

Do you have faith that the Lord can see you through? Are you trusting God with some or all of your heart?

. . . and lean not on your own understanding . . .

How many times do we try in our flesh to understand what we are going through?

. . . in all your ways acknowledge Him . . .

The Lord wants us to recognize Him as our powerful and almighty God.

. . . and He shall direct your paths.

The Lord is faithful to direct our paths, time and time again!

The Lord wants us to trust Him with everything, including: our marriages, children, finances, jobs, and even the small, everyday things.

If we cannot trust Him in the little things, how can we trust Him in the bigger things?

Cynthia Cortez
Calvary Chapel Guadalupe
Guadalupe, California

January 16

My Refuge

~

You are my hiding place; You shall preserve me from trouble; You shall surround me with songs of deliverance. Selah
Psalm 32:7

We all have day-to-day cares that can be draining to our spiritual lives. Luke 8:14 paints a picture of the Word being planted; but then the cares, riches, and pleasures of life choke it. These cares—especially the itsy bitsy, seemingly insignificant ones—can choke and spiritually drain us just as effectively as the major ones.

Look at Psalm 100. I know it is hard to thank God when we are going through tough times, but Satan wants to rob us of the joy He has given; so being thankful to God takes our mind off what Satan wants us to think about. Hebrews 13:15 says, "Continually offer the sacrifice of praise to God," and during those times it is a sacrifice replacing our cares with thanksgiving. Soon, the Lord's peace and presence will come, and the attacks will not be able to withstand the overwhelming flood of God's love. Being a believer in Jesus Christ does not mean we will not have troubles, trials, and temptations. We will go through storms. Jesus will protect us within the storm and give us His peace amidst the troubles. Our refuge in Christ comes from the peace He gives us inside of the storm.

How can we combat these cares? By seeking refuge in Him. By letting Jesus surround us with songs of deliverance.

April Hoffman
Calvary Chapel Yarnell
Yarnell, Arizona

January 17

Rise and Shine

My voice You shall hear in the morning, O LORD; in the morning I
will direct it to You.
Psalm 5:3

I am an early bird and I love to be awake before the sun comes up. In the
stillness of the morning, I am more able to hear God speak to me than
when I'm in the midst of a busy day. My thoughts are clear and my heart
is open.

Do you have a special place and time to meet with the Lord on a daily
basis? If not, find that place and time today and cherish it with all your
heart. God's Word tells us in James 4:8, "Draw near to God and He will
draw near to you." "And you will seek Me and find Me, when you search
for Me with all your heart" (Jeremiah 29:13).

Lynette Johnston
Calvary Chapel Santa Cruz
Santa Cruz, California

January 18

My Jesus, My Hero

And we have seen and testify that the Father has sent his Son to be
the Savior of the world.
1 John 4:14 NIV

Many times God reveals Himself during our frail moments. He shows us our need for something greater than ourselves—our need for a Savior. We all like to think about heroes and watch them "save the day."

Our country's recent tragedies on 9-11 prove our need and desire for true heroes. Was there anyone who didn't feel thankful and proud of the men and women who risked their lives trying to save others? These people have become modern day heroes. Still, our heroes' lives are frail and their deeds momentary.

There's only One who is truly worthy of the title Savior. *Jesus is my Hero.* He's a strong tower to run into, a rock to stand on, and a shield about me. These are a few names of my Hero.

My Savior and Hero allowed Himself to be nailed to the cross, covering my sins.

My Redeemer and Hero rose from the dead, declaring His victory over death.

My Everlasting Father and Hero has gone to prepare a place for me so that I can be with Him forever.

My Prince of Peace and Hero sent a Wonderful Counselor, the Holy Spirit, so that I am never alone again, never without guidance and direction to walk through this life.

Jesus wants to be your hero too!

Lori Marse
Calvary Chapel Boynton
Boynton Beach, Florida

January 19

Grace Under Pressure

And He said to me, "My grace is sufficient for you, for My strength is
made perfect in weakness."
2 Corinthians 12:9

Ever since the day we were born we have been told what we can or cannot
do. So, when we were old enough to talk, our first words were, "I can't
wait until I grow up." Now our glorious days of "all grown up" are here.
Hooray! Right?

Adulthood has arrived with even more pressures upon us than we
could have ever imagined. Sometimes it is all too much to bear. That's
when we find ourselves saying, "If I hear one more word out of your
mouth I'll . . ." or "If that phone rings one more time I'll . . ." Scream?
Cry? Break down? Explode? One or all of the above? Why not, none of
the above? We need to trust the Lord and know that His grace is sufficient
when we are at the end of ourselves.

Listen closely to my prayer, O LORD; hear my urgent cry. I will call to
you whenever trouble strikes, and you will answer me.
Psalm 86:6–7 NLT

In trouble? Need help? Call upon God. Stop and pray to Him. He will
offer His perspective if you C.A.L.L.

C—Compose yourself and rely on Him.
A—Apologize, if necessary, to man and God.
L—Love unconditionally.
L—Listen to the Lord and then to others.

Carey Franquiz
Calvary Chapel Miami Lakes
Miami Lakes, Florida

January 20

At Jesus' Feet

She had a sister called Mary, who sat at the Lord's feet listening to
what he said.
Luke 10:39 NIV

A few years ago, my sister treated me to a wonderfully relaxing pedicure at a luxurious spa—an experience I'll never forget! For a glorious half hour, my pedicurist was totally devoted to pampering my tired feet!

Mary, the sister of Martha, expressed her devotion to the Lord by being at His feet. Mary is mentioned three times in the Gospels and each time, she is at the Lord's feet! In the popular account of Mary and Martha in Luke 10:39, we find Mary sitting "at the Lord's feet listening to what he said." She is quietly absorbing all He is teaching her.

Sometime later, Mary's brother Lazarus died, and in despair, Mary fell "at his feet" (John 11:32 NIV). In a time of crisis, Mary was seeking Jesus. Then, just days before Jesus' crucifixion, Mary took her expensive perfume and "poured it on Jesus' feet and wiped his feet with her hair" (John 12:3 NIV). In servant-like humility and costly devotion, she anointed and blessed her Lord before His burial.

Do you long for more of Jesus? Are you in crisis? Do you desire to bless the Lord? Whatever circumstances you're in, take some time today and sit at His feet—listening, seeking, and worshiping your Lord!

Come, let us bow down in worship, let us kneel before the LORD our
Maker.
Psalm 95:6 NIV

Becky Hallman
Calvary Chapel Kauai
Kapaa, Hawaii

January 21

Grimy Pans, Grimy Hearts

❦

Create in me a clean heart, O God.
Psalm 51:10

Cleaning a broiler pan is a difficult task—yet God used this task one day to speak to my heart. The grime was baked on so thick, it looked permanent! To begin with, I poured hot soapy water over it. I scrubbed it with a brush, and it began to come off. I soaked it for a while in hot water, and I took a stiff brush and applied pressure to get the embedded stains out. Then I took a dull knife to scrape off the last bits. Finally, the pan was clean and shiny, ready for use.

I couldn't help thinking about the similarity of that pan to my heart. Sometimes it seems impossible to purify years of my own grime. But God pours His Spirit over me and loosens the darkness. Little trials of adversity are like abrasive polish. He'll often draw me close and encourage me to "soak" in His presence. After a period of waiting, God often puts the scrubber on me again. Harder and deeper testing and trials often hurt. Deeply embedded habits and attitudes are painful to eradicate. But God's mercy in allowing these fiery trials cleanses me to the core!

Like the pan, my heart can shine and reflect Jesus. Each time I struggle with a grimy heart, I remember God's steadfast love towards me, carefully changing me from glory to glory.

Teresa Muller
Calvary Chapel Carmel Valley
Carmel, California

January 22

The Command with a Promise

"Honor your father and mother" which is the first commandment
with a promise—"that it may go well with you and that you may enjoy
long life on the earth."
Ephesians 6:2–3 NIV

There may be times in our lives when we are tempted to show disrespect to our parents. Most parents have problems and experience failures. As children, we can react with frustration and disrespect.

With my own father, I had become disappointed over time, and I lost respect for him. One day, the Lord knocked on the door of my heart. He showed me that I needed to change my attitude towards my father. Once I did, the most amazing thing happened. My father changed his attitude towards me. For the rest of his life we had a loving relationship.

God wants us to honor our parents because of who they are, rather than for what they have done. In the same way, our heavenly Father loves and forgives us because of who we are in Jesus Christ.

For the eyes of the LORD run to and fro throughout the whole earth,
to shew himself strong in the behalf of them whose heart is perfect
toward him.
2 Chronicles 16:9 KJV

Kara McDaniel
Calvary Chapel Arlington
Arlington, Texas

My Delight Is in Him

Blessed is the man . . . [whose] delight is in the law of the LORD, and
in His law he meditates day and night. He shall be like a tree planted
by the rivers of water, that brings forth its fruit in its season, whose
leaf also shall not wither.

Psalm 1:1–3

Living in the middle of a desert that is experiencing a drought, I often
look upon the barrenness of the land with sadness. Yet, when we consider ourselves, how often do our spiritual lives resemble the desert—dry,
cracked, and fruitless?

Psalm 1:2–3 tells us that as we delight in the Word of God and meditate upon it, we will become nourished, refreshed, and fruitful. Delighting
in the Word is more than simply doing our Bible reading for the day. It
is looking forward to and enjoying our time with the Lord above all else.
Afterwards, it is savoring those tasty morsels and meditating upon them
throughout the day.

When you have a free moment, where do your thoughts go? May we
shift the focus of our hearts and minds off ourselves, our schedules, and
our 'to do' lists and onto the Word of God, that our delight might be continually in Him and His Word.

Then we will be like that tree planted by the rivers of water.

Amber Knapp
Calvary Chapel Green Valley
Henderson, Nevada

January 24

God's Cafe

I have treasured the words of His mouth more than my necessary
food.

Job 23:12

My grandfather used to take my sisters and me to a first-class French res-
taurant every now and then that served seven courses of the finest food—
in fact, food so delicious that we would skip breakfast and lunch to get
the most enjoyment out of dinner at the café. By 4:00 p.m. on the day
we were to have dinner there, we would get so hungry that my sisters and
I would grab a bag of potato chips and eat just a few to tide us over. Of
course, we couldn't eat just *one*, so soon we would finish the whole bag
and realize the big mistake we had made. Sitting at the French café, we
wouldn't dare admit that we weren't that hungry, so we would stare at our
plates hoping no one would notice.

Imagine being so full of junk food that you couldn't possibly enjoy the
most delicious gourmet meal! When my spiritual appetite is low, or when
I am stuffed on spiritual junk food, God often corners me, "Why don't
you desire Me and My Word with a passion like others have?" He reminds
me how at times when my appetite was at its peak, in weakness I have
filled it with the wrong things. At these moments, I have learned firsthand
that the flesh profits me nothing—it is the Spirit that gives life!

Jeremiah warned the people about going anywhere but to God for
fulfillment:

For My people have committed two evils: they have forsaken Me, the
fountain of living waters, and hewn themselves cisterns—broken
cisterns that can hold no water.

Jeremiah 2:13

What do you turn to for a quick fix—food, TV, shopping, running
to a friend? Whatever it is will leave you hungrier still. Jesus alone is the

bread of life (John 6:35). Partake of Him and you will be satisfied. Wait on Him to fulfill you in His timing. As Amy Carmichael said, "You've never known passion or fulfillment till you have felt the fire of God."[5]

> "Blessed are those who hunger and thirst for righteousness, for they shall be filled."
> Matthew 5:6

Karen Pulley
Calvary Chapel Old Bridge
Old Bridge, New Jersey

January 25

Following Closely

Then Jesus said to His disciples, "If anyone desires to come after Me,
let him deny himself, and take up his cross, and follow Me."
Matthew 16:24

From the moment Jesus apprehends our life, He places a desire in us to draw closer to Him, but with that desire comes a challenge—to deny ourselves.

Have you denied yourself lately? Is there an area in your life right now in which you are having a difficult time knowing what to do? Are you so full of pride that humbling yourself is out of the question? Or have you turned down an opportunity to minister because you've decided you have done too much already? Maybe the Lord has given you directions to do something now, but in your "wisdom," you have put it off until you feel like it.

Every day you need to decide to follow Jesus and deny yourself. Close to Him is where you want to be. There you are able to hear, understand, and admire what matters most to Him. His example is perfect and His grace sufficient.

Denying yourself is hard by definition, but it will bear much fruit.

"I am the vine, you are the branches. He who abides in Me, and I in
him, bears much fruit; for without Me you can do nothing."
John 15:5

Take time to draw close to Him today. You will be blessed!

Marie Taylor
Calvary Chapel Aurora
Aurora, Colorado

January 26

Suffering Together

For to you it has been granted on behalf of Christ, not only to believe
in Him, but also to suffer for His sake. . . . Let each of you look out
not only for his own interests, but also for the interests of others.
Philippians 1:29; 2:4

There is great benefit for the kingdom of Christ that comes from our
suffering for His sake. It has been granted to us—given as a gift. The
American Heritage Dictionary defines *grant* as: "to consent to; to accord as
a favor." We must look on suffering as a purposeful experience.

The Lord recognizes our need for comfort during suffering. The
Scriptures tell us, "if there is any consolation in Christ, if any comfort
of love, if any fellowship of the Spirit, if any affection and mercy . . ."
(Philippians 2:1), then we are to come together to comfort, love, and
persevere through suffering together. We must be likeminded, looking
out for the good of our brothers and sisters at all times. We must consider
others as better than ourselves. We will be ripped apart standing alone;
it is only as we remain together that we will indeed stand. Suffering will
kill our joy, hope, and desire to live and glorify Christ if we do not lift up
one another's arms (Exodus 17:11–13) and bear one another's burdens
(Galatians 6:2).

Standing together during suffering will bring glory to God and joy
and strength to us.

Debi Schneider
Calvary Chapel Vail Valley
Vail, Colorado

My Secret Place of Prayer

"But you, when you pray, go into your room, and when you have shut
your door, pray to your Father who is in the secret place; and your
Father who sees in secret will reward you openly."
Matthew 6:6

As a child, I prayed by my bed or with my parents. During my early teen
years, I sought God mainly at the altar of my church. I cried out to Him
sometimes silently and at other times audibly. My need to communicate
with Him grew greater each year; I was desperate to do His will.

Before marriage, I spent hours in prayer, as I did not want to fail in
His plan for me in South America. During those many years, I found over
thirty places of prayer in many different countries. Years ago I made a list
of them.

There are many places to pray, and many Scriptures tell us how to
pray, but there are no excuses to cease from praying. First Thessalonians
5:17 says, "Pray without ceasing."

Whether your secret place of prayer is in your bedroom, in your favorite chair, in a tiny computer cubicle at work, in a field, in your car, or in
an airplane, pray!

The effectual fervent prayer of a righteous man availeth much.
James 5:16

Rachel Naomi Farrel
Calvary Chapel Golden Springs
Diamond Bar, California

January 28

Skirting the Issue

❧

Therefore gird up the loins of your mind, be sober, and rest your hope fully upon the grace that is to be brought to you at the revelation of Jesus Christ.
1 Peter 1:13

Being raised in a tiny Dutch town has taught me to value the definition of "neat and tidy." Unfortunately, I'm not it. Though somewhat amazed by women who seem inherently put together inside their smart clothes and manicured nails, I've opted for the lower maintenance (I like to call it "natural") look.

Natural was "in" two thousand years ago. Men tucked their robes up into their sash belts, not for appearances, but to run, fight, or work unhindered. I can picture myself as the guy twenty yards behind, having to fix my sandal or tuck in parts of my robe falling down.

Like tying up unmanageable robes, we can sweat and strain to get one besetting habit under control, only to find that another inevitably comes undone. We need the Lord to help us detangle from the snares of sin, and only He can grant us the right motivation to do it—for an eternal crown.

The next time you're late, lugging a purse, balancing the mail, and carrying a cup of coffee (which just spilled on the front of your cream-colored sweater), remember no amount of human resolve alone can keep us Christians focused, tucked in, and running our race swiftly. We must rely in faith upon the One who created us.

Humbly ask that the Lord would help you in your weakness, and that the God of all order would keep your heart, mind, and life aligned with His—in perfect peace.

Cristin Novak
Calvary Chapel Prague
Santa Ana, California

Lord Help Us! We Need a Miracle

"Ask, and it shall be given you."
Matthew 7:7 KJV

"We're never going to find a parking place; there are way too many cars here. Lord, Help us! Dad's in pain and we need a miracle!" Immediately, a car pulled out of a parking place in front of us, and I pulled into one of the best handicapped parking places in the whole UC Davis Medical Center complex. The third passenger in our car was my father's certified nursing assistant: a non-Christian. "Wow! That was sure something," she said. I was then able to share with her that prayer is powerful, telling her that this happens all the time because God really does care for us.

My dad was facing his second of three injections for his collapsing, disintegrating spine. This provision also encouraged him and removed his anxiety before the procedure because, as a believer, he was reminded that God was with us.

The testimony from this answered prayer is an example of what Moses wanted Israel to experience.

> For what great nation is there that has God so near to it, as the LORD
> our God is to us, for whatever reason we may call upon Him?
> *Deuteronomy 4:7*

La Von Fromm
North Valley Calvary Chapel
Yuba City, California

January 30

Maranatha!

The Lord is at hand.
Philippians 4:5

Tucked here in the fourth chapter of Philippians is a priceless gem of truth that deserves your attention today. In five short words, we're told that the Lord is at hand. This means that Jesus is coming back soon! Just as the bride waits anxiously and prepares for her groom, so too must we wait with anticipation for Jesus to return. When you fully embrace this truth, you will live differently. Every decision will be affected, every thought will be considered, and every action will be weighed because you won't want to be left behind! You won't want to find yourself unprepared to meet your heavenly Bridegroom.

Knowing that the Lord is at hand will definitely affect the way you treat others. Jesus loved people. He lived for them and He died for them. When He walked on this earth, He made it evident that they were precious to Him. How do you feel about people? Do you treat them with gentleness or are you harsh and demanding? Do you insist on your rights or do you see in every situation a chance to die to yourself? Do you forgive easily or do you keep score of wrongs done to you? Are you judgmental and critical or accepting of those who are different from you? If you truly believe that the Lord is at hand, then you will be considerate of others.

Gail Mays
Calvary Chapel South Bay
Gardena, California

January 31

Awesome God

⤳

"Consider the lilies of the field."
Matthew 6:28

As an artist, I often think about the touch of the Master's hand in our world. One of my favorite verses is Matthew 8:27, ". . . even the winds and the sea obey Him."

It's amazing to me that the Creator of the universe not only controls the winds and the seas, and keeps the planets from bumping into each other, but He can also create the most delicate, fragile lilies of the field, in fragrant, magnificent colors.

I can labor hours, perhaps days to create only a two-dimensional painting of a flower. No fragrance, no delicate petals to touch, only a dim reflection of my Creator's divine handiwork.

Michelangelo said, "A true work of art is but a shadow of the divine perfection."[6] How true! He also said, "Art is a gift from God and must be used for His glory."[7] God gives each one of us gifts. What is your gift? Some have the gift of teaching, and some have the gift of hospitality; as for me, I will continue to paint and hope that a glimmer of His divine creativity will shine through my gift. I pray that He will shine through your gift as well.

Whatever your gift is, give it back to the Lord for His glory, and He will bless and multiply it abundantly!

Connie Friedman
Calvary Chapel Lancaster
Smoketown, Pennsylvania

February = Love

We love Him because He first loved us.
1 John 4:19

Because of Valentine's Day, Americans spend millions of dollars on cards, candy, and flowers to express their love to one another. As Christians, not only is it appropriate to consider our love for others, but to ponder God's love for us as well. There is no better example of love than what Jesus did for us on the cross. I challenge you to spend time each day meditating on His love for you, personally. On the 14th, why not send the Lord a love letter, telling Him how much you cherish Him? Get up an hour earlier just to spend extra time in fellowship and prayer with your beloved Savior. Be creative this month—bless the Lord in new ways. I know God will be pleased!

FEBRUARY

F His love is Forever! (Jeremiah 31:3)
E His love is Enough! (Psalm 107:9)
B His love is Beautiful! (Psalm 27:4)
R His love is Redeeming! (Ephesians 1:7; Galatians 4:4–7)
U His love is Unbreakable! (Romans 8:35–39)
A His love is Awesome! (Psalm 146:6–7)
R His love is our Refuge! (Psalm 57:1)
Y His love is for You! (John 3:16)

Kelly Bell
Calvary Chapel Murrieta
Murrieta, California

February 2

Dead Man Talking

Therefore if any man is in Christ, he is a new creature; the old things
passed away; behold, new things have come.
2 Corinthians 5:17 NASB

Remember the expression, "Dead men tell no tales"? We often find the
opposite to be true in our daily lives as Christians. Romans 6:4 paints a
word picture of what it's like to always be in the ditch spiritually—as in
not being able to get past who we were before Christ began His transforming work in our lives. It's a bit like dragging around your old, dead self—a
lifeless mannequin—propping it up, and then talking from behind it, like
a ventriloquist. I'm sure you'll agree—it's kind of a ridiculous concept.

Why is it so hard to believe we are being transformed (Romans 12:1–
2)? In order to be an active participant in the transformation process, we
must read and believe His Word, and then walk in it! After all, God has
given us everything we need for life and godliness (2 Peter 1:3–4). Leave
your dead self alone because God promises us that He will finish the work
He started in you (Philippians 1:6).

Judy Daniel
Calvary Chapel Cheyenne
Cheyenne, Wyoming

February 3

Pleasing Our Father

≈

. . . find out what pleases the Lord.
Ephesians 5:10 NIV

My two young sons love to bring me fresh roses from our garden, and I relish their simple act of devotion. They know what pleases me! Similarly, as dearly loved children of God, we are exhorted to "find out what pleases the Lord" (Ephesians 5:10).

As I recently meditated on Ephesians 5 and various passages that mention "pleasing the Lord," two truths hit home. One thing that delights our Father is a thankful heart. He loves to hear us thank and praise Him for who He is and what He has done. The Psalmist David thanked God even when he was in pain and understood that the sacrifice of praise would please God more than the sacrifices of animals (Psalm 69:29–32).

A second thing that pleases our Father is living a life of love. Ephesians 5:1–2 exhorts us as children to imitate our Father by living a *"life of love."* The simple acts of kindness and compassion we show our family members and others bring joy to our Father's heart.

You can please your Father today! Take a few moments and thank Him for His goodness and faithfulness in your life. Then ask Him to show you how you can, in practical ways, love others today.

And we pray this in order that you may live a life worthy of the Lord
and may please him in every way.
Colossians 1:10

Becky Hallman
Calvary Chapel Kauai
Kapaa, Hawaii

February 4

The Countdown

He has made everything beautiful in its time. Also He has put eternity
in their hearts.
Ecclesiastes 3:11

Remember how time moved so slowly as you were growing up? You waited and waited for high school, then you waited for your first car, your first job, then college. Eternity seemed far away. But now it appears someone turned the hands of time forward and now it's spinning out of control!

The psalmist says, "So teach us to number our days, that we may gain a heart of wisdom" (Psalm 90:12). You see, time hasn't changed; we have. But "Jesus Christ is the same yesterday, today, and forever" (Hebrews 13:8).

He is not held by time; He sees the whole picture. He has put an awareness of the future in our hearts. When we number our days, we are making every minute, every hour, and every day count for God. We are growing in wisdom. We are "redeeming the time, because the days are evil" (Ephesians 5:16).

So whether we are at work, at home changing diapers, or on the mission field, we can be keenly aware of God's presence in our lives as we number our days. Let us live each day for His glory!

Sally Lee
Calvary Chapel Kingman
Kingman, Arizona

February 5

Love One Another

～≋～

"This is my command: Love each other."
John 15:17 NIV

It was the end of the pastors' wives retreat. We were all singing the last worship song after Communion. I had felt particularly burdened that day. I was carrying the weight of the world on my shoulders and no one knew.

A young pastor's wife leaned forward and softly whispered in my ear, "Your shoulders are very broad. They are carrying many burdens. They are wasted burdens. Give them to God and do what you know to do best: love the people."

There was my answer! It was God's job to take the burdens of people and my job to simply love them. That was the key. After all, He loved us first (1 John 4:19) and then set our example.

To love others is not a *suggestion* found in the Scriptures. It is a *command* from God. First Peter 4:8 states, "Above all, love each other deeply" (NIV). It is not possible to love others too much. It is with love that we win people to Jesus and His love. Let us continue to love one another. "Love covers over all wrongs" (Proverbs 10:12 NIV).

Jean McClure
Calvary Laguna
Irvine, California

February 6

Go Ahead! Let the Walls Fall

Then she let them down by a rope through the window, for her house
was on the city wall; she dwelt on the wall.
Joshua 2:15

Rahab was a woman with unshakable faith. She didn't allow position, politics, poverty, or parents to shake her world. Her faith in a God she only heard about helped her to stand in a falling world.

So then faith comes by hearing, and hearing by the word of God.
Romans 10:17

The Word tells us that her house was literally built on the wall of Jericho, which was about to become a sidewalk. By faith, at the end of a trumpet sound and a few loud shouts, the wall did fall, and great was its fall. Still standing, however, was her hope for a future. She rested her faith in two spies and in a scarlet rope. It wasn't much, but it was enough!

When you are all shook up, and you forget what it took to get you where you are today, listen to others who tell of God's wonders, or remember this lost lady who stood alone in her faith and believe, as she did,

The LORD your God, He is God in *heaven above and on earth beneath.*
Joshua 2:11, emphasis added

Then perhaps you can say, "Go ahead; let the walls fall. I'm ready."

Kathy Salaiz
Calvary Chapel West Covina
West Covina, California

Jewels from Jesus

And they shall be mine, saith the LORD of hosts, in that day when I make up my jewels; and I will spare them, as a man spareth his own son that serveth him.
Malachi 3:17 KJV

There is a tradition of giving rings to mothers and grandmothers. On such a ring are set individual stones to remember the birth month of children or grandchildren. Each stone represents a unique child, and each child represents years of loving service and sacrifice.

Our Lord is busy making something like this to present to each of us. Instead of a ring, we understand it to be a crown of jewels. Every crown, like every person, will be different. Its stones will represent times of service and sacrifice that were pleasing to the Lord.

Think of it: Your life of service and sacrifice will one day be remembered by jewels set in a crown and presented to you by your Lord.

What will we do with our crown of jewels? While worshiping Jesus in heaven, we will toss them at His feet as we cry,

Thou art worthy, O Lord, to receive glory and honour and power: for thou hast created all things, and for thy pleasure they are and were created.
Revelation 4:11 KJV

Pam Pensiero
Calvary Chapel Hanford
Hanford, California

February 8

True Beauty

❧

Do not let your adornment be merely outward—arranging the hair,
wearing gold, or putting on fine apparel—rather let it be the hidden
person of the heart, with the incorruptible beauty of a gentle and
quiet spirit, which is very precious in the sight of God.
1 Peter 3:3–4

One of the most popular programs on television today is *Extreme Makeovers*.
The world is fascinated with those who are completely transformed by
drastic surgeries, weight loss, hair styling, and wardrobe changes.

As Christians, the temptation is to follow the world's view of beauty
and to seek to be changed externally. Yet 1 Peter 3:4 tells us "the hidden
person of the heart" is far more precious in God's sight.

Proverbs 31:30 says, "Charm is deceitful and beauty is passing, *but
a woman who fears the LORD, she shall be praised*" (emphasis added). True
beauty that is lasting comes from a reverential fear of God.

Let Him give you the "ultimate" makeover that will never sag, wrinkle,
or fade away—a beauty that results from an intimate, personal, and vital
relationship with the living God.

June Hesterly
Calvary Chapel Costa Mesa
Santa Ana, California

24-Karat Saints

I will . . . refine them as silver is refined, and test them as gold is
tested. They will call on My name, and I will answer them.
Zechariah 13:9

TV personality Arthur Godfrey once watched a blacksmith divide scrap
metal into two separate piles: some on his right and the rest on his left.
Godfrey asked what the piles were for. The smithy replied, "Some of the
metal will be useful when put through the fire, coming out refined and
perfected. But the other stuff can't take the heat, so I toss it into the junk
heap."

That experience forged a favorite prayer Godfrey uttered during fiery
trials. He believed God's goal was to make him pure—a 24-karat saint—
so he'd say, "Lord, the fire, not the junk heap!"[8]

Has God placed you in a heated situation? Perhaps an unfaithful
spouse, a prodigal child, or an unrelenting illness ignited it. Instead of
asking God, "Why me?" consider, "Why not me?" Since Jesus was refined
by the furnace of affliction, then why not us? May you and I pray, "Let
affliction come, for it reveals that God has chosen me. Whatever forms the
flames take, help me see 'the Son of God' in the midst of them. Make me
as pure as 24-karat gold. Lord, the fire, not the junk heap!"

His eyes were bright like flames of fire. His feet were as bright as
bronze refined in a furnace.
Revelation 1:14–15 NLT

Lenya Heitzig
Ocean Hills Community Church
San Juan Capistrano, California

February 10

God First

❧

Pick me up and throw me into the sea. . . . For I know this great
tempest is because of me.
Jonah 1:12

Jonah realized that a storm at sea had come because of his disobedience,
and he saw it affecting those around him.

When I began a business selling kitchen products, I made a promise
to God. I wouldn't book any home parties for Thursday evenings, which
was our Bible study night. God blessed that little business with many sales
and a stream of parties.

One evening a woman approached me about holding her party on
a Thursday. "I'm sorry." I replied resolutely. She implored and wouldn't
budge, "That's the ONLY night that will work for me!" She was looking
for a way to welcome her myriad of friends and relatives to a "house-
warming." She assured me it would be large and profitable. "All right," I
broke down, "I suppose one Thursday won't hurt."

Three days before the party the woman told me she had at least sixty
confirmed RSVPs. The evening of the party, she had decorated with candles and lace. All manner of scrumptious delights were planned. Then
we waited for the guests. Only two showed up. "I don't understand," the
hostess fretted sadly, "They said they were coming for sure!"

Inwardly Jonah's words haunted me. "Throw *me* overboard." It wasn't
the hostess's fault, I realized. It was God reminding me that blessings can
only come when He is first in our lives and when we are living our lives
according to His will.

What I have vowed I will make good.
Jonah 2:9 NIV

Joni Woolley
Calvary Chapel Alpha
Alpha, Michigan

February 11

The Doorway to Heaven

Therefore He says: "Awake you who sleep, arise from the dead, and
Christ will give you light."
Ephesians 5:14

Recently, a friend's relative entered into eternity. This young grandmother
was killed in a tragic accident. At the funeral, my friend watched as the
woman's little granddaughter looked into the casket. The little girl pro-
claimed, "There's grandma sleeping; can I crawl up and take a nap with
her?"

The Bible speaks of death in the same way. Jesus said,

"Make room, for the girl is not dead, but sleeping."
Matthew 9:24

For the believer, death is not a "good bye" but a "see you later." It is
the final doorway. When our loved ones pass from here to eternity, if they
knew Christ, it is a "see you later" for us.

What a glorious place heaven will be! We will be reunited with those
who have gone before us, and we will have new improved bodies, ones fit
for eternity. So, we don't have to fear that last doorway.

The first doorway—Jesus—should precede the final doorway. Have
you considered Him who died for you? Listen to His invitation to you:

"I am the door. If anyone enters by Me, he will be saved, and will go in
and out and find pasture."
John 10:9

If you have not accepted that invitation, I urge you to do so today.
Jesus is the doorway to heaven!

Sally Lee
Calvary Chapel Kingman
Kingman, Arizona

February 12

Dwelling in Unity

Behold, how good and how pleasant it is for brethren to dwell together
in unity!
Psalm 133:1

Every day we face situations that test our hearts. Paul tells us in Romans 12:18, "If it is possible, as much as depends on you, live peaceably with all men." Unity begins with us. We need to take our eyes off ourselves and put them on Jesus, the only One who can change us.

Unity is a foundational building block in any relationship. I find that God uses my family—the people closest to me—to reveal the importance of unity. Dwelling in unity begins with loving someone unconditionally, without any reservation in your heart. It's the love you have for your child when you hold them for the first time. Unity is then sustained by looking out for the good of others, not just yourself (Philippians 2:4). It's not always easy, because everyone involved in a relationship has to embrace these two principles. Only God, through His Spirit, can enable us to fulfill this high calling of unity.

Are you dealing with some strife at home, at work, or at church? Is the Lord speaking to you about a relationship that needs attention? Don't allow the Enemy to rob you of joy and bring division. Daily invite the Lord to apply unconditional love and selflessness to your heart and continue to enjoy the goodness and pleasantness of dwelling in unity!

Valerie Calisher
Calvary Chapel Santee
Santee, California

February 13

That Good Part

❧

"One thing is needed, and Mary has chosen that good part, which will
not be taken away from her."
Luke 10:42

Today women have many opportunities to "be all they can be!" Life is
filled with places to go, people to meet, and things to experience. Busy.
Busy. Busy.

But with these opportunities come a responsibility to make wise
choices.

Luke tells of a time when Jesus came to Martha's house. Martha over-
extended herself taking care of her guests' physical needs. Her sister Mary
chose to sit at the feet of Jesus and fill her life with His words. When
Martha complained, Jesus' gentle rebuke made her stop and consider how
she was misplacing her priorities. Her choice caused her not to be able to
receive what Jesus wanted to give her. Martha could have made the same
choice Mary made.

And so can we.

As you prepare to go out into your busy world today, take time to
choose that good part. Sit at the feet of Jesus. Fill your life with His words.
Confess and repent of sin. Ask Him to take control of your day and guide
you. Tell Him you love Him. Don't forget He promises "that good part"
will not be taken away when we choose Him.

Tot Landry
Calvary Chapel Casa Grande
Casa Grande, Arizona

February 14

A Box of Candy Hearts

❧

I have loved you with an everlasting love.
Jeremiah 31:3

The message of love has been sounded through the ages, but none is more beautiful than the message God gives us of His "agape" love.

By this we know love, because He laid down His life for us.
1 John 3:16

One year for Valentine's Day, I was the recipient of a box of little, multi-colored, candy hearts. They were embossed with sayings that represented the world's view of love. Sayings such as "cutie pie," "you're mine," "I'm yours," "u 4 me," and "sizzle" were but a few of the ideas expressed in vivid dye. One even said, "I luv u."

God's blessing of love to us is similarly written across the hearts of His people. The messages, scrolled in blood, read: "I will never forsake you;" "I will never mislead you;" "I will never forget you;" "I forgive you;" "I am the way;" "I am with you;" "I will comfort you;" "I'm never too busy for you;" "I am always yours;" "you are always mine." The world's sayings on candy hearts will fade in time, but the very source of love, our heavenly Father, loves us with an amazing and unending love.

Behold what manner of love the Father has bestowed on us, that we should be called children of God!
1 John 3:1

Jan Cotten
Country Chapel of Midland-Odessa
Midland, Texas

February 15

Count It All Joy?

Count it all joy when you fall into various trials, knowing that the
testing of your faith produces patience.
James 1:2–3

The Bible tells us we are to be joyful in all types of trials. But what about the difficulties of this life such as chronic illness, the death of a loved one, a wayward child, or a broken relationship? Perhaps you are like me and your first reaction is despair.

When difficulty comes, how can we count it all joy? James 1:17 says that "Every good gift and every perfect gift is from above, and comes down from the Father of lights, with whom there is no variation or shadow of turning." These trials don't seem "good" at the time they occur. But the word *good* in James 1:17 represents the very character of God; He alone is good! The word *perfect* is the result of all God causes or allows to touch our lives. He is perfecting us through various trials and conforming us into His image. If you are a child of God, know it is all good!

Today, as you focus upon Jesus, remember God's perspective in all these things. Second Corinthians 4:18 says, "We do not look at the things which are seen, but the things which are not seen. For the things which are seen are temporary, but the things which are not seen are eternal."

Sally Van Wick
Calvary Chapel Bible Fellowship
Temecula, California

February 16

Come Aside into a Quiet Place and Rest Awhile

~≈~

"Come ye yourselves apart into a desert place, and rest a while."
Mark 6:31 KJV

The disciples went on an evangelistic journey. It was a physically, emotionally, and spiritually challenging trip of faith, for they could take no provisions with them. They couldn't even take Jesus with them! They were armed with His words and His power as they went about healing the sick, casting out demons, and preaching the good news. Afterwards, when they gathered with Jesus for debriefing, the needy people still flocked to them.

Ministry can take a lot out of a person. The disciples needed a retreat. Jesus was sensitive to their need. "And he said unto them, 'Come ye yourselves apart into a desert place, and rest a while.'" The disciples might have set their hopes on the deserted place they were sailing to, "Oh boy! A retreat!" But their rest was in the ship with them.

Time spent with Jesus brings rest to His busy servants. Each day He beckons you to join Him in the ship. Go apart with Him. Listen to His Word. Be still and give Him your undivided attention. Pour out your heart and confess your failings. It will change the course of any day, and you will begin it rested and refreshed.

Their strength is to sit still.
Isaiah 30:7 KJV

Jeanie Matranga
Calvary Chapel Downey
Downey, California

February 17

Hearing from God

Call upon Me and go and pray to Me, and I will listen to you. You will
seek Me and find Me, when you search for Me with all your heart.
Jeremiah 29:12–13

A little girl came to her mother one day asking, "Mama, are you sure God
really speaks? Why doesn't God ever speak to me?"

The mother said to her little girl, "It's true—God does speak, and He
will make Himself known to those who sincerely seek Him. He is the only
One you can take at His Word. Take your Bible to a quiet place and just
call out to Him. Tell Him everything you're feeling, doubting and believing. Then, be still: wait and listen." While the little girl did as her mother
suggested, Mama prayed.

Sometime later, the little girl came running wide-eyed with her Bible
open in her hand, proclaiming, "Mama, He spoke to me! God really spoke
to *me*!" With pleasure, Mama asked, "Tell me, what did He say to you?"

The little girl carefully and slowly read out loud, "Call to Me, and I
will answer you, and show you great and mighty things, which you do not
know" (Jeremiah 33:3).

As the daughter grew, she got caught up in the cares of this world and
strayed from her Lord. But her Mama still prays for her, believing God,
and taking Him at His Word.

Refrain your voice from weeping, and your eyes from tears; for your
work shall be rewarded, says the LORD, and they shall come back from
the land of the enemy. There is hope in your future, says the LORD,
that your children shall come back to their own border.
Jeremiah 31:16–17

Barbara Gil
Calvary Chapel of the Redwoods
Smith River, California

February 18

Doing Spiritual Battle

No one engaged in warfare entangles himself with the affairs of this
life, that he may please him who enlisted him as a soldier.

2 Timothy 2:4

Jesus may have our hearts, but if He doesn't have our minds, our lives will
be defeated. We need to acknowledge that we are in a spiritual battle, war-
ring with our flesh and against Satan. The Bible clearly defines warfare:

Our flesh wars against us:

But each one is tempted when he is drawn away by his *own* desires
and enticed.

James 1:14, emphasis added

Satan wars against us:

We do not wrestle against flesh and blood, but . . . against the rulers
of the darkness of this age, against spiritual hosts of wickedness in
the heavenly places.

Ephesians 6:12

Romans 12:2 tells us to stop being pressed into the mold of the world,
and instead to be "transformed by the renewing" of our minds. As our
minds are transformed by the Spirit, we will more easily recognize the flesh
arising in us or Satan attacking us in various situations. So, as we acknowledge the spiritual warfare and verify that it is our flesh or Satan, then we
can learn to do as 2 Corinthians 10:5 tells us: "[to cast] down . . . every
high thing that exalts itself against the knowledge of God," and instead
bring "every thought into captivity to the obedience of Christ." We can
know if anything coming into our minds is from our flesh or from Satan
by subjecting our thoughts to our offensive weapon—His Word.

Therefore submit to God. Resist the devil and he will flee from you.

James 4:7

Sherry Merrihew
Calvary Chapel Oklahoma City
Oklahoma City, Oklahoma

February 19

Be Joyful!

❦

Rejoice in the Lord always.
Philippians 4:4

Be joyful in Jesus! Read Philippians 4:4–7. As believers, we can be full of joy knowing that no matter what happens to us, Jesus Christ is with us. The Lord is with you! Rejoice in the Lord! Be joyful!

Be Joyful! "Rejoice in the Lord always." Philippians 4:4
Read: 1 Thessalonians 5:16
Be Ready! "The Lord is at hand." Philippians 4:5
Read: Matthew 24:42
Be Anxious for Nothing! "Be anxious for nothing." Philippians 4:6
Read: Matthew 6:25–34
Be Praying! "In everything by prayer." Philippians 4:6
Read: 1 Thessalonians 5:17
Be Thankful! "By prayer . . . with thanksgiving." Philippians 4:6
Read: 1 Thessalonians 5:18
Be Peaceful! "The peace of God will guard your hearts." Philippians 4:7
Read: John 14:27

Lord, let me rejoice in You always! I want to be ready for Your soon return. Let me trust in You and be anxious for nothing. I want to bring everything to You in prayer. Please give me a thankful heart. You are the Prince of Peace; fill me with Your peace today. Lord, make me a woman of prayer and a woman of Your Word. In Jesus' name, amen.

Suzie Larson
Calvary Chapel Caldwell
Caldwell, Idaho

February 20

Delight Yourself in the Lord

Delight yourself in the LORD; and He will give you the desires of your
heart.
Psalm 37:4 NASB

Oh, how wonderful our God is! His Word is so true! He longs to bless us
and give us the desires of our hearts. All we have to do is delight ourselves
in Him. To *delight in* means, "to take great pleasure in."

Do you take great pleasure in your Lord today? Do you spend time
alone with Him, or do you just visit Him once a week on Sunday? Do you
listen for His voice and obey His Word? Have you sat down and shared
with Him all that is on your heart?

Commit your way to the LORD, trust also in Him, and He shall bring
it to pass.
Psalm 37:5

Dear friend, no matter what you're going through in life, whether it is
divorce, death, sickness, or tragedy, you can commit your life to the Lord
and trust in His plan and purpose for you. He loves you, and He knows
what it is like to hurt and suffer. He will be with you through all of these
things, just as He has been with me. Continue to delight yourself in Him
and trust Him, even if things don't go your way, for He longs to bless you
and give you the desires of your heart.

Elyse Hittle
Calvary Chapel Payson
Payson, Arizona

February 21

Dying Moment by Moment

But put on the Lord Jesus Christ, and make no provision for the flesh, to fulfill its lusts.
Romans 13:14

I so often wish that the things we lay on the altar would stay there. They always seem to get up and creep back off the altar. Seldom is it a simple matter of saying, "Lord, I give You these struggles and temptations. Take them from me; let me be more like You," and poof, they disappear! They may be gone for a time, but often it seems we turn around and there they are again.

It is essential to understand that placing things on the altar is a day-by-day, moment-by-moment offering. The more we do it, the easier it becomes, but yielding to the Holy Spirit must never stop. We have to be constantly aware that we are giving these things up to the Lord. If we aren't consistent, they will find their way back into our lives, and eventually overtake us.

Continually turn to the Lord and His Word—this has to be our way of life.

Rest in the LORD, and wait patiently for Him.
Psalm 37:7

Bonnie Botsford
Horizon North County
Rancho Santa Fe, California

February 22

God Is Merciful

He has showed you, O man, what is good. And what does the LORD
require of you? To act justly and to love mercy and to walk humbly
with your God.
Micah 6:8 NIV

We simply do not have the qualifications to approach a perfect God. Our
humanity cannot stand up against the blinding magnificence of His complete perfection. That is why we desperately need God's grace AND His
mercy!

> Micah 7:18–20—He hurls our iniquities into the depths of the sea.
> Luke 1:46–55—His mercy extends to those who fear Him.
> Luke 6:35–36—He is our example of unconditional mercy.
> Romans 9:14–16—His mercy does not depend on man's desire or effort.
> Ephesians 2:3–9—He is rich in mercy.
> Titus 3:5–7—His mercy is generous, through Jesus Christ our Savior!

These attributes of grace and mercy are the basis for our approach to
the throne of God. He not only gives us what we do not deserve (grace—
unmerited favor), but He does NOT give us what we DO deserve! That
is because of His mercy, without which we could never approach Him. In
the book of Micah, we are called to imitate that attribute: What does the
LORD REQUIRE of you? Do justly, love mercy, and walk humbly with
your God.

When we realize the depth and breadth of His mercy, we are humbled.
Could someone use your mercy today? Slander, lack of forgiveness, and
gossip could all fall under the category of "unmerciful." Run away from
these things!

Donna Riley
Calvary Chapel La Mesa
La Mesa, California

February 23

What's That Smell?

For we are to God the fragrance of Christ among those who are being saved and among those who are perishing.
2 Corinthians 2:15

"The fragrance of Christ"—isn't that marvelous? Living in the Philippines, I am keenly aware of fragrances—or rather odors. It is typically 90/90 each day. That is, 90 degrees and 90 percent humidity! With only a fan to cool you, things can get kind of, well, "sticky." It takes great effort to stay smelling nice or at least not to smell bad. I may bathe several times a day, use body powder, antiperspirant, deodorant, and cologne. I've got the whole odor arsenal! Even so, it doesn't always last.

In my diligence to keep my outward body clean and non-offensive, I must also keep my inward body (my heart) clean before the Lord because the truth inside always comes out and permeates the outside around us.

As I *bathe* my family and myself in prayer and am *washed* in His Word, the "fragrance of Christ" becomes stronger and begins to pour out to those around us. It's absolutely intoxicating!

May it be so, Lord, that in all we do and everywhere we go, may those around us smell the sweet fragrance of Christ in us and be drawn to Him each day.

Lorie Ramsey
Calvary Chapel Bible Fellowship
Iloilo City, Philippines

February 24

Beauty for Ashes

For He is like a refiner's fire.
Malachi 3:2 KJV

One day while burning a Y2K bag (paper trash compacted into a brown paper bag, stapled shut) in the fireplace, I asked God to purify me and clean me out. While praying, I noticed that the outer layer of bag was almost gone. The trash inside was producing a nice glow with some pretty colors.

He began to show me the clutter I had accumulated. There was no need to remove the staples or pull out every item and examine it. He just had me drag it to the curb of my heart to be picked up by Him. "Once I burn it, you can't have it back again," He said, "but I'll give you something in return."

I thank God that Jesus is the "redemption center" where I can bring the rubbish of my life, my heart, and my past—and get "beauty for ashes."

. . . to give unto them beauty for ashes . . . that they might be called
trees of righteousness.
Isaiah 61:3 KJV

Mary Pultro
Calvary Chapel on the King's Highway
Philadelphia, Pennsylvania

February 25

PB and J

And we know that God causes all things to work together for good to those who love God, to those who are called according to His purpose.

Romans 8:28 NASB

"Peanut, Peanut butter, . . . Jelly!" goes the children's song. I can almost taste the chewy, slightly sweet lunchtime staple many of us grew up on. It always satisfies, and depending upon the jelly, brand of peanut butter, and type of bread, each PB and J sandwich picks up different nuances of flavor, becoming a unique delicacy.

Early in my Christian walk, I learned the importance of memorizing Scripture for meditation, prayer, conviction of sin, correction of behavior, and overall training in right living before God. Like PB and J, Scripture memory is something I grew up on. One of the first verses I memorized was Romans 8:28. Often, the Holy Spirit will bring this verse, or others like it, back to mind with an entirely new application or a different nuance of meaning. When I learned this verse, the phrase "all things work together for good" was important in my life. Recently, the Holy Spirit has been stressing the phrases "to those who love God" and "according to His purpose." I thought this old staple was thoroughly worn out. But God is bringing out a fresh, unexplored sweetness from it, and all the phrases are working together for good in me.

The Lord's lovingkindnesses indeed never cease, for His compassions never fail. They are new every morning; great is Thy faithfulness.

Lamentations 3:22–23 NASB

Jeneane Herrera
Calvary Chapel Las Vegas
Las Vegas, New Mexico

February 26

Forgive

Jesus said, "Father, forgive these people, because they don't know what
they are doing."
Luke 23:34 NLT

I am a wife, mother, and grandmother, and I've learned that people who
live in intimacy hurt and offend each other. We know we need to forgive
when this happens, but sometimes it's hard. Pain gets in the way, shame
gets in the way, and humiliation gets in the way. Remember the circumstances of Luke 23:34? Jesus was dying on the cross. "And the people stood
looking on" (verse 35). When Jesus hung on the cross, people stopped and
stared. The expression "looking on" can be translated "to look intensely,"
or "to stare." Have you ever seen a traffic accident? People stop and stare.
People get some kind of perverse pleasure in seeing someone else in pain.

I have recently gone through the ordeal of breast cancer. This required
several trips to the doctor and to the hospital. I do not like getting un-
dressed in front of strangers. It is humiliating. Can you imagine how humiliating it was for Jesus to hang on the cross, practically naked, with everyone staring at Him? But Jesus forgave them. Jesus was in pain hanging
on the cross. Jesus was humiliated hanging on the cross. In spite of pain
and in spite of humiliating circumstances, we can forgive those who hurt
us. The presence of pain does not mean we are excused from extending
forgiveness to others.

Instead, be kind to each other, tenderhearted, forgiving one another,
just as God through Christ has forgiven you.
Ephesians 4:32 NLT

Mary Geraci
Calvary Chapel South Denver
Littleton, Colorado

February 27

Cling to Him

❧

To console those who mourn . . . to give them beauty for ashes.
Isaiah 61:3

It was 6:30 a.m. and my husband and I sat in the hospital room, holding our five-day-old son, Jacob, for the first, and the last time. We said our good-byes in a blur of tears and pain. The questions came flooding in: "Didn't You hear our cries, Lord?" "If You love me, why did You let this happen?" "Why Lord, why?"

What do we do when life brings those horrible, sickening blows that wound us to the core? At these times, more than any other, we must cling to what we know of God. When Moses was in the cleft of the rock and the Lord spoke to him, He revealed His compassion, grace, and lovingkindness (Exodus 34:6). Beloved, He does not desire that we hurt. His heart aches with ours, as would any loving parent's when their child grieves. Sin, death, and suffering are not part of His original plan, but are a result of the fall. But thankfully, He is ultimately in control. We can only see one little jagged, seemingly broken, piece of the mosaic, but He sees it all, from eternity to eternity. If we commit our hurts and disappointments to Him—even those "mortal wounds"—He will take the tiny pieces of our shattered hearts and fill all the cracks and crevices with His healing Spirit. He will then bring forth strength and beauty that never would have been possible had not the wounding come.

Cling to Him. He will show His tender mercies and endless love and bring beauty from ashes.

Cherrise Denham
Calvary Chapel Troy
Troy, Missouri

February 28

Are We Ready for War?

Put on the full armor of God so that you can take your stand against
the devil's schemes.
Ephesians 6:11 NIV

We need to be prepared for battle every day if we are going to be an example for our children. Just before this classic verse in Ephesians, Paul instructs us in human relationships. He says, "Wives—submit; Husbands—
love; and Fathers (and Mothers)—do not provoke your children to wrath
or resentment" (see Ephesians 5:22–6:4).

These are areas where the Enemy infiltrates our homes. The Christian
home was designed by God to be a refuge and stronghold against the
Enemy, but Satan will never give up his attempt to undermine it. So
Christians, put on your armor! We have a real Enemy, and he is not flesh
and blood. We cannot fight with carnal weapons. The spiritual weapons
that we fight with are mighty to the pulling down of strongholds. Our
God is good to give us just what we need, just when we need it. My prayer
is that we would "never tire of doing what is right" (2 Thessalonians 3:13
NIV)—everything depends upon it. Our very homes and families hang
in the balance. Our obedience is crucial for others to see. Hold fast to the
Lord. Put on the full armor of God and stand. Submit and love. He is our
strength. And He will always enable us to obey Him.

Peggy Kravig
Calvary Chapel Downey
Downey, California

March 1

Abide and Obey

"I am the vine, you are the branches. He who abides in Me, and I in Him, bears much fruit; for without Me you can do nothing."
John 15:5

Jesus promised an abundant and fruitful life as a result of being empowered by the Holy Spirit. The Spirit-filled life is a life surrendered to Christ. As He lives in us and through us, He gives us continual victory over the flesh. He has provided all we need by His Spirit. Our responsibility is simply to abide and obey.

Abiding and obeying produces an abundant and abounding fruit that is fragrant, sweet, and attractive to a world that needs Jesus. Are you abiding, obeying, and abounding?

June Hesterly
Calvary Chapel Costa Mesa
Santa Ana, California

March 2

Standing on His Promises

And He said, "My Presence will go with you, and I will give you rest."
Exodus 33:14

Have you ever experienced a season where your life seemed to be turned upside down? The Bible might call it "sifting." The Lord said to Peter, "Satan has asked for you, that he may sift you as wheat" (Luke 22:31). My season of sifting came this summer when my husband was out of the country on a mission trip. My mother-in-law had emergency surgery, and it seemed that she would not survive. That itself seemed to be a burden I could hardly carry. Then my father called and informed me that my mother had broken her hip, was bleeding internally, and needed emergency surgery that same day. The sifting had begun, but the Lord so faithfully carried me through. As I made my way to the hospital for surgery number one, I heard the Lord say to me, "My presence will go with you, and I will give you rest." He filled me with that peace which surpasses all understanding and commanded me "do not fret—it only causes harm" (Psalm 37:8).

Are you anxious about something today? Do you need His perfect peace? Rest assured, your Savior is with you to be your peace and strength. His encouragement to you is,

Be strong in the Lord and the power of His might.
Ephesians 6:10

Thou wilt keep him in perfect peace, whose mind is stayed on thee.
Isaiah 26:3 KJV

Sheila Walker
Calvary Chapel Living Word
Irvine, California

Did God Really Say That?

The LORD has kept me from having children.
Genesis 16:2 NIV

He said to the woman, "Did God really say? . . ."
Genesis 3:1 NIV

Sarah struggled to believe God's promise that she would have a child. Eve questioned God's intentions. Since the garden, Satan has been trying to get us to question what God has said. When we doubt God's promises, we are forgetting the character of God. When we take our focus off the loving, faithful character of God, we begin to think He is withholding good from us.

Is there an area in which you are struggling to believe God? Are you finding it difficult to wait on Him? Is there something He has not given or done for you? Don't wrestle with doubt. Remind yourself of the faithfulness of your God. Hide God's Word in your heart, especially Scripture that speaks of His love and faithfulness. Deepen your relationship with Him. He keeps His promises and He loves and provides for His children.

"For I know the plans I have for you," says the LORD. "They are plans
for good and not for disaster, to give you a future and a hope."
Jeremiah 29:11 NLT

Holly Robinson
Calvary Chapel Oldsmar
Oldsmar, Florida

March 4

Who Are You Waiting for?

My soul waits for the Lord more than watchmen wait for the
morning.
Psalm 130:6 NIV

With every crossroad we come to, either we choose to seek the Lord with
our whole hearts and wait for His lead, or we proceed ahead, reacting
out of our own limited knowledge and understanding. Then we ask, but
only after we request that He bless us and work things out as we think
He should. What is *God's* instruction to us? Why is it that *my* soul doesn't
always wait for the Lord more than watchmen wait for the morning?

Psalm 34:10 says, "The young lions lack and suffer hunger; but those
who seek the LORD shall not lack any good thing." We will suffer fleshly
choices if we lack spiritual food. If we are not in communion with Jesus
through our reading and meditation on His Word every day, we will not
be sufficiently built up in our faith to make the right choice to wait on the
Lord during those difficult and uncertain times. As a result, we will make
fleshly choices.

Let us be like David and say with our whole hearts,

But it is for you, O LORD, that I wait; it is you, O Lord my God, who
will answer.
Psalm 38:15 NRSV

Be strong, and let your heart take courage, all you who wait for the
LORD.
Psalm 31:24 NRSV

Katie Babich
Calvary Chapel Susanville
Susanville, California

March 5

S.I.N.

Then Jesus was led up by the Spirit into the wilderness to be tempted by the devil. . . . Then Jesus said to him, "Away with you, Satan! For it is written, 'You shall worship the LORD your God, and Him only you shall serve.'" Then the devil left Him, and behold, angels came and ministered to Him.
Matthew 4:1, 10–11

We are *all* born with it. We *all* do it. Why is it when I think I've got a handle on a particular area of sin in my life, I'm tested again? You would think I would pass the test by now. The truth is, as long as we are in this body of flesh, there will always be temptations, and we will constantly be tested. However—there is hope!

Jesus gave us His perfect example to follow. Matthew 4:1–11 shows us how Jesus dealt with temptation. He used God's Word. Our power to overcome temptation comes from the *use* of Scripture: applying God's Word to our lives and abiding in His promises.

I know if I find myself in S.I.N. it is because Scripture Is Neglected. Before you find yourself in S.I.N., *use* Scripture. Don't neglect it. Seek the Lord and meditate on His Holy Scriptures so He may show you how to use "the sword of the Spirit, which is the word of God" (Ephesians 6:17).

Karen Zachary
Calvary Chapel Camarillo
Camarillo, California

March 6

The Key to Following Christ

And the peace of God, which surpasses all understanding, will guard
your hearts and minds through Christ Jesus.
Philippians 4:7

How encouraging it can be for us to realize that God wants to guard our hearts. Actually, the one whom He is often guarding our hearts from is ourselves.

Some of the biggest issues in our lives are the ones we bring upon ourselves through the damaging emotions of anger, fear, loneliness, and worry. But the key to following Christ is faith in allowing Him to reign and rule over these emotions with the new life that He has come to give and the power and ability He has to provide. This new life comes only when we die to ourselves and daily live anew in Christ. Doing so doesn't mean that we can't or won't experience emotions; it just means that in all things, we have to look to Christ as our example.

The root of anger, fear, loneliness, and worry is selfish thinking that takes place in our lives when we are focused on ourselves and on our own needs. But the root of love, joy, hope, and peace is found through the presence of Jesus Christ in our lives. The key to following Him today is found in remaining faithfully focused on Him.

But without faith it is impossible to please Him.
Hebrews 11:6

Bonnie Botsford
Horizon North County
Rancho Santa Fe, California

Camel or Deer?

As the deer pants for the water brooks, so pants my soul for You, O
God. My soul thirsts for God, for the living God.
Psalm 42:1–2

Did you know that the average woman's body is fifty to sixty percent water, and it needs constant replenishing? That's why you see so many people carrying around water bottles.

When you are thirsty, your body is already beginning to dehydrate. Thirsting is a gift from God. We know that we need water to sustain our bodies *physically*. In the same way, we need the living water that God gives to sustain us *spiritually*.

But how do you satisfy that need? Well, are you like a camel or a deer? Camels can go three months without drinking water. They are self-sufficient because they have big humps on their backs that store water. They were made for desert living! A deer, on the other hand, knows that in order to survive, she has to drink water every day.

In your spiritual life, to which do you relate? Are you like a camel that drinks only occasionally, or are you like a deer that needs to drink every single day? Have you allowed the attitude of self-sufficiency to rob you of your daily thirst for God? In this respect, you weren't made for desert living! May you be like a deer and see your need to daily come and drink!

Karen Stangel
North Shore Christian Fellowship
Haleiwa, Hawaii

No Matter What

The LORD does whatever pleases him, in the heavens and on the earth,
in the seas and all their depths.
Psalm 135:6 NIV

When things are going well and life seems great, it's easy to say, "God can do whatever He pleases with me," or to consider myself, "crucified with Christ." But what about those times when things aren't so rosy? Am I still willing to follow Jesus no matter what? What if . . .

I really want something and God says, "No"?

(. . . no matter what?)

God allows me to live a life of pain and suffering?

(. . . no matter what?)

The person I love most in this world dies?

(. . . no matter what?)

I have to examine my heart. Is God really sovereign in all areas of my life, or do I remain faithful only if God fits into *my* plans and agenda? I need to determine my response *before* the next time my life isn't going the way I'd planned, so that I will have already decided in my heart to say, "No matter what, Lord, I will follow You."

Linda Sasso
Calvary Chapel Boise
Boise, Idaho

The Beginning of Knowledge

Fear the LORD your God and serve him. Hold fast to him and take
your oaths in his name.
Deuteronomy 10:20 NIV

Fearing God is recognizing, reverencing, and responding to who He is, the King of kings and Lord of lords. Without reverencing Him above all in our lives, we cannot serve Him and in turn serve others. It is His desire to change us from the selfish beings that we are to the selfless reflection of His Son who came to conform us into His image.

I'm often reminded of our early days in ministry when I struggled with separation from family and friends, and the transition in lifestyle (moving eight hundred fifty miles from Southern California to a small town in the desert of southern New Mexico with only one single-story shopping mall!). That experience taught me how to appreciate the days of simple blessings and allowed the Lord to draw me closer as I served Him. Those things that used to compete for my attention were far away, and I experienced the freedom of allowing Him to direct me in serving my husband, children, and church. I thank God for counting me worthy to serve Him and praise Him for teaching us through the example of His Son, our Savior Jesus.

Direct me in the path of your commands, for there I find delight.
Turn my heart toward your statutes and not toward selfish gain.
Turn my eyes away from worthless things; preserve my life according
to your word. Fulfill your promise to your servant, so that you may
be feared.
Psalm 119:35–38 NIV

Mary Ortega
Calvary Chapel of Las Cruces
Las Cruces, New Mexico

March 10

Are You Covered?

⌘

[Put on] the whole armor of God.
Ephesians 6:13

My husband was at a retreat, and the children and I were alone. Though we live deep in the woods, isolated from neighbors, I'm normally not afraid when he's gone. But on this Friday night, I'd just spent the evening with friends. Somehow, our conversation had turned to stories of peeping Toms and home intruders. I was nervous by the time I returned home, and quickly locked all the doors and windows before putting the children to bed. With the house tightly secured and my cordless phone on the bed next to me, I felt safe enough to drift off to sleep.

The next morning, realizing I'd left my Bible in the car, I unlocked our front door and swung it open. A familiar jingling noise greeted my ears: my keys dangled in the lock. I'd left them hanging there—all night.

Sometimes we're like that with our armor. We remember the belt of truth, but leave our feet uncovered. Or we shod our feet with the gospel of peace, remember the belt of truth, the helmet of salvation, the shield of faith, and the sword of the Spirit, but we forget to put on Christ. We leave the breastplate of *His* righteousness behind—and leave our hearts vulnerable to attack.

Don't forget your covering today. Make sure you've got your *whole* armor.

Shannon Woodward
Calvary Chapel Marysville
Marysville, Washington

March 11

Separation Anxiety

Be still, and know that I am God.
Psalm 46:10

As my husband prepared for a three-week mission to India, the thought of just dropping him off at the airport and waving a nonchalant goodbye was more than I could stand. My heart was so heavy. I wasn't ready for this. And God understood.

By God's provision, a visitor's pass took me to the gate and I was able to see him off. What a blessing! As we carried on casual conversation with others, I became aware of Larrie next to me. He was close enough to touch and just knowing that brought comfort.

What a picture of Jesus! Hebrews 13:5 says, "I will never leave you nor forsake you." In life's busyness and trials, He is there. And you can *know* His presence smack dab in the middle of it all. Shift your focus off your circumstances. Let the eyes of your heart seek His presence. "Be still and know." Hear again His words, "I will never leave you nor forsake you."

As I write, Larrie is still gone but I know when he gets off that plane, we'll be looking for one another, and when our eyes meet, our hearts will rejoice!

Jesus, too, is coming back. When He does, He'll be looking for you, His beloved!

"I will come again and receive you to Myself; that where I am, there you may be also."
John 14:3

Rhonda Palmer
Calvary Chapel Henderson
Henderson, Nevada

March 12

Before You Ask

"In this manner, therefore, pray: Our Father in heaven, hallowed be
Your name."
Matthew 6:9

As my quiet time with the Lord ended one morning, I headed to my son's
room with great anticipation of our time alone together. It was hard not
to be disappointed when instead of the usual sweet greeting and precious
hug, I encountered a list of wants and questions. So I stopped him in
mid-sentence and explained that I would go out and come back into the
room so we could start our time together on a more affectionate note with
a warm greeting and a hug.

You can imagine my surprise when I bumped into the Lord in that
hallway. I almost knew before He spoke to my heart what He would say.
"Diane, I feel the same way." I had to consider how often I had started my
prayer times with requests and questions, rather than a proper greeting of
affection and esteem that would befit my Lord, my Creator, the Sovereign
of the Universe, my Friend, my Abba, my Daddy.

I realized that morning that it was time not just for my son to start
over, but for me to go back out of the throne room and reenter with the
praise, adoration, honor, and worship my Holy Father deserves.

"God is Spirit, and those who worship Him must worship in spirit
and truth."
John 4:24

Diane Coy
Calvary Chapel Fort Lauderdale
Fort Lauderdale, Florida

March 13

Why Ask?

Let your requests be made known to God.
Philippians 4:6

On a recent trip to Alaska, my husband and I took the tour through Denali National Park to see Mount McKinley, the tallest mountain in North America. While waiting for the bus into the park, several other vacationers commented about how the spectacular mountain is usually shrouded in clouds, often leaving tourists disappointed. I prayed a little prayer that God would let me see the top on this once-in-a-lifetime trip.

The bus driver started telling us about the surroundings and warning us that we probably would not see the top of *the* mountain. I prayed again and really felt that God whispered to my heart, "You'll see it!" When the mountain came into view, it was shining in all its splendor—all the way to the snowy top! The gasp of appreciation was audible on the bus.

What about the people who saw it and did not pray? Yes, they were blessed, but I enjoyed something very special in the privacy of my heart. Because my Father and I discussed this matter, our fellowship was exquisitely sweet and very personal. I was blessed because I had *asked*. How awesome it is to have fellowship with the God of the universe regarding things that are important to me. Invite Him into your day.

Dianna Michaels
Calvary Chapel Spring Valley
Las Vegas, Nevada

March 14

The Joyful Walk of Obedience!

Dear friends, if our hearts do not condemn us, we have confidence
before God and receive from him anything we ask, because we obey
his commands and do what pleases him.
1 John 3:21–23 NIV

One thing that brings the greatest joy to my heart is when my young
boys willfully obey and please me. When a child chooses to lovingly obey,
there's an instant communion between mother and child that brews a
sweet harmony of the souls. All other challenges of parenting seem to mo-
mentarily drift silently away. The greatest gift God uses to teach us more
about ourselves is children. I am overjoyed when my children obey me,
and yet God desires and commands the same from me, His child.

God's plan for His children is that we will submit every aspect of our
lives to Him, that daily we would live our lives expressing the life of Jesus
in our character, our conduct, and our conversation. A joyful walk of obedience is doing what God says to do, when God says to do it, the way He
says to do it. By this, our children will know that we love God.

And this is love: that we walk in obedience to his commands. As
you have heard from the beginning, his command is that you walk
in love.
2 John 6 NIV

Kellie Farag
Calvary Chapel Lake City
Coeur d'Alene, Idaho

March 15

Leading Little Ones in Battle

All the men of Judah, with their wives and children and little ones,
stood there before the LORD.
2 Chronicles 20:13 NIV

The enemy is rapidly approaching for battle and King Jehoshaphat gathers the nation together before the Lord to seek Him. The Lord encourages the people:

Do not be afraid or discouraged because of this vast army. For the
battle is not yours, but God's.
2 Chronicles 20:15 NIV

As mothers, we need to lead our little ones to stand before the Lord when the battles come. We need to teach our children that the Lord will fight those battles for us as we seek Him. Take time to ask your little ones what they are struggling with; be faithful to pray and read God's Word together.

Take up your positions; stand firm and see the deliverance the LORD
will give you.
2 Chronicles 20:17 NIV

Lori Cook
Calvary Chapel La Habra
La Habra, California

March 16

The Fragrance of Christ

*. . . through us diffuses the fragrance of His knowledge in every place.
For we are to God the fragrance of Christ.
2 Corinthians 2:14–15*

I love the entrance of spring, the season of new birth. I welcome the warmth after the last snow, the parade of ducklings and baby birds, the longer hours of daylight, and the green budding of the trees. A beautiful display of spring flowers represents seeds that have fallen, broken, and died to grant new life, diffusing fragrance in every place.

Each sweet-smelling aroma is a reminder that a seed has died. What a beautiful analogy of Jesus' body, the Seed, who was broken for us!

*This is My body which is broken for you.
1 Corinthians 11:24*

*But if it die, it bringeth forth much fruit.
John 12:24 KJV*

*And walk in love, as Christ also has loved us and given Himself for
us, an offering and a sacrifice to God for a sweet-smelling aroma.
Ephesians 5:2*

Come to Him with a surrendered heart, one full of brokenness; die to your old self, and allow His fragrance to be released in you to a dying world that your might bring forth much fruit.

Vi Goodrich
Horizon Christian Fellowship
Indianapolis, Indiana

"This is My commandment, that you love one another as I have loved you."
John 15:12

While recently flipping through a magazine, my eyes focused on the phrase, "love them anyway." These words took me back to a relationship that had gone sour because of a big misunderstanding.

I remember it was so easy for me to focus on how "I was wronged" and how all my pain was justified. As I stewed and gloated in my own self-righteousness, Jesus quietly reminded me of how much He'd forgiven me of. He showed me all the times I'd sinned and brought hurt to Him, yet His forgiveness was still given to me so freely. In that very moment, my eyes filled with tears as I wept and felt His deep compassionate love for me.

Do you have unforgiveness in your heart toward someone today? Go to that difficult person and make it right. Allow God's love, peace, and forgiveness to tear down the wall of dissention between you, and "love them anyway."

But He, being full of compassion, forgave their iniquity, and did not destroy them. Yes, many a time He turned His anger away, and did not stir up all His wrath; for He remembered that they were but flesh.
Psalm 78:38–39

Norma Pittman
Calvary Worship Center
Colorado Springs, Colorado

March 18

Pardon Me!

He who covers his sin will not prosper, but whoever confesses and
forsakes them will have mercy.
Proverbs 28:13

First John 1:5 tells us, "God is light and in Him is no darkness at all."
That means nothing is hidden in Him. Light exposes all things; it cannot
hide or cover darkness. It only radiates brightness.

When you turn on a light in a dark room, it shines so that you may
see clearly. Light helps us not to hurt ourselves or stumble unnecessarily.
It provides security and strength. Light dispels all darkness, all fear. God
is Light—our Light. In Him we find safety and surety. Light reveals all
hidden things.

God's Light is so powerful that it is able to show us any secret areas
in our lives—externally and internally. He is faithful to show us secret
chambers in our hearts that we weren't aware of, so that we can be free.
And when Jesus sets us free, we are totally released from sin. That kind of
freedom causes us to live lives that emulate His Light.

The more our light shines, the more radiant we become in Jesus, and
the more our lives bring glory to Him. Matthew 5:16 states "Let your
light so shine before men, that they may see your good works and glorify
your Father in heaven." That should be our purpose for living. So keep
shining for Jesus!

Angela Tomasso
Calvary Chapel Westside
Spencerport, New York

In the Secret

". . . Your father who sees in secret will reward you openly."
Matthew 6:6

I finally decided that the best time for me to have my devotional time was going to be when my baby was taking a nap and my four-year-old was choosing an activity of her own. But her activity would have to be a silent one because Mommy needed to have her devotions. As time went by, she caught on to what I was doing. I realized one day that she was watching me and imitating everything I was doing. Her words brought about deep conviction.

She smiled, and with a soft tender voice, told me, "Mom, when I grow up, I want to be like you." With my heart pounding loud and tears close at hand, I thought, "Who would want to be like me?" Caressing her soft cheeks, I told her, "You grow up to be the best woman of God ever."

You see, devotions can become another "check-off" on our "to-do list." We can lose the whole meaning of devotions in our lives, but "time well spent" can result in a life that others want to imitate.

Patricia M. Zuniga
Calvary Chapel Vida Nueva
Las Vegas, Nevada

March 20

Walking Partners

If we walk in the light as He is in the light, we have fellowship with
one another.
1 John 1:7

If you've ever had the opportunity of walking with someone on a daily
basis, you know how important a walking partner can be. They help to
keep the pace up when you might be tempted to slow down. Ordinary
scenery seems much more enjoyable when shared with someone else,
and then there is the stimulating conversation! For the Christian, spiritual walking implies a step-by-step, day-by-day journey with Jesus Christ.
Each day is filled with new challenges and choices as we yield to His direction and plan for our lives.

Did you know that God has created a tailor-made walking path just
for you? He promises that it will take you directly to the planned designa-
tion, and He Himself will be your personal "walking partner." The road,
He says, will be straight but not always smooth. And yet, His presence
will always be evident to lead you along in your walk of faith. He desires
to walk with you on this journey; you only need to draw near to Him and
follow His lead!

Kym Hindt
Calvary Chapel Houston
Friendswood, Texas

March 21

Be Content No Matter What!

I have learned, in whatsoever state I am, therewith to be content.
Philippians 4:11 KJV

Are you searching for contentment in your life? Have you looked for it in things or even in people, only to find that there's no joy there? That's not a surprise. The things of this world, even the relationships found in this world, cannot meet your deepest needs or fulfill the dreams of your heart. The Lord is the only One capable of doing that.

Whatever your current circumstances might be, good or bad, you need to view them as an opportunity to deepen your relationship with Jesus. God will always use whatever situation you're in to draw you closer to His side. It is possible to live above your circumstances. You can detach yourself from those harmful, anxious concerns that always seem to swallow you up and cause you to fall apart. How? By trusting the Lord, knowing that He'll never take you through anything that is not absolutely necessary; by accepting His plan and cooperating with Him; by choosing to be content; and by seeing Him in all that comes your way.

Determine in your heart and mind that you are going to be content no matter what comes your way because God is in control!

Gail Mays
Calvary Chapel South Bay
Gardena, California

March 22

The Mirror

Do not merely listen to the word, and so deceive yourselves. Do what it says. Anyone who listens to the word but does not do what it says is like a man who looks at his face in a mirror and, after looking at himself, goes away and immediately forgets what he looks like. But the man who looks intently into the perfect law that gives freedom, and continues to do this, not forgetting what he has heard, but doing it—he will be blessed in what he does.

James 1:22–25 NIV

It is our nature to want to look into a mirror each day before we leave the house for work, school, chores, or an appointment. We check the mirror to see our reflection and to see what might need to be fixed in order to be presentable. The mirror does not make us beautiful or ugly, it simply shows us what we really look like. Once we acknowledge what we see, we set about the task of making the necessary repairs or improvements.

Spending time studying and meditating on the Word of God is like looking into God's mirror. If we ask the Lord, He will show us what our hearts are truly like. As a mirror uses light to reflect our true image, God's Word, the only true Light, is a mirror to our soul.

God is never surprised with the discoveries we make about ourselves. He wants us to acknowledge the truth about ourselves and ask Him to do the work in us that only He can do. We cannot fix or change ourselves, but we have a God who delights in changing us into the image of His dear Son.

What do you see when you look into the mirror of God's Word? Do you need forgiveness today? Do you need a Savior? Thanks be to Jesus Christ—He is all we need!

Peggy Kravig
Calvary Chapel Downey
Downey, California

March 23

Got God?

The King of Glory
Who can tell the wonders of His might?
He rules over nations;
But we, His saints, are His Delight

For you are a people holy to the LORD your God. The LORD your God
has chosen you out of all the peoples on the face of the earth to be his
people, his treasured possession.
Deuteronomy 7:6 NIV

What an honor to be chosen of the Lord—to be considered a "treasure" to
Him! When I think of the value that He places on me, it causes me to bow
my heart to Him and ask "Why me, Lord? Who am I that You should see
me as a jewel, a treasure? And if I am a jewel to You, well, Lord You know
how chipped and imperfect I am. What would You want with me?"

"I have loved you with an everlasting love" (Jeremiah 31:3 NIV).
"I have eternal pleasures that await you" (see Psalm 16:11 NIV).
"I am preparing a heavenly home . . ." (John 14:1–4 NIV).

Jesus' love for us is so great that He was obedient unto death on the
cross for our sins of pride, selfishness, rebellion, disobedience. He endured the beatings, the nails, the humiliation, the pain, so that we can live
eternally with Him in heaven (John 3:16). He has given us the joy of our
salvation and a treasury of blessings!

First Corinthians 2:9 says that our minds cannot even conceive the
things that God has prepared for us. He has made us His treasure and has
blessed us with His amazing love.

Patti Bottger
Calvary Chapel Lakeside
Lakeside, California

March 24

Ratios to Be Respected

After the number of the days in which ye searched the land, even forty days, each day for a year, shall ye bear your iniquities, even forty years . . .
Numbers 14:34 KJV

For every day the people of God spied the land in disbelief, they spent a year wandering in the desert. How can someone reap a year of trouble for just disobeying the Lord for one day?

How can just one signature on a loan result in years of indebtedness? How can just a small compromise of flirting result in sexual sin that devastates a family for years? How can that one program put suggestions in your head that could result in perspectives that damage your life for years? How can one day of reading that romance novel plant a year of imaginations and lustful thoughts?

Our days are very important. They make up our years and our years make up our lives.

Teach us to number our days, that we may apply our hearts unto wisdom.
Psalm 90:12 KJV

If we realize that the way we handle even small things can have radical consequences, we might very well . . . "continue in the fear of the LORD all the day" (Proverbs 23:17 RSV).

The Lord created days, giving us a pace in which to live consecrated lives. May we listen today for the Lord to order our steps, and may we respond in obedience. Not only can rebellious decisions reap years of negative consequences, but individual steps of obedience can reap years of blessings.

Maureen Schaffer
First Love Calvary Chapel
Whittier, California

March 25

All Day Long

⤋

I call on you all day long. Bring joy to your servant, for to you, O
Lord, I lift up my soul.
Psalm 86:3–4 NIV

Sometimes life is so busy! Up at 6:15, shower, dress, read a short section
of Scripture, dash off a quick prayer, prepare breakfast, supervise chores
and home schooling, plan meals, throw in a load of laundry, and answer
the never-ending stream of phone calls.

After one particularly busy and difficult day, I moaned to my husband,
"Where is the peace and the joy that's supposed to overflow from my life?"
He hugged me and promised to supervise the kids the next afternoon so I
could spend some extended time with the Lord.

Psalm 86 helped me see that I needed to make some changes. If I
wanted to experience joy and peace in the midst of my busy life, then I
must call on the Lord all day long and open my heart and mind to the
Spirit's voice. I need to continually lift up my soul to the Lord. I don't
need solitude to communicate with the Lord . . . I just need to call out to
Him and have a heart tuned in to hear His voice.

You are God my Savior, and my hope is in you all day long.
Psalm 25:5 NIV

Carrie Turansky
Calvary Chapel Mercer County
Mercer County, New Jersey

Listen, Recognize, Obey

And Samuel said, "Speak, for Thy servant is listening."
1 Samuel 3:10 NASB

As David was "a man after God's own heart," we should desire to be women after God's own heart. We need to get to a place in life where we truly desire to have the ears of Samuel—ears that hear and recognize only God's voice the first time He speaks.

During the beginning of Samuel's ministry, God had to call him three times before he responded (1 Samuel 3:8). But as we move on to chapter 16, Samuel has matured. He recognized God's voice, then immediately listened and obeyed when God told Samuel to anoint David as king despite his own intuition or feelings (Samuel had thought that Jesse's son Eliab would be anointed king).

May we all be able to listen, recognize, and obey God when He speaks.

For the Lord does not see as man sees; for man looks at the outward
appearance, but the LORD looks at the heart.
1 Samuel 16:7

Barbara Gil
Calvary Chapel of the Redwoods
Smith River, California

My Heart Stands in Awe

But my heart stands in awe of Your word.
Psalm 119:161

What is more precious to you than anything in the whole world? What do you love?

I love Your commandments more than gold, yes, than fine gold!
Psalm 119:127

God's Word is more precious than gold. The very heart of God is written in a book so that we can soak in His every Word and have life in His name. Every year, as I read it from cover-to-cover, my heart stands in awe. Every morning I pray, "Lord, give me Jesus."

The apostle John wrote in 1 John 1:1–4 that he had seen with his own eyes the Word of Life, his hands had handled the Word of Life, he bore witness of the Word of Life, and was declaring Him then to us.

But these are written that you may believe that Jesus is the Christ, the
Son of God, and that believing you may have life in His name.
John 20:31

Read Psalms 19 and 119 and list all the descriptions of the Word. Schedule a daily habit of studying the most incredible, heart-changing book you'll ever read. May God's Word be more precious to you than anything else in the whole world. May your heart stand in awe of His Word!

Vi Goodrich
Horizon Christian Fellowship
Indianapolis, Indiana

March 28

How Do I Look?

Looking unto Jesus the author and finisher of our faith.
Hebrews 12:2 KJV

Now that I am about to turn forty-six, I am noticing little changes on my body, particularly on my face. What used to be called "beauty marks" are now large, unsightly moles. I have wrinkles around my mouth and eyes, and recently I've noticed that my right eyelid is beginning to sag. It was really bothering me for about a week, when I decided to turn my obsession into a prayer. I came across Proverbs 4:25–26 during morning devotions:

> Let your eyes look straight ahead, and your eyelids look right before you. Ponder the path of your feet, and let all your ways be established.

God spoke to my heart, reminding me that His thoughts and ways are much higher than mine. God didn't care about my sagging eyelid as much as He cared about my spiritual vision. He lovingly convicted me that my real problem was my perspective. I was looking at my past with resentment, my present with fear, and my future with dread. I looked up and read the postcard that hangs in my prayer closet:

> Look back . . . thank Him;
> Look around . . . serve Him;
> Look forward . . . trust Him;
> Look up . . . expect Him.

My right eyelid still droops, but my spiritual vision is now repaired—and that's what matters anyway!

Lynette Mello
Calvary Chapel Livermore
Livermore, California

March 29

Where Do You Run?

The name of the LORD is a strong tower; the righteous run to it and
are safe.
Proverbs 18:10

My husband, answering the call from the Lord, moved us twenty-five hundred miles from the comfort of family and friends to southern Utah. We hadn't lived here six months when Jeremiah, our youngest son, developed a serious infection. His body was rejecting necessary hardware that had been placed in his chest a year before our move.

Following the doctor's orders, the nurse at the local clinic inserted a PIC line into Jeremiah's arm. She explained the procedure for administering his medication over the next six weeks, emphasizing the importance of punctuality. The realization of the severity of this infection, along with the four-week lapse until our health insurance kicked in, caused me to run, not to my Jesus, but to my husband Joe, saying, "Where is God in this?"

He led me to Jesus, reminding me of His presence, and reminding me that He is to be our strength. (Psalm 46:7). Joe led us in prayer, then called the hospital. Within fifteen minutes, it was official: our son met all the criteria necessary to receive this lifesaving medication for free.

I learned a valuable lesson that day. The strength and peace found in Joe, I was to find in Jesus. Had I failed a time of testing? No—I had passed, for I learned to run to God—not to man.

Terri Carroll
Calvary Chapel Cedar City
Cedar City, Utah

March 30

Worry

~~~

"For this reason I say to you, do not be anxious for your life . . ."
Matthew 6:25 NASB

So many concerns can consume our lives that we may often find ourselves spending more time worrying about our present circumstances than we do enjoying what God has already provided for us. Single people wonder when they'll meet their future mate, young marrieds can be concerned with starting a family, parents of teens often worry where their kids are and if they'll keep walking with Jesus. We then reach midlife, face the empty nest, and wonder what our purpose for living is, as we then turn the corner to watch our aging parents reach the place where they become dependent on us.

What worries you today? Have you missed today's blessings for tomorrow's concerns? Matthew 6:33 tells us to "Seek first His kingdom and His righteousness; and all these things shall be added to you" (NASB). Jesus promises to take care of us, but we must put Him first in our lives and then trust Him to meet our needs according to His will.

Finally, brethren, whatever is true, whatever is honorable, whatever is right, whatever is pure, whatever is lovely, whatever is of good repute, if there is any excellence and if anything worthy of praise, let your mind dwell on these things.
Philippians 4:8 NASB

Becky Brown
Calvary Chapel Central Phoenix
Phoenix, Arizona

March 31

Satisfied from Above

My people shall be satisfied with My goodness, says the LORD.
Jeremiah 31:14

To live in America is to be continually bombarded with advertisements. Although annoying at times, these distractions do serve one useful purpose: they incessantly remind us how dissatisfying life is apart from Jesus Christ. The unregenerate man continually searches for the latest gizmo on the market, hoping that it will finally bring lasting satisfaction to his empty soul. There always seems to be something newer, bigger, or faster—like a carrot dangling before his eyes.

Maybe you too have found yourself caught up in the striving of this culture. Perhaps you have been looking again to circumstances, relationships, material possessions, or even ministry to fill the holes in your heart.

Run back to Jesus, my friend. Abide in Him and allow His everlasting love to consume you. As you rest in your Father's arms today and allow Him to meet your every need, your heart will once again rejoice in complete contentment. For "my God shall supply all your need according to His riches in glory by Christ Jesus" (Philippians 4:19).

For He satisfies the longing soul, and fills the hungry soul with goodness.
Psalm 107:9

Kathy Morales
Calvary Chapel Lone Mountain
Las Vegas, Nevada

April 1

Fool's Gold

───❧───

"The devil . . . speaks from his own resources, for he is a liar and the father of it."
John 8:44

Isn't it interesting how something evil can look so attractive? As he did with Adam and Eve, the Enemy can make the bondage of sin look like freedom. Satan tempted them to eat the fruit and that which Eve thought was going to satisfy and make her happy turned out to be bondage. And you know what? Satan laughed his head off at Adam and Eve. If anyone knew that we can never be equal to God, Satan did, but he knew that he could tempt us to want to become like God and we would fall for it hook, line, and sinker.

John 8:44 says that Satan is a liar; lying is his native tongue. Satan will tell us that something is "gold," but we have to remember that everything he says is a lie. What looks like gold might just be the shiny mineral, pyrite. During the gold rush days, people would mistake pyrite for gold. When they took it to experts to be analyzed, it turned out to be worthless. What Satan offers is the same. It might glitter and catch our eyes, but it is not valuable. Isn't it interesting that another name for pyrite is "fool's gold?"

Rose Beal
First Love Calvary Chapel
Whittier, California

April Snow

Purge me with hyssop, and I shall be clean: wash me, and I shall be
whiter than snow.
Psalm 51:7 KJV

I love to meditate on Jesus—His resurrection and our promised new life—
through the visuals of spring. One April day, an untimely snow storm
moved me deeper still. The massive amounts of fallen snow reminded me
of Isaiah 1:18:

> Come now, and let us reason together, saith the LORD: though your
> sins be as scarlet, they shall be as white as snow.

As I watched all the budding branches and flowers bend with the
heaviness of the snow, I realized, by their physical weightiness, the greater
significance of the cross. When Jesus sees me, He sees white. The purity
we've received in the Lord's eyes is far more significant than my hopes of
having new life.

When I accept His payment for my sin, Jesus covers me like a blanket of snow. My new life would not be the same without His covering.
I would still have my filthy rags of self-righteousness, accomplishments,
pride, rationalizations, or excuses. Apart from His Holy Spirit, I am simply a fool, but in Him I am honored (Proverbs 26:1). He not only takes
us, He takes us as His own beloved (Ephesians 1:6).

Reason with Him, and allow Him to cleanse your heart.

> Create in me a clean heart, O God; and renew a right spirit within
> me.
> *Psalm 51:10 KJV*

Additional Reading: Psalm 51:7–17; 147:15–18; Psalm 148:7–14

Francesca Osigian
Calvary Chapel Asheville
Asheville, North Carolina

April 3

Amazing Grace

❧

My grace is sufficient for you, for My strength is made perfect in weakness.
2 Corinthians 12:9

The word *grace* was used by the Greeks to speak of beauty, like the beauty of a rose in full bloom. Later they used it to refer to something that gives beauty, like parents giving just the right gift to their child and then seeing the child radiate with joy. God's grace gives us that kind of beauty.

Shortly after being diagnosed with Adenoid Cystic Carcinoma, a rare form of breast cancer, I decided not to ask the question "Why?" but instead, "Lord, how do You want to use this illness to glorify Your name?" In the middle of my twenty-eight-day stay in the hospital, my veins started collapsing from the toxicity of the medications. The IV specialist asked my husband Bob to sing a song as she administered *another* needle into one of my few useable veins. As tears rolled down my cheeks, Bob started singing "Amazing Grace." Immediately, I felt peace, courage, and healing fill my body and soul. Miraculously, I didn't feel the needle. With tear-filled eyes, my nurse said, "I'm shaking—that was so beautiful." The next morning my previously high temperature had dropped down to normal.

I experienced Jesus' compassion and grace that night as my husband sang "Amazing Grace," and I was comforted in the reminder that His grace is sufficient for me.

LaVon Fromm
North Valley Calvary Chapel
Yuba City, California

April 4

Giants versus Faith

And Caleb stilled the people before Moses, and said, Let us go up at
once, and possess it; for we are well able to overcome it.
Numbers 13:30 KJV

Here we see an incredible example of what focusing on our fears can do
in the long run in our lives. Those sent in to spy out the land for Moses,
except Caleb and Joshua, reaped a lifetime of wanderings but days of disbelief.

When we take our days, our precious days, and focus on how we
are "not able to go up against the people; for they are stronger than we"
(Numbers 13:31 KJV), and we bring up an evil report within our medita-
tions, we become like these men and set ourselves up for the consequences
of unbelief.

The Lord tells us that "without faith it is impossible to please him . . ."
(Hebrews 11:6 KJV). Many times the giants in the land—and they may
truly be giants—blind us to a confidence we have available in Christ, a
confidence that is well able to dominate the voices and pressures facing us.
Faith is not faith unless it matches itself against what is seen.

Won't you make a concentrated effort to take every thought captive
today and echo Caleb's conclusion after he saw the incredible obstacles
and chose to put his faith in the Lord?

Only rebel not ye against the LORD, neither fear ye the people of the
land . . . the LORD is *with us*: fear them not.
Numbers 14:9 KJV, emphasis added

Maureen Schaffer
First Love Calvary Chapel
Whittier, California

April 5

Grace upon Grace

⟨✦⟩

For the grace of God . . . has appeared to all men, teaching us
that, denying ungodliness and worldly lusts, we should live soberly,
righteously, and godly in the present age.
Titus 2:11–13

In Galatians 5:17, Paul tells about the struggle within every born-again
believer.

For the flesh lusts against the Spirit, and the Spirit against the flesh;
and these are contrary to one another, so that you do not do the
things that you wish.

We are all faced with this dilemma.

We are *commanded* in Galatians 5:16 to "walk in the Spirit." The good
news is that God never commands us to do anything without providing
the resource! Titus 2:11 says we have been given *grace* for salvation. But it
doesn't stop there. Once we are saved, we can boldly go before the throne
of grace for daily living—grace to help in time of need, grace upon grace.
Grace to teach us to say no to the flesh. Grace to teach us to glorify God in
all that we do. When we try to obey His commands in our own strength,
that is pride, and we eventually fail.

There is only one way to obtain grace. Peter says in 1 Peter 5:5 that
"God resists the proud, but gives grace to the humble."

I pray you will humbly go before the Lord and seek His grace for
whatever struggle you may have today.

Sally Van Wick
Calvary Chapel Bible Fellowship
Temecula, California

April 6

But Lord, How?

He said to me, "My grace is sufficient for you, for my power is made
perfect in weakness." Therefore I will boast all the more gladly about
my weaknesses, so that Christ's power may rest on me.
2 Corinthians 12:9 NIV

As a pastor's wife, I've always felt a very strong call on my life to help other
women with their Christian walk. However, I was sick for years with an
illness that barely allowed me to get out of bed. I was before the Lord,
sobbing, asking how I could minister to other women. "Have You made
a mistake?" I was sure He had, because I was incapable of fulfilling the
burden placed upon my heart. He was faithful to remind me His callings
are irrevocable (Romans 11:29).

I was miserable trying to do it in my own strength. I asked the Lord to
take me home to Him. God spoke clearly, "Read Philippians!" Paul also
wanted to be with the Lord, but God told him it was necessary to remain
in the body to benefit the people for their progress and joy in the faith.

I've found that in allowing my weakness to bring death to the flesh,
Christ's power is sufficient for me.

When I am weak, then I am strong.
2 Corinthians 12:10 NIV

For to me, to live is Christ and to die is gain.
Philippians 1:21 NIV

Kimberly Chikeles
Calvary Chapel Saint Paul
Saint Paul, Minnesota

April 7

Broken Things

The sacrifices of God are a broken spirit; a broken and contrite heart,
O God, you will not despise.
Psalm 51:17 NIV

When we are broken and grieving over our sin, God notices! A broken spirit and a contrite heart are precious to Him. A few years ago, I had a collector plate on my piano that a gust of wind had knocked off and broken. When my daughter Johnna saw me ready to toss it in the trash, she told me that I should glue it. I didn't think it was worth gluing as the picture on it would be marred. At that she remarked, "Mom, I love the things of yours that you have glued back together because it means that you loved it enough to put it back together." My heart melted.

I could only ponder God's heart that afternoon, how He loves the areas in my life that have been put back together. The fact that they are there, with their scars and memories, only reminds me that God loved me enough to put me back together.

Are you in a time of brokenness? Perhaps there is a sin in your life that you still find yourself grieving over. Surrender your heart into the hands of your heavenly Father who loves to put you back together again. You are not worthless; you are precious to Him!

Lynda Kelly
Calvary Chapel Bullhead City
Bullhead City, Arizona

When God's Plan Seems Impossible

Oh, the depths of the riches both of the wisdom and knowledge
of God! How unsearchable are His judgments and His ways past
finding out!
Romans 11:33

"For My thoughts are not your thoughts, nor are your ways My ways,"
says the LORD. "For as the heavens are higher than the earth, so are My
ways higher than your ways, and My thoughts than your thoughts."
Isaiah 55:8–9

When I look at some of the circumstances in our lives and the ways the
Lord causes us to trust Him, these are the passages of Scripture that come
to my mind.

And as I look at Joshua's life, the testing of his faith, and the miraculous way God destroyed the enemy, I praise and thank the Lord for His
great and simple ways—the ways that confound the wise. God gave Joshua
a simple plan: march around Jericho once each day for six days, and on
the seventh day march around seven times, blow the trumpets, shout, and
the walls of the city will fall down flat (Joshua 6:1–5).

Just think that plan through! It doesn't make sense! It's not logical! It
is impossible, even ridiculous, yet Joshua didn't try to figure it all out. He
simply trusted and obeyed.

What do you do when the Lord gives you a plan or direction that
seems simple, even ridiculous, and doesn't look like it would make any
difference at all?

We are to trust the Lord and lean not on our own understanding.
When we do, the walls will fall down.

Karin Kyle
Calvary Chapel Modesto
Modesto, California

April 9

Clearing the Clutter

Therefore, . . . let us lay aside every weight, and the sin which so easily ensnares us, and let us run with endurance the race that is set before us.
Hebrews 12:1

My son had acquired quite a few toys. Since our home was small, I decided to pack some up to clear the clutter and preserve their novelty. I placed them in a cardboard box in the living room with the intention of putting the box away. That never happened, and every day I would walk around that box. You would think that the mere size, which took up half of the walking space, would have prompted me to action, but a strange thing happened. I walked around that box so many times that I didn't even see it anymore. It had become part of the décor.

In life we can become immune to the box of things that we know the Lord wants us to pack away for another season. They may not necessarily be bad things, just things that keep our lives so cluttered that we don't leave space for the Lord. The Bible calls them weights that hinder our ability to run the race. I decided that day to move the box, and through prayer, to pack up my clutter, make room to run, and enjoy the newness of my relationship with God.

Diane Coy
Calvary Chapel Fort Lauderdale
Fort Lauderdale, Florida

April 10

Confident in Jesus

❧

[Jesus] said to them, "Why are you fearful?"
Matthew 8:26

So many times when we are going through trials, we become consumed with them. But our faithful God tells us to "be strong and of good courage." That admonition certainly is a total contradiction to the nature of our flesh. Right away, we start worrying, and if we don't stop, we soon lose our peace entirely and carry on as if Jesus is totally unaware of what is going on.

We are a privileged people to have the Holy Spirit indwelling us. How awesome that Jesus is in us, that He is for us, and that He even knows our troubles before we do. In His faithfulness, He has prepared a plan to get us through our trials. When clouds come, we cannot see the sunshine; when seeds are planted, we cannot see the flowers. Yet in time, the clouds do pass and the sun shines; the seeds do produce beautiful flowers. So it is with our lives; our trials aren't in vain or designed to hurt us, but are happening for a purpose, to prosper us.

Today ask Jehovah to give you His courage to face your trouble in His strength. He is devoted to you and sees you as precious. He will see you through every storm. I pray you have the courage to trust our almighty God for whatever your need is today.

Angela Tomasso
Calvary Chapel Westside
Spencerport, New York

April 11

The Jesus You Can Trust

Behold, your King is coming to you, lowly, and sitting on a donkey.
Matthew 21:5

What is the first impression that comes to your mind when you think about God? Maybe you imagine someone who is angry, unapproachable, and far away. If so, you are not alone. God understands this and so He sent Jesus. Jesus came near and lived low. He was the best the Father had to offer, and yet He placed Himself on the lowest shelf.

Now close your eyes and imagine yourself in the crowd as Jesus drew near. This scene is called the triumphal entry, and yet, it is far from the world's perspective of a victorious and authoritative ruler coming into power.

He came into Jerusalem riding a borrowed donkey—small, untrained, and unimpressive. As He rode along, even the children could touch Him and look into His eyes. People responded by taking off their outer garments. There was an atmosphere of abandon and vulnerability. Worship was spontaneous. Cries of adoration came from deep within their hearts.

Consider perhaps the most important concept of this verse: "Your [lowly] King . . . is coming to you." Matthew tells us to "behold." This image of our gentle Savior needs to sink into the deepest part of our being.

As Jesus approached the city, He stood over it and wept, "O Jerusalem, Jerusalem, . . . how often I have longed to gather your children together, as a hen gathers her chicks under her wings, but you were not willing" (Matthew 23:37 NIV).

Jesus was so close to Jerusalem, but Jerusalem was so far from Jesus. Today, the same choice is set before you—intimacy or distance. The almighty God has come to be your Prince of Peace. Will you draw near to

Him? Will you reach out to touch Him, to see Him as He really is? Will you take off the outer cloaks that isolate and insulate the real you? Will you let Him ride into your day? Will you give Him a "triumphal entry"?

Debbi Bryson
Calvary Chapel Church Planting Missions
Oceanside, California

April 12

Christ's Ambassadors

He has committed to us the message of reconciliation. We are therefore Christ's ambassadors, as though God were making his appeal through us.

2 Corinthians 5:19–20 NIV

An ambassador's assignment is to represent personally and accurately a kingdom and its leader. This entails an honest representation of his leadership, including his character and values.

Incredibly, it is our high calling and great privilege, as disciples of Jesus, to take the message of reconciliation to the world. As those who have experienced the miracle of being restored to favor with our heavenly Father, we have been given the responsibility of representing Him to those who are still estranged from Him.

As we take the good news to a lost and dying world, we need to keep in mind the sober duties of our appointment. We must remember that we are representing our King. It is up to us to display His heart and character to those we meet. In order to do so, we must first know Him. The only way to know someone well is to spend time with him or her. He has given us His Word, and He desires to spend time with us. As we spend time alone with Him in worship, prayer, Bible study, and meditation, we begin to know His character and His heart.

As we interact with others daily, and as they watch us, are we accurately depicting Him?

Dea Gros
Calvary Chapel Silver City
Silver City, New Mexico

April 13

What Are You Waiting For?

Wait on the LORD; be of good courage, and He shall strengthen your heart.

Psalm 27:14

We live in an instant generation: a culture of fast food, multi-tasking, and immediate gratification, with drive-up tellers, drive-through restaurants and pharmacies, cell phones, and lattes-to-go. We don't have to do much waiting . . . or do we?

Perhaps in the busyness of daily life, these conveniences help us to get the "business of life" accomplished. But what about those long-term items we wait for? What are *you* waiting for? A husband? Children? A healing? A loved one to come to Jesus?

Ephesians 5:15–16 says "See then that you walk circumspectly, not as fools but as wise, redeeming the time, because the days are evil." The Lord does not always reveal His time frame, although He has every detail of your life covered. In His time, all will be fulfilled. He's waiting to see what *you* will do with this time He is giving *you* to *wait*.

Do you want to be courageous? Do you want to experience ongoing strength straight from the mighty One Himself? Thank Him for these opportunities to watch Him work as you wait on Him!

"Occupy till I come."
Luke 19:13 KJV

Lynn Fernandez
Calvary Chapel Twin Cities
Bloomington, Minnesota

April 14

Jesus—Our Servant King

. . . and took upon him the form of a servant . . .
Philippians 2:7 KJV

Jesus said, "If you want to be great in the kingdom, you must become a servant of all" (see Mark 9:35; 10:44). So, seek greatness. Seek to be a servant. Remember what Jesus did on the night before He went to the cross? He dined with His disciples and washed their feet, including those of the man who was about to betray Him! He wanted to place within their hearts and minds a picture of servanthood they would never forget. When He finished, He commissioned them to go and wash one another's feet. In essence, He sent them into the world to follow His example of servanthood. For the true disciple, the only response to this commission is obedience. How far will you go to be obedient to the Lord?

It's a joy to wash the feet of those you love and care about, but what about the difficult ones? Is there a Judas in your life, someone who has hurt or betrayed you? Maybe there's someone you love and they've rejected you. No matter what the circumstances, you are commissioned to wash their feet. That's the true test of genuine servanthood! The example Jesus gave was one that included all—not just those that you're sure will appreciate you and accept your love—but all. Being a servant will never make sense to you, but it makes perfect sense to God.

Gail Mays
Calvary Chapel South Bay
Gardena, California

April 15

My Great Gain

But godliness with contentment is great gain.
1 Timothy 6:6 NIV

That is not the same jingle I hear from the radio and TV ads. "I deserve a break today; I can have it my way; and I can get it before the end of the day!"

God tells me true wealth is in striving for His good character, and in it, happily finding all my desires satisfied. I can do this when the next Mervyn's sale begins; I just avoid the mall to keep my lust for stuff in check. But trusting God for my difficult circumstances is a greater challenge. I find myself begging God to change my life rather than asking Him to change me. As I speak only to God about my concerns and ask for His help to practice godly character traits of "love, joy, peace, patience, kindness, goodness, faithfulness, gentleness, and self-control" (Galatians 5:22 NASB), I stumble into freedom from cares about my uncomfortable state. I have no worries. I exchange contentiousness for contentment, and concern about the things around me for more of Him. My status is rich in Jesus because God has become my "great gain." I am completely satisfied.

The LORD is my shepherd, I shall not want. He makes me lie down in green pastures; He leads me beside quiet waters. He restores my soul; He guides me in the paths of righteousness for His name's sake.
Psalm 23:1–3 NASB

Jeneane Herrera
Calvary Chapel Las Vegas
Las Vegas, New Mexico

April 16

Thirsting for More

"But whoever drinks of the water that I shall give him shall never
thirst."
John 4:14 NASB

Do you find yourself thirsting for something fresh and new in your life,
but you aren't sure what it is that you need? Jesus said in Matthew 5:6,
"Blessed are those who hunger and thirst for righteousness, for they shall
be satisfied" (NASB).

The Samaritan woman filled her life with other men, until Jesus came
into the picture. Jesus didn't abandon her because of her choices or lifestyle, but He met her where she was, and as a result, she allowed Him to
fill that void. The world is constantly tugging at us to seek greater satisfaction, but Jesus desires that we find our fulfillment in Him. Take time to
go to Jesus and ask Him to fill any emptiness you may have with more of
Him.

As the deer pants for the water brooks, so my soul pants for you,
O God.
Psalm 42:1 NASB

Becky Brown
Calvary Chapel Central Phoenix
Phoenix, Arizona

April 17

Consider It All Joy

And the peace of God, which transcends all understanding, will guard
your hearts and your minds in Christ Jesus.
Philippians 4:7 NIV

I once heard the story of a man who was going through physical and spiritual trials, one upon another. He began to feel sorry for himself. Then, one day, while sitting in a college classroom, he noticed that one of his classmates had an ear-to-ear smile on her face. This continued for many weeks. The trouble was that he knew that she, too, was going through trial after trial. A few months later, he stopped her and asked how she could be so happy while going through trials. She turned to him and said, "It is my Father's will that I be joyful always." Just then he realized that he had taken his eyes off Jesus.

How about you? Are you going through something that has caused you to take your eyes off of Jesus? First Thessalonians 5:16–18 says, "Be joyful always; pray continually; give thanks in all circumstances, for this is God's will for you in Christ Jesus" (NIV). I've learned in the past to keep my eyes off my situation and on Jesus.

For the joy of the LORD is your strength.
Nehemiah 8:10 NIV

Leisa Carter
Calvary Chapel Lake Havasu City
Lake Havasu City, Arizona

April 18

Moved with Compassion

But when He saw the multitudes, He was moved with compassion
for them.
Matthew 9:36

Though we live in a world filled with pain and suffering, we often get caught up in our own little worlds, obsessed with *self*. A life of *self* causes us to be blind and unaware of the sufferings of others. Many times, because it is easier, we just choose not to see.

Jesus set the example to follow. He denied Himself, looking to the needs of others first. He took time to truly see and to be aware of others. He did not just see people, He saw hearts in need and was moved with compassion. His heart was stirred to take action.

How can we do this? We deny *self*. When this process begins, our eyes will see as Jesus sees—with a heart of compassion. That compassion must also move us to take action. We can act through prayer or with direct contact. Our actions may not result in changing a suffering world or even the multitudes. But if we are willing, we can bring comfort to many, one soul at a time.

Blessed be the God . . . of all comfort, who comforts us in all our
tribulation, that we may be able to comfort those who are in any
trouble, with the comfort with which we ourselves are comforted
by God.
2 Corinthians 1:3

Mary Grigsby
Calvary Chapel Golden Springs
Diamond Bar, California

April 19

Eternity in Our Hearts

He has also set eternity in the hearts of men . . .
Ecclesiastes 3:11 NIV

You know, missionaries have always been seen as birds of another feather. And maybe in some ways it's true. But when it comes right down to it, we all have wants, dreams, and desires. As God began tugging at my heart to serve Him in Colombia, South America, the question arose, "Will I obey?"

For a missionary, the hardest adjustments aren't so much changes in food, language, or culture. The most painful thing is leaving family behind.

One day before my departure, my father said to me, "Hallie, the Indians in Arizona need Jesus too; why do you have to go so far away?" I answered him, "Daddy, if I wasn't absolutely sure of eternity, I could never leave. But I know this life is but a breath, and what is eternal lasts forever. We have all eternity to be together."

May we always keep that hope, and may our treasures always be in Him.

"For where your treasure is, there your heart will be also."
Matthew 6:21 NIV

Hallie Martinez
Calvary Chapel Golden Springs
Diamond Bar, California

April 20

Keep It Simple, Sister!

These searched for their family records, but they could not find them
and so were excluded from the priesthood as unclean.
Ezra 2:62 NIV

When Jeff and I got married thirty years ago, we had a tiny little house. But I had a "junk drawer" that held all those little "things" that I just knew I would use someday. As our family grew, so did the junk drawer. Soon it became the "junk closet" and then the "junk garage." Why did I feel the need to save all that stuff? I began to realize that trying to organize the clutter was keeping me from precious devotional time with the Lord. I've found that clutter can't be organized, it just needs to be given away.

After the Jews were freed from Babylonian captivity, they needed the papers that proved who the priests were; but they had lost them in that worldly city. The clutter of Babylon and captivity had stolen what was really precious. Are you lost in the clutter of your home? Is God's Word mixed in with a pile of papers and junk? Do you feel captive by all your "things?" Remember, we're pilgrims passing through. It's all going to burn anyway.

Karyn Johnson
Calvary Chapel Downey
Downey, California

April 21

Walk Not in Their Way[10]

My son, if sinners entice thee, consent thou not. . . . My son, walk not thou in the way with them; refrain thy foot from their path.
Proverbs 1:10, 15 KJV

What kind of company do you keep? Are you spending time with friends who compromise their walks with the Lord? Are you tempted to walk in *their* ways with them?

My husband and I have seen many who have compromised their walks by ungodly friendships, ignoring counsel. They thought they would be able to handle it. They thought they would not get taken down, that *they* would be the strong ones. Now they no longer walk with the Lord, or they are suffering consequences that God never intended for them.

Are you playing with fire in the Enemy's territory? Stop, and refrain your foot from his path.

Can a man take fire in his bosom, and his clothes not be burned?
Proverbs 6:27 KJV
Wherefore let him that thinketh he standeth take heed lest he fall.
1 Corinthians 10:12 KJV

Patricia Maciel
Calvary Chapel Downey
Downey, California

April 22

What Shall I Wear Today?

"... Wherewithal shall we be clothed?"
Matthew 6:31 KJV

Fashions make a statement. Every time we step out in public, we are making a statement. Without words it seems almost impossible to have that much power over our communication. But fashion does. What image comes to mind when you think of *Victoria's Secret?* Sexy, fit bodies, beauty, wealth, and acceptance. The power of suggestion tears right through our desires and straight into our lusts—just as the Serpent's words deceived Eve.

Eve's sin matches ours to a tee—she wanted something that she did not have. The Serpent's goal was to get Eve's eyes off her blessings and onto desires she didn't know she had. As a result, she was led into sin.

For all that is in the world, the lust of the flesh, and the lust of the
eyes, and the pride of life, is not of the Father, but is of the world.
1 John 2:16 KJV

Instead of putting your desires first, perhaps take a brief moment to check what *really* represents you best.

Thou art clothed with honour and majesty.
Psalm 104:1 KJV

If the words of my mouth are saying, "Christ first," then my dress should be too.

Let the words of my mouth, and the meditation of my heart, be
acceptable.
Psalm 19:14 KJV

Cara Earp
Calvary Chapel Arcadia
Arcadia, California

April 23

Conversations with God

Pray continually.
1 Thessalonians 5:17 NIV

Do you put prayer in time slots—praying each morning, at bedtime, and at meals in between? God wants to be in continual communication with us as He was with Jesus Christ, not scheduled into our days like a luncheon date. This means praying whenever the Holy Spirit prompts us to lift up a person or situation in prayer. Often the telephone will ring and someone will have a concern or problem. A homeless man walking down the street might grab our attention, or we will remember a friend's job interview or surgical procedure at the appointed time, or be blessed by good fortune or circumstances. All are promptings for prayer.

Recently I spoke with a man who had kayaked over six thousand miles from Mexico to South America. The purpose of his trip was to remove the distractions of modern American life so that he might communicate more effectively with God. For most, stepping away from the demands of work, family, ministries, social obligations, and household tasks is not an option. Yet, these very demands provide incentive for prayer. Newspaper headlines, delays at the check-out stand, traffic jams, piles of laundry, and soccer games are all reasons to have conversations with God.

Susan Cort Johnson
Calvary Chapel Westwood
Westwood, California

April 24

I'm with You Always

He will not leave you nor forsake you.
Deuteronomy 31:6

In February 2001, my husband Joe almost died in our hotel room. He was shaking hard, as if he was having a seizure, and his body became twisted. After turning the light on and getting a clear look at his appearance—his purple face and eyes rolling backwards—I panicked. I told God, "I'm scared; I don't know what to do; I don't even know where we are!"

That's when I lost it. Joe reassured me, "Honey, be strong: just pray!" I begged the Lord not to let him suffer if He were going to take Joe home and asked Him to wait until we returned home; but I acknowledged that His will be done. Then I heard a voice say, "Don't be afraid, I'm with you. I will never leave you nor forsake you." There was no doubt in my mind that I was hearing God's voice. I regained strength, courage, and peace of mind knowing He was with me.

Wherever you are, whatever your situation or difficulties, you can be assured of this: God is with you.

Surely the arm of the LORD is not too short to save, nor his ear too dull to hear.
Isaiah 59:1 NIV

Is any one of you in trouble? He should pray.
James 5:13 NIV

Ruby Sinnott
North Park Christian Fellowship
San Diego, California

April 25

Press On

～⁓～

... Christ in you, the hope of glory.
Colossians 1:27 KJV

Riding on a plane several years ago, I read a book about a man who desired a victorious Christian walk and about how God accomplished that in him. Desiring a closer walk with Jesus, I began to pray, asking God to take all of me: my hands, my feet, every area of my life. I asked that I would know that He truly lives inside of me and that through my life, His will and purposes might be accomplished.

We must absolutely surrender to His will, bringing every sin to the cross of Christ, no matter how small we may think it is. No sin is worth broken fellowship with our Savior.

Christ dwells within us as believers, giving us power over sin and temptation through the Holy Spirit as we yield ourselves to Him. Victory comes only because Christ dwells within. Can you say along with Paul:

> Brethren, I count not myself to have apprehended: but this one thing I do, forgetting those things which are behind, and reaching forth unto those things which are before, I press toward the mark for the prize of the high calling of God in Christ Jesus.
> *Philippians 3:13–14 KJV*

It is time for us to heed the call of God and press on to higher ground.

Sandi Chappell
Calvary Chapel Greece
Rochester, New York

April 26

Actions Speak Louder Than Words

But be ye doers of the word, and not hearers only, deceiving your own
selves.
James 1:22 KJV

When Bill and I lived in Southern California some twenty-five years ago, my friend Pat taught me the basic principles of quilting. Since that time I've made a few quilts, mostly for my family. It seems as though there is always a quilt that I'm working on, one on my quilt frame being basted, and thoughts in my mind of the one I'll do next.

Most quilters have a fabric stash and buy fabrics according to their color value—that is, light, medium, or dark. Clearly though, what good is that stash of mine if I never actually make a quilt with it? No one would ever experience the beauty, warmth, and comfort a quilt can give.

It's like that with the Word of God. You can stash it away by memorizing verses and cut it apart by studying the Greek and Hebrew, parsing the verbs, and getting involved with Bible study, and yet, never experience the beauty, warmth, and comfort of God's Word. It's only in applying His Word to your life experiences that you get the full benefit that God has provided for you. Otherwise, you live the Christian life "deceiving your own selves." Actions speak louder than words, especially when it comes to calling yourself a Christian and living in such a way that others know you are a Christian.

Rosemary Gallatin
Calvary Chapel of the Finger Lakes
Farmington, New York

April 27

A Peaceful Princess

Find rest, O my soul, in God alone; my hope comes from him.
Psalm 62:5 NIV

Since I was a little girl, I have been spoon-fed Cinderella stories. Most likely you have too. The conditioning process has taken root, and we are now programmed to believe that when we get married, our handsome prince charming is going to take away all hardship, and we will live happily ever after. Such thinking is self-serving (James 3:14–16). Expecting another person to kowtow to all our desires or to meet all our emotional needs is unrealistic. What happens when prince charming is a royal pain and there is trouble in "paradise" (1 Corinthians 7:28)? If your expectation is in your husband, you will be disappointed. Hope deferred makes the heart sick (Proverbs 13:12), unfulfilled desires lead to quarrels (James 4:1–12), and anger can lead to severe emotional anguish and mental instability (Psalm 73:21–22).

Sarah, whose name means "princess," had a completely different perspective. Her hope was not in a romantic, thoughtful husband, but in God. Sarah laid down her rights to be treated like a princess and instead chose to be a servant (1 Peter 3:5–6). Sarah was a peaceful princess. You too can be a woman with a gentle, peaceful spirit if you are willing to lay down your rights to be the "princess" and instead choose to put your hope in God.

Nancy Charles
Calvary Chapel Charleston
Charleston, South Carolina

April 28

Fingerprints

❧

You knit me together in my mother's womb.
Psalm 139:13 NIV

Too frequently in our lives, we seem to take a "world's eye" view of ourselves and others. We see only how we fall short of what is perceived by the world as beauty and success. We need to look at ourselves, as well as others, from God's perspective and with God's love.

Daily, we leave our fingerprints on many things. But our fingerprints don't just jump off our fingers; we have to touch things in order to leave a mark. We are God's handiwork: each a special creation made by His hands, each a work in progress. Just as we leave fingerprints on those things we touch, God leaves His fingerprints on our lives as He works in us. When He comforts us, His touch is gentle, leaving light prints. As He is molding us, He may need to use more firmness or stronger pressure, leaving heavier prints. In order for God to leave His mark on you, you have to be "in touch" with Him. God, our Creator, is always working in our lives, if we let Him. His fingerprints on our lives, and on the lives of those around us, should encourage us and remind us:

He who has begun a good work in you will complete it.
Philippians 1:6

Look for the fingerprints.

Kim Kuykendall
Calvary Chapel Williams
Williams, Arizona

April 29

Encouraging and Uncompromising

Therefore, when we could no longer endure it, we thought it good to be left in Athens alone, and sent Timothy, our brother and minister of God, and our fellow laborer in the gospel of Christ, to establish you and *encourage* you concerning your faith, that no one should be shaken by these afflictions; for you yourselves know that we are appointed to this.
1 Thessalonians 3:1–3

Therefore, my beloved brethren, be *steadfast, immovable, always* abounding in the work of the Lord, knowing that your labor is not in vain in the Lord.
1 Corinthians 15:58, emphasis added

As a Christian, the words *encouraging* and *uncompromising* come to mind as principles to live by daily.

If we are to be anything for our Lord, we are to be *encouraging* to others and *uncompromising* before the Lord. The apostle Paul used both of these words in his letters to the churches.

We are to be *steadfast* "in the work of the Lord."

We are to be *immovable* "in the work of the Lord."

We are to be *always* "in the work of the Lord."

There isn't room for anything that is discouraging and compromising. As for me, this means that everything I do and say must be glorifying to God.

Marcia Montgomery
Calvary Chapel Prescott
Prescott, Arizona

April 30

There Is Peace and Power in His Name

Put on the whole armor of God, that you may be able to stand against
the wiles of the devil.
Ephesians 6:11

Having peace in adversity is only possible in the presence of God, which He grants us by His grace. Peace is not the absence of adversity. I think a lot of people say, "I have peace in my life," when in reality, there is no adversity in their lives. But the absence of trials is not true peace. True peace is not based on circumstances. Having peace in our trials can only happen when God is the foundation and support of our life (John 16:33).

If you do not have peace, then you have guilt or you have fear. Guilt and fear come from the Enemy because God does not give us these things. The Bible says, "He Himself is our peace" (Ephesians 2:14). No matter how difficult things get, our God is able to bring about beautiful blessings to our lives. Remember to do these three things: Read God's Word daily, pray, and always keep your focus on Jesus.

> Be anxious for nothing, but in everything by prayer and supplication,
> with thanksgiving, let your requests be made known to God; and the
> peace of God, which surpasses all understanding, will guard your
> hearts and minds through Christ Jesus.
> *Philippians 4:6–7*

Bonnie Botsford
Horizon North County
Rancho Santa Fe, California

May 1

When God Is Silent

God withdrew from Hezekiah in order to test him and to see what
was really in his heart.
2 Chronicles 32:31 NLT

Before marriage, I experienced a season of intimacy with Jesus during
which He shared His secrets with me in prayer. Reading His Word was
like hearing the audible voice of God speaking poignantly to the circumstances I faced. I felt like a super saint—immovable!

After a whirlwind wedding, we sojourned to Albuquerque. Everything
changed; oceans and succulent seafood gave way to deserts and spicy chili.
Somewhere in the midst of the upheaval, God's presence changed too, like
the sun obscured by clouds. Reading my Bible was like reading the phone
book. My prayers were as dull as a plastic knife. As I cried out to God, I
discovered, "In my prosperity I said, 'I shall never be moved.' LORD, by
Your favor You have made my mountain stand strong; You hid Your face,
and I was troubled" (Psalm 30:6–7).

I'd taken God's favor for granted, assuming it was something I had
achieved. When He hid His face, my mountain of spiritual pride crum-
bled. I felt like a silly saint—inflatable!

Sometimes God is silent. For Hezekiah, God's withdrawal was a test
designed to discover what was in the king's heart during pain, not just
prosperity. For David, God's distance was a reminder that without God
we can do nothing. What is God saying to you through His silence?

Lenya Heitzig
Ocean Hills Community Church
San Juan Capistrano, California

May 2

Submission

For the husband is the head of the wife as Christ is the head of the
church.
Ephesians 5:23 NIV

Submit to my husband? Out of the question! After all, my husband can't
find the salt or balance the checkbook. Wouldn't submission make me a
doormat?

One day I invited Jesus into my heart and into my marriage. He
brought His attributes of love, forgiveness, self-sacrifice, and submission
into our home.

The Lord began to work on my heart. Submission didn't make me
less of a person. In fact it became a sign of spiritual maturity. I wanted to
please God and be obedient to Him.

God sent me a wonderful man to cherish, respect, support, and lift up
in prayer. I finally realized that if I love God and my husband, I need to
submit to my husband's authority, given to Him by the Lord. My proper
role is by his side as his helper, partner, lover, and best friend.

February 22, 2003, Bill and I celebrated our twenty-eighth wedding
anniversary. Our desire is for Jesus to be glorified in our lives and marriage.
Inviting Jesus into your heart and home can make all the difference.

Do you want your husband to love and cherish you? Do you want
harmony and peace in your home? If so, try this:

Wives, submit to your husbands as to the Lord.
Ephesians 5:22 NIV

Debbie Crawford
Calvary Chapel Somerset
Somerset, New Jersey

The Deception

There is a way that seems right to a man, but its end is the way of
death.

Proverbs 16:25

Haven't we all said at one time or another, "But it seems so right?" When
a person is deceived in their way of thinking, Isaiah 44:20 says, "He feeds
on ashes, a *deluded* heart *misleads* him; he cannot save himself, or say, 'Is
not this thing in my right hand a lie?'" (emphasis added). Proverbs 14:12
says, "There is a way that *seems* right [appears to one's own judgment to be
right] to a man, but in the end it leads to death" (emphasis added).

Delusion or deception is like looking at a person in a full-length mirror. As you look at the reflection, if you are standing very close to it, you
cannot tell if you are looking at the real person or the image in the mirror.
The person who is deceived looks at the image and is convinced that it is
real, but it is in fact *not real*, it is only an *image*, a *false perception*, an *illusion*, and it is the exact opposite of *truth*. It is a *lie*.

The only way that the deceived person would be able to recognize that
it is the illusion that they are looking at is by pulling back from that thing.
If they move far enough back, they will be able to see what is real (truth)
and what is illusion (lie). It is vital to step away from the thing you are
confused about, or the person that is bringing confusion so the Lord can
reveal to you whether it is a truth or a lie. Stand back from the mirror and
align it to God's Word.

Is there something or someone in your life bringing you confusion? It
is time to align your thinking to His thinking, to God's Word. He is the
standard that we measure everything by. His Word is truth and He will
lead you into all truth! (John 16:13).

Peggy Kravig
Calvary Chapel Downey
Downey, California

A Wise Woman

> This man's name was Nabal, and his wife, Abigail, was a sensible and beautiful woman. But Nabal, a descendant of Caleb, was mean and dishonest in all his dealings.
> *1 Samuel 25:3 NLT*

The word *sensible* can be defined as having understanding, common sense, and even a sharp mind. David had sent some men to deliver a message to Abigail's husband, Nabal, to which he responded rudely. The ten men returned to David and told him what Nabal had said. David was poised for revenge.

Upon hearing the news, Abigail flew into action. She prepared a meal for David and his men. (We all know that the way to a man's heart is through his stomach.) She thought quickly, understood the situation, and was quick to cut David off before he cut her husband up!

While traveling to meet David, I can almost imagine Abigail asking the Lord for words of wisdom. She gave him the food that softened his heart. We all need an Abigail in our lives, or maybe God has called us to be an Abigail—to speak wise words from the Lord and to perform kind deeds. She was beautiful on the outside, but she was also very sensible and wise. Even David thanked God for Abigail's good sense, and when Nabal died, he came back to ask for her hand in marriage. May the Lord help us to be as wise, understanding, and sensible as Abigail.

Angela Pierce
Calvary Chapel of the Front Range
Fort Collins, Colorado

May 5

Spotlight Living

❧

Who is she who looks forth as the morning, fair as the moon, clear as the sun, awesome as any army with banners?
Song of Solomon 6:10

Do you remember the beams of light that would shine into the night skies back in the '60s, '70s, and '80s? They would draw attention to some sort of sale or grand premiere. We who are the church of Jesus Christ are to shine in such a way that others are drawn to Him because of us.

Today we seldom see spotlights in the night skies, and I fear the church is also losing its light. In this passage of Scripture, a lady is noticed for all the right reasons. She reflects the light of the "Bright and Morning Star," she radiates the warmth of Jesus' love, she proudly wears the emblem of godliness, and she's not afraid to fight for what is holy and just!

Like it or not, as Christian women, we are in the spotlight. If we are not drawing attention to Jesus, but to ourselves, we may as well pull the plug and go back into obscurity!

The night is almost gone; the day of salvation will soon be here. So don't live in darkness. Get rid of your evil deeds. Shed them like dirty clothes. Clothe yourselves with the armor of right living, as those who live in the light.
Romans 13:12 NLT

Kathy Salaiz
Calvary Chapel West Covina
West Covina, California

May 6

Fill My Cup, Lord

Satisfy us in the morning with your unfailing love, that we may sing
for joy and be glad all our days.
Psalm 90:14 NIV

I collect teapots and teacups. Every time I go into the Ross department store, I find myself in the knickknack section, looking to see if they have any new *Roy Kirkham* teacups to add to my collection. Of course, I don't need any more, but that doesn't matter, because I like them and have an incurable desire for more. So, I just keep on buying them and stacking them away in my cupboards.

You and I are a lot like a teacup. However, God has no intention of searching for us only to store us away in a cupboard. He wants to fill us and put us to use. You see, apart from being filled, a teacup has nothing to offer on its own. It's in need of an outside source to pick it up, fill it, and then use it.

Psalm 90:14 is a great Scripture to pray in the morning before you get out of bed. It puts your focus on Him. You have to do so every day because if you are anything like me, you leak! Simply pray, "Fill my cup, Lord." Allow Him to fill you with His resources and make you useful for His service.

Karen Stangel
North Shore Christian Fellowship
Haleiwa, Hawaii

May 7

Purpose in Your Heart

Yet I will rejoice in the LORD, I will joy in the God of my salvation.
Habakkuk 3:18

No matter what your circumstances might be, now is the time to purpose in your heart to rejoice and keep faith in the Lord.

Hard times fall on everyone. No one is exempt from trials. Habakkuk 3:17 says, "Though the fig tree may not blossom, nor fruit be on the vines; though the labor of the olive may fail, and the fields yield no food; though the flock may be cut off from the fold, and there be no herd in the stalls—*yet I will rejoice in the LORD*" (emphasis added).

So now, the choice is yours. Will you remain faithful to the God who loves you so much that He made a way for you to be with Him throughout all eternity just by receiving, accepting, and believing in His Son Jesus Christ?

In receiving Jesus as our Savior, we rest in the promise that "He Himself has said, 'I will never leave you nor forsake you'" (Hebrews 13:5). Those words bring great comfort, even in the midst of trials.

May He grant you according to your heart's desire, and fulfill all your
purpose.
Psalm 20:4

Barbara Gil
Calvary Chapel of the Redwoods
Smith River, California

May 8

Under the Spreading Vine

Then the LORD God provided a vine and made it grow up over Jonah
to give shade for his head to ease his discomfort, and Jonah was very
happy. . . . But at dawn the next day, God provided a worm, which
chewed the vine so that it withered.

Jonah 4:6–7 NIV

I lost a friend this past year. She was indeed a delightful vine in my life,
supportive and concerned about all I did. It was great to be with her, and
I relied heavily upon her sustaining friendship, leaning on her strength
during many difficult times.

Suddenly she was gone. "God!" I whimpered, thrashed, begged, and
cried over and over. "Why? How could You?"

It took awhile for me to still my aching heart long enough to see God's
finger pointing at people I had forgotten and other relationships I had
neglected (or had neglected to develop). Life had been easy while I had
my vine to keep me refreshed.

The Ninevites were a stone's throw away from Jonah as he clamored
on about his "loss." Why didn't he go there? Surely in the city there were
plenty of shade trees and plenty of people who had just repented and who
were ready for his friendship—ready to be discipled. He couldn't see them
for his own loss.

Let God lift your eyes to see beyond your loss to the "lost" all around
you.

Should I not be concerned about that great city?

Jonah 4:11 NIV

Joni Woolley
Calvary Chapel Alpha
Alpha, Michigan

May 9

Martha

But Martha was distracted by all the preparations that had to be
made.
Luke 10:40 NIV

One night God gave me a dream. I was in church worshiping with white
gloves on. It was hard for me to lift my hands because the gloves were very
heavy. I took them off. Then I saw a white haired, older man sweeping the
church floors with a broom.

Early on in the ministry, there were times when my agenda and ideas
ran before the Lord and I would yell back, "Bless this one, Lord!" I had
gotten caught up in "much serving" (Luke 10:40), the busyness of ministry. Service and work came before prayer and spending time with the
Lord. My personal relationship with Jesus suffered. I didn't have God's
balance in my life and thus every area of my life suffered.

I believe God was the white haired man in my dream. God said that
He would build the church in His time, in His way. Did I stop to ask God
for direction, for strength, for His plans? I had to admit that no I didn't,
not all the time, because I was too busy and distracted with jumping ahead
and "doing" rather than "listening." I had to take off my white gloves.

She had a sister called Mary, who sat at the Lord's feet listening to
what he said.
Luke 10:39 NIV

God can seem very far away when we don't sit at His feet. Our first
priority is to protect our personal relationship with Jesus Christ.

I needed to ask God for forgiveness. Each day, we need to sit at the
Lord's feet and listen to what He says.

Debbie Crawford
Calvary Chapel Somerset
Somerset, New Jersey

May 10

And Now I Know You Really Love Me!

I have loved you with an everlasting love.
Jeremiah 31:3

I can still remember being overwhelmed with a love for God when I was a little girl. Though I was not yet a Christian, I was raised in a religious home and had been introduced to the belief that there really is a God, and that He loves me. As I grew older, this knowledge of God's love for me seemed to get crowded out by many distractions. Finally, as a young college student, it seemed that those days were so far behind me that I actually forgot how much He loved me. Like so many others, I made my mistakes and found myself in a place that I thought I would never get to. It was at that place that God once again broke into my troubled life. The word He said to me was simply this: "I have loved you with an everlasting love." Just think, when I did not even care if He loved me and when I was not interested in Him at all, He was still there, gentleman that He is, calling out to me in His sweet, loving, patient way: "Honey, I love you. I will never leave you, I will never hurt you, and I will always love you . . . I have loved you with an everlasting love."

If you have been disappointed in life, perhaps by someone you have loved, and if you have gotten to the point of feeling that you just aren't worth loving, please remember God's Word to you today. "I love you, I will be true to you, and My love for you is for always and forever." He loves you with an everlasting love. What a great and loving God we serve!

Marie Rosales
Calvary Chapel Chino Valley
Chino, California

May 11

Sweeter Also Than Honey

More to be desired are they than gold, yea than much fine gold;
sweeter also than honey and the honeycomb.
Psalm 19:10

Have you ever chewed a piece of Juicy Fruit gum? It tastes so very good, but after it has been chewed thoroughly, all of the flavor has been extracted and it is time for a new piece.

Honey in this passage of Scripture is figurative of God's Word in our lives. Honey is sweet, never sour or bitter. It was considered very desirable in ancient times. It was to be enjoyed and savored.

The honeycomb is where the honey is stored inside the beehive. The bees carefully and precisely construct the honeycomb out of wax. In some cultures, chunks of honeycomb dripping with honey are chewed until every last drop of honey is extracted, just like we would chew a piece of gum.

Do you do this with God's Word? Do you enjoy it and look forward to your time in it? Is it a special treat for you in the midst of your busy schedule?

When was the last time you took a portion of Scripture and really chewed on it? Let me encourage you to chew and meditate on His Word continuously until you have extracted every last bit of its sweetness.

Jolene Jones
Calvary Chapel of Skagit Valley
Mount Vernon, Washington

May 12

Resort in Jesus

Be my strong refuge, to which I may resort continually.
Psalm 71:3

Last summer my husband and I went to the island of Molokai. I was looking forward to our trip to this island because there is nothing to do but relax and enjoy the beauty of God's creation. We were both in need of some R & R, and that is exactly what we found there!

The Lord pointed out to me one morning that I didn't need to fly to Molokai in order to relax and get some rest. Of course, there is nothing wrong with going on vacation and getting away. Nevertheless, the point was clear: the Lord has a resting place for our souls.

This verse says that we have a resort in Jesus! Isn't that a wonderful idea? The added bonus is that we can enjoy this resort *continually*. This word speaks of "duration, without interruption, at all times." We never have to pack our bags and leave this resort. The door to this guesthouse is always open, and it's free!

The next time you are in need of a getaway in order to get some rest, remember to tap into your resort in Jesus. May it be more than a wonderful idea. I pray that you will delight in the peace of His presence continually.

Karen Stangel
North Shore Christian Fellowship
Haleiwa, Hawaii

May 13

A Weed-Free Garden

See to it that no one misses the grace of God and that no bitter root
grows up to cause trouble and defile many.
Hebrews 12:15 NIV

Although I was generally happy with the way my new garden had turned
out, I was surprised to see the number of weeds that had sprouted up. Some
apparently appeared overnight! I had mistakenly believed that applying a
good layer of mulch would keep these undesirable plants at bay. Now the
only remedy was to yank out each weed by the root.

Sometimes in our lives we discover that we've allowed seeds of bitterness to take root in our lives. We may try to cover them up with the
mulch of good works, such as church attendance, tithing, et cetera, but
God knows our hearts. The only solution is to yank out the bitterness and
give it to our Father in heaven. He is able to cleanse and restore, and His
grace truly is sufficient for us.

How do we prevent weeds from taking root in our hearts? Start each
day in the Word of God and in prayer. Ask your heavenly Father to reveal
to you any seeds that He didn't plant, and then remove them. You'll be
pleased with the results!

Search me, O God, and know my heart; test me and know my anxious
thoughts. See if there is any offensive way in me, and lead me in the
way everlasting.
Psalm 139:23–24 NIV

Carla Brown
Calvary Chapel Columbus
Columbus, Ohio

May 14

Sharing in the Blessing

Devote yourselves to prayer, keeping alert in it with an attitude of
thanksgiving.
Colossians 4:2 NASB

When I was a little girl, I loved helping my dad with his chores. Whether
it was handing him tools while he fixed the car or helping him wash the
car with my own little bucket and sponge provided by my loving father, I
delighted in working with him! My sweet daddy always showered me with
enthusiastic praises for even the smallest job when I gave my best effort.
He knew very well that it would bring me great joy as we shared in the
wonderful result.

So it is with our heavenly Father when we participate with Him
through prayer as He works in our lives and the lives of those we love and
pray for. He certainly could complete His work efficiently without any
help from us, but He desires that we share in the wonderful blessing. So
cherish and treasure this great and wonderful opportunity the Lord has
given you to share in His work. And don't forget to spend some time just
thanking and adoring your sweet Daddy.

Cherisse Denham
Calvary Chapel Troy
Troy, Missouri

May 15

Fragrance

But thanks be to God, who . . . manifests through us the sweet aroma
of the knowledge of Him in every place.
2 Corinthians 2:14 NASB

Springtime. That's the time of year when I find myself walking through
the garden, enjoying the sweet fragrance of the flowers blooming. Lilacs,
roses, hyacinth, Lily of the Valley, can you smell them? Take a deep breath
and enjoy!

What a wonderful picture of what our lives should be like to those
around us. Do we reflect Christ's love, kindness, goodness, and gentleness? Are others attracted to these things in us? When others are in our
presence, do they sense the sweetness of peace and joy?

As we walk with Christ and allow His Spirit to lead us, God will mani-
fest that fragrance of Christ through us, in every place.

What a privilege to be used as He "draws all men to Himself" (see
John 12:32).

Lisa Ulman
Calvary Chapel of Kalamazoo Valley
Kalamazoo, Michigan

May 16

As It Turned Out

❧

Always be prepared to give an answer . . .
1 Peter 3:15 NIV

Have you ever found yourself aware that you were exactly where God had prepared you to be at a particular moment in time? When Ruth and Naomi returned to Bethlehem at the time of the barley harvest, Ruth said, "Let me go to the fields and pick up the leftover grain behind anyone in whose eyes I find favor. . . . As it turned out, she found herself working in a field belonging to Boaz" (Ruth 2:2–3 NIV). God pointed Ruth in the right direction to go into the appropriate field and prepared Boaz to take note of her instead of routinely taking care of business.

My husband and I were in desperate spiritual and emotional condition in the early 1980s because we had not surrendered our hearts to Jesus. Amazingly, we found ourselves at a Christian music concert. "As it turned out," the Lord pointed us to just the right seats, located next to a godly Christian girl who was prepared to "take note" of us that night, pray with us, and give us good counsel on getting into church.

We're never quite sure when God will plant someone right in the middle of our path for us to notice. Lord, prepare us by Your Holy Spirit today!

Always be prepared to give an answer to everyone who asks you to give
the reason for the hope that you have.
1 Peter 3:15 NIV

Sue LeBoutillier
Calvary Chapel Ontario
Ontario, Oregon

God Already Knows

It shall come to pass that before they call, I will answer; and while
they are still speaking, I will hear.
Isaiah 65:24

It is a wonderful thing to know that the Creator of all things loves me so
much that He wants to hear from little old me. And not only does He
want to hear from me, He also wants me to hear Him. Imagine that! The
one true God desires to speak to me!

If the all-knowing God (Psalm 139:4) already knows what we're going
to say, why should we pray? Maybe just to bring Him good pleasure, for
He loves to hear us call upon His name and He desires to have a relation-
ship with us. Or maybe because we need to hear ourselves call out to Him.
There are times we don't even know what we're going to say. Then when
His sweet Holy Spirit comes and makes sense of our groanings and utter-
ances, we are brought back to that place of peace, that place of knowing
God is in control.

Now close this book and just talk to Him. He's waiting to hear from
you. "Life is fragile: handle it with prayer."

Then you shall call, and the LORD will answer; you shall cry, and He
will say, "Here I am."
Isaiah 58:9

Barbara Gil
Calvary Chapel of the Redwoods
Smith River, California

A Daily Walk with God

So all the days of Enoch were three hundred and sixty-five years.
Enoch walked with God; and he was not, for God took him.
Genesis 5:23–24 NASB

In a moment, in the twinkling of an eye, we will be caught up with our Lord and Savior Jesus Christ. I love to think of this truth daily, and look to the Lord, waiting and watching for His soon return—walking with God each and every day, just as Enoch did.

Isn't it interesting that "all of the days of Enoch were three hundred and sixty-five years"? There are 365 days in a year, just as there were 365 years in Enoch's walk with God. Every day is an opportunity to walk with God, living in anticipation of that glorious event called the rapture, when Christ takes us out of this world, just as God took Enoch.

Thus, we are to walk as heavenly women.

He hath shewed thee, O man, what is good; and what doth the LORD
require of thee, but to do justly, and to love mercy, and to walk humbly
with thy God?
Micah 6:8 KJV

May we be like Enoch, who lived godly each and every day until the day God took him to heaven.

Vickie Stahl
Deschutes Christian Fellowship
Bend, Oregon

May 19

In His Presence Is Fullness of Joy

The one thing I ask of the LORD—the thing I seek most—is to live in
the house of the LORD all the days of my life, delighting in the LORD's
perfections and meditating in his Temple.
Psalm 27:4 NLT

David had his priorities right. His foremost desire was to be in the presence of the Lord day after day. He knew the peace and joy that follows a life lived in the presence of Jesus. Have you been struggling with your priorities? God's grace is sufficient to bring you back to Him. His mercy never fails. Come back to your first love, remember He is the lover of your soul, and He created you for the very purpose of fellowship with Himself.

"Greater love has no one than this, that one lay down his life for his
friends."
John 15:13 NASB

Lay your life at His feet today and see the transformation that takes place.

My heart has heard you say, "Come and talk with me." And my heart
responds, "LORD, I am coming."
Psalm 27:8 NLT

Jolene J. Cesmat
Calvary Chapel North Bend
North Bend, Washington

May 20

A Life without Christ Is a Wasted Life

LORD, make me to know my end, and what is the measure of my days,
that I may know how frail I am.
Psalm 39:4

Read Psalm 39:1-7

As a mother of six, I often wonder just how my own mother was able to raise four daughters—each a year apart—keep an immaculate house, and have sit-down dinners every night with the whole family. I hardly remember my parents arguing, and every Sunday we went to church as a family. My mother sewed and baked to earn extra money. She also made much of our clothing. Remembering all the wonderful parties and holiday celebrations she hosted brings back fond memories. I asked my mother how she did it. She pondered the question and said, "I sacrificed a relationship with you girls. I was so busy trying to keep an orderly home and bring in extra money that I missed out on school activities and being more available for you." My mother looks back and sees wasted years because of choices she made. She believed that if she had developed a relationship with us, we would not have made some of the choices we made while growing up.

I spent my motherhood years trying to have a relationship with my children. I home schooled all my children and stayed active with them. I taught them about the Lord and included them in everything we did. Yet, each one of my children went down the same road I did, a road of rebellion and bad choices. I look back and see a lot of wasted years. My focus was on my children. My mother's focus was on an orderly home. Neither of us made Christ our focus. We tried to do things right, but without Christ being the center of our lives, we ended up with wasted years!

A life without Christ would be a wasted life. True life begins with Christ. He is the One who helps us through this journey of life. To be able to look back as Paul did and say, "to live is Christ, and to die is gain" (Philippians 1:21) brings ultimate fulfillment. My mother and I had fruit from our labor, some good and some not so good, but to live for Christ is gain—no waste at all. Spend time with Him! Get to know Him! Have daily devotions and an active prayer life. We cannot change a person's life, but we can have an abundant life in Jesus Christ.

Doreen Marinelli
Calvary Chapel Cape Cod
Sandwich, Massachusetts

May 21

The Lord's Battle

"Remember the Lord, great and awesome, and fight." . . . [And] God
. . . brought their plot to nothing.
Nehemiah 4:14–15

The Lord has given each of us a section of the wall to build and protect, just as He gave the Jews through the leadership of Nehemiah. Often that section is within our own homes or ministry. We come against much opposition, especially as we "set our hands to this good work" (see Nehemiah 2:18).

The Enemy would love to thwart us in our usefulness at home or in ministry. God has given us an effective weapon against this Enemy:

For the weapons of our warfare are not carnal but mighty in God.
2 Corinthians 10:4

When Nehemiah encountered opposition, his reaction was: "Nevertheless we made our prayer to our God. . . . Our God will fight for us" (Nehemiah 4:9, 20).

What battle are you facing today? Do you feel overwhelmed and powerless? So did Jehoshaphat. He prayed:

For we have no power against this great multitude that is coming
against us; nor do we know what to do, but our eyes are upon You.
2 Chronicles 20:12

Are your eyes upon Jesus? He is our only source of power and strength. Come to Him right now in humility and faith. The battle belongs to the Lord!

Jennifer Hayden
New Beginnings Christian Fellowship
Evansville, Indiana

May 22

Come Up Here

❧

Come up here, and I will show you things which must take place after
this. Immediately I was in the Spirit, and behold, a throne set in
heaven, and One sat on the throne.

Revelation 4:1–2

How is it that John was "immediately" in the Spirit? Didn't it take some
time? A worship song or two? Weren't the kids wanting breakfast, the dog
barking, or the phone ringing? Wasn't there laundry to do or a kitchen to
clean? While these duties and distractions didn't plague John, they're all
too familiar to us as wives and mothers. Most of us could replace the word
"immediately" with "occasionally" or "periodically." But it doesn't have to
be that way!

John heard the Lord's voice calling him to come, and he obeyed.
Jesus told His disciples to rise and pray, lest they enter into temptation
(Matthew 26:41). The key to hearing His voice and walking in the Spirit
is to rise before the distractions do!

As a result of John's obedience, he saw the One who is seated on the
throne. You too can see the One who sits on the throne every day, but it
may require that you rise before the distractions do, and listen to His still
small voice calling you to "come up here."

Michelle Randall
Calvary Chapel Brandon
Brandon, Florida

May 23

Keep Me Fishing, Lord

❧

"Follow Me, and I will make you fishers of men."
Matthew 4:19

At times, I have had a broken heart for those who do not know Jesus, and I ask God to give me opportunities to plant seeds. He is faithful in giving me a burning desire to share the gospel through His love so that the lost may come to know Jesus. Yet, there have also been times in my walk when I have been consumed with my personal life and the ministry God has given me. But my true prayer is that we, as believers, would always have a burden for the lost and always be fishing for them.

I often think to myself, "If I knew someone was going to die in a tragic car accident, would I try to stop him or her from getting into that car?" Of course I would! If that person did not know our precious Lord, they would die without Him. Therefore, we must share with them the good news of Jesus so they too can have everlasting life.

Maybe it's been awhile since you went fishing. Follow Jesus, He will lead you, showing you where and how to again be a "fisher of men."

And how shall they preach, except they be sent? as it is written, How beautiful are the feet of them that preach the gospel of peace, and bring glad tidings of good things!
Romans 10:15 KJV

Lorraine Velasquez
Olive Branch Calvary Chapel
La Mirada, California

May 24

Holiness Is an Action Word

You are to be holy to me because I, the LORD, am holy, and I have set
you apart from the nations to be my own.
Leviticus 20:26 NIV

The Lord has set us apart to be holy. But, living a holy life cannot be
achieved by a passive, just-sit-there lifestyle. There is an action that
needs to take place on our part. Not that we are saved by works, because
Ephesians 2:8–9 states we are saved by grace. We aren't talking about salvation here, we're talking about holiness. We must be actively conscious
of living a holy life because it doesn't come naturally. Let's look at our part
from Colossians 3:1–17 (NIV):

(verse 1) . . . *set* your heart
(verse 2) . . . *set* your mind
(verse 5) . . . *put* to death
(verse 8) . . . *rid* yourself
(verse 12) . . . *clothe* yourself
(verse 13) . . . *bear* with/*forgive*
(verse 14) . . . *put* on love
(verse 15) . . . *let* the peace of Christ
(verse 16) . . . *let* the word of Christ
(verse 17) . . . whatever you *do, do* it all in the name of the Lord

So, the next time you feel this "Christian thing" just isn't working, ask
yourself, "Am I doing my part?"

Linda Sasso
Calvary Chapel Boise
Boise, Idaho

May 25

The Best Dressed Woman

As God's chosen people, holy and dearly loved, clothe yourselves with
compassion, kindness, humility, gentleness and patience.
Colossians 3:12 NIV

I had less than two hours to spend at the mall, and I faced an almost impossible task: find the right dress to wear for my son's wedding. As mother of the groom, I'd be meeting many people and posing for countless photos. I wanted just the right outfit, one that made me look ten pounds thinner and ten years younger. It couldn't clash with the wedding colors or outshine the bride, a very unlikely outcome in my budget bracket.

I shot off a quick prayer and attacked the racks. To my surprise, I found the perfect dress at the first store. My daughters agreed it was a winner, and I quickly completed my purchase.

How about you? Does choosing just the right outfit leave you glaring at the mirror and feeling discouraged? Don't worry! There is one way to dress that never goes out of style and always wins the approval of friends and family. Wrap yourself in compassion and kindness, slip on a little gentleness, and don't forget to tie on some patience. When you display those qualities, no matter what you're wearing, you'll look beautiful!

Put on the new self, created to be like God in true righteousness and
holiness.
Ephesians 4:24 NIV

Carrie Turansky
Calvary Chapel Mercer County
Mercer County, New Jersey

Wake Up and Smell the Flowers

Therefore He says: "Awake, you who sleep, arise from the dead, and
Christ will give you light."
Ephesians 5:14

Somewhere along life's walk, we have forgotten to stop, look up at Him,
and appreciate the amazing blessings of God. We have not remembered to
pause and smell the flowers!

But Paul urges us awake because God will give us light! God's light
makes us grateful and wise in this life.

Romans 12:2 teaches us, "Do not be conformed to this world, but be
transformed by the renewing of your mind, that you may prove what is
that good and acceptable and perfect will of God."

Perhaps today you might wish to pray: "Dear Lord, if I am asleep, if I
am discontent, or if I have failed to cherish Your many blessings, awaken
me that I might walk in Your light."

Wherefore be ye not unwise, but understanding what the will of the
Lord is.
Ephesians 5:17 KJV

Becky James
Calvary Chapel Prescott
Prescott, Arizona

May 27

A Bold Entrance

Let us therefore draw near with confidence to the throne of grace, that
we may receive mercy and may find grace to help in time of need.
Hebrews 4:16 NASB

We live in times in which we can pick up the phone and call our friends
or our pastor, or we can try to figure things out on our own. So often we
forget our Creator and Redeemer, who shed His blood on the cross for us.
He is our help, full of grace, full of mercy, full of abounding love. He is
the King over all creation and our loving Father. He knows what we think
and what we need even before we ask Him.

The Spirit Himself intercedes for us with groanings too deep for
words; and He who searches the hearts knows what the mind of the
Spirit is.
Romans 8:26–27 NASB

We can share all our hopes, desires, fears, hurts, and needs—*anything*—with God, and we can come boldly before the throne of grace. He
hears us, and He loves us so much. When we see how He works in our
lives through prayer, it builds our faith.

So, come boldly to your Father, with confidence and expectation.

Jenny Gonzales
Calvary Chapel Cerritos
Cerritos, California

May 28

Damage Control

Do not let any unwholesome talk come out of your mouths, but only
what is helpful for building others up according to their needs, that it
may benefit those who listen.
Ephesians 4:29 NIV

Have you ever done a study on the book of James? What an awesome
book—small, but filled with precious jewels for living a Christ-centered
life. James 3 is totally devoted to a very small part of the body called
the tongue—this one little part that can destroy a person in a matter of
seconds. James 3:9 tells us, "With the tongue we praise our Lord and
Father, and with it we curse men, who have been made in God's likeness"
(NIV).

As I struggle daily with the misuse of my tongue, I know that I'm not
alone. I have also learned that when I try to change myself, I fail. Paul
wrote in Romans 7, "I do the things I don't want to do and don't do the
things I want to do" (see verses 15–20). If you are not speaking love and
encouragement to others with your tongue, please ask God daily to change
you and help you to bridle your unruly tongue. I have written Ephesians
4:29 on an 8"x10" piece of paper, and placed it on my refrigerator to help
me remember how much power is in that one small part of my body.

Other Scriptures about the tongue:

Proverbs 10:19; 15:4; Matthew 12:36–37; James 3

Karen Letzring
Calvary Chapel Oxford
Oxford, Mississippi

May 29

Forget It!

∽

. . . forgetting what lies behind and reaching forward to what lies ahead, I press on toward the goal for the prize of the upward call of God in Christ Jesus.
Philippians 3:13–14 NASB

"If only I had . . . if only they hadn't . . . too bad it happened that way . . . I feel like giving up . . ." Three things Paul tells us to do in order to know Christ, to be more like Him, and to be all He has in mind for us: forget, reach, and press.

Forget those things that keep you from moving forward in faith and spiritual growth. Dwelling on the past can stunt the work God has for you today.

Through the LORD's mercies we are not consumed, because His compassions fail not. They are new every morning.
Lamentations 3:22–23

Reach forward and move ahead in the plan Jesus has for your life. Be determined to stay focused on Jesus' will for your life, and choose to do today what will move you ahead toward your life goals in Jesus Christ.

. . . because of the hope which is laid up for you in heaven.
Colossians 1:5

Press on. Even when it's hard or you're tired or discouraged, do the next thing for Jesus Christ.

And let us not grow weary while doing good, for in due season we shall reap if we do not lose heart.
Galatians 6:9

Kim Fine
Calvary Chapel Farmington
Farmington, New Mexico

May 30

Bonding Effectively

Evening, and morning, and at noon, will I pray, and cry aloud . . .
Psalm 55:17 KJV

Evening, morning, noon, and many times in between, the nursing infant cries out for nourishment and companionship. That tiny life spent nine months in the safety and warmth of its mother's womb. When life in the world is thrust upon the child, the intimacy is disrupted, and the child now has to cry out for the food and nourishment that so effortlessly was received in the womb.

God specifically designed the physical nourishment of an infant to take place in several feedings throughout day and night so that the crucial bond between mother and baby would be nurtured. This is a picture of the bonding that needs to take place between God and His children.

While the first prayer time in the morning is so essential for the Christian, bonding is most effectively established with several daily sessions in the Word and communication with Jesus throughout the day and night. Notice that He is always with you; speak to Him about all that you're involved with. Consult His Word often. Are you awake at night? It's a perfect opportunity to commune with Him and listen to His still, small voice.

. . . and he shall hear my voice.
Psalm 55:17 KJV

Jeanie Matranga
Calvary Chapel Downey
Downey, California

The Success of Failure

Take now your son, your only son Isaac, whom you love, and go to the land of Moriah, and offer him there as a burnt offering on one of the mountains of which I will tell you.

Genesis 22:2

What kind of faith can do this? It is not the kind of faith that is gained overnight. It is the kind of faith that has been refined through testings of fire.

God called Abraham away from his country and his father's house, and though he delayed, he went—*faith*. There was famine in the Promised Land so Abraham went to Egypt—*failure*.

Abraham separated from Lot, trusting God to choose for him—*faith*. God made a covenant with Abraham, "He believed in the LORD, and He accounted it to him for righteousness" (Genesis 15:6)—*faith*. There was the Hagar and Ishmael event—*failure*.

God told Abraham a son would be given through Sarah; Abraham fell on his face and laughed, "Oh, that Ishmael might live before You!" (Genesis 17:18)—*failure*. The Lord appeared to Abraham and spoke again that Sarah would bear a son; Abraham didn't laugh this time—*faith*. But before Sarah conceived Abraham journeyed south, and out of fear, he told Abimelech that Sarah was his sister—*failure*.

By the time God came to Abraham and told him to sacrifice Isaac, Abraham's faith was not only a product of his success but also of his failures. He had learned that God never failed him. His promises came to pass. He could be fully trusted. There was no reason to fear, no reason to doubt. Abraham completely trusted the Lord. He was swift to obey; he rose early the next morning (Genesis 22:3). Abraham concluded that God was able to raise Isaac up, even from the dead (Hebrews 11:19). Abraham knew God too well; He could not go back on His promise—He would fulfill it.

That is the kind of faith that was needed when Abraham faced this test: a faith born out of failures and victories.

Every failure in our lives can be successful if we grow in our faith. Remember, you are a work in progress.

> Being confident of this very thing, that He who has begun a good
> work in you will complete it until the day of Jesus Christ.
> *Philippians 1:6*

Karin Kyle
Calvary Chapel Modesto
Modesto, California

June 1

The Day Roy Rogers Died

Wilt thou not revive us again?
Psalm 85:6 KJV

It was a difficult time in my life. My heart was heavy because my prodigal son was at his lowest—far from God. There seemed no end in sight, no chance, no hope. Having read some lyrics from a popular CD, I was shocked at how evil this generation had become, how faithless and far from the Lord.

The same day, the newscaster announced that the great Western hero of the '50s, Roy Rogers, had died. My father loved Roy Rogers, so we used to watch Westerns together. The news program proceeded to take a look at the life of Roy Rogers. Far from the proud, spoiled celebrities of today, he was truly a star. On Christmas and other holidays, he would visit children's hospitals and entertain the kids. He spent countless hours helping underprivileged children in every way possible, all without pay. I thought to myself, "What a true role model that man was. He was so humble, so full of integrity, and in many ways, squeaky clean."

Then I thought about the "role models" promoted for our children today—men who beat their wives, punks who exploit women with filthy lyrics, teens who make millions of dollars only to spend it on themselves, drugs and sex pushers—and the flood just broke. I wept, feeling truly broken.

Since that day, revival has been the passion of my life. I long to see the Spirit of God poured out upon all of us so that we can truly feel His presence. I pray for revival like the days of old, when people would weep openly, confessing their sins to God; Christians would spend sincere time in prayer and in God's Word, and as a result, would reap the fruits of holy, sanctified living. In those days, bars and theaters closed down, and even police officers had nothing to do, so they formed singing quartets. Imagine that!

If you want to be stirred up to pray for revival, just take a look at our youth. Read books on revival, and I guarantee it will stir you to pray like David, "I will not let my eyes sleep . . . until I find a place to build a house for the LORD" (Psalm 132:4–5 NLT).

> Revive Thy work in the midst of the years.
> *Habakkuk 3:2 NASB*

Karen Pulley
Calvary Chapel Old Bridge
Old Bridge, New Jersey

June 2

Be Zealous and Repent

"As many as I love, I rebuke and chasten: be zealous therefore, and repent."
Revelation 3:19 KJV

It never feels good to be rebuked or corrected. That's because our flesh has been busted! And when it is busted, it can only do one of two things . . . ignore the rebuke and continue on with its bad self or repent by receiving the correction and actually turn and do what is right. Ahh . . . to do what is right! Now, that feels good: to obey God and follow Him, to allow Him to change us by letting Him stop us in our tracks and correct us at any time. The love of our heavenly Father feels so good when we choose to receive His chastening, and as a result, His blessing.

"Be zealous." Now there's something we need to work on. We can be zealous to share God's Word, zealous to help a friend, or zealous to pray for souls; but what about being zealous to repent? To actually be ready and open to correction with the same joy and excitement in our hearts that we would in our service to the Lord. Let's not drag our feet or throw a fit when God busts us, but let's work on being zealous and repenting with a thankful heart, knowing it is because our God is good and loves us so very much.

Patricia Maciel
Calvary Chapel Downey
Downey, California

June 3

Be Not Dismayed—A Wonderful Promise

No man shall be able to stand before you all the days of your life; as I was with Moses, so I will be with you. I will not leave you nor forsake you.

Joshua 1:5

At 6:30 a.m. on a cold and stormy morning, I drove down a lonely country road, heading south to a very important 9:00 a.m. meeting. It was imperative that I look and act my very best. I was physically hurting, and the major surgery I would undergo to correct the cause of my pain was still weeks away.

The Lord had given me the most wonderful Scripture in the middle of the night.

Do not fear or be dismayed; tomorrow go out against them, for the LORD is with you.

2 Chronicles 20:17

At the time the Lord reminded me of the promise of His presence, the most spectacular rainbow appeared across the sky above my car. I felt the presence of the Lord. As God was faithful to King Jehoshaphat and his army as they faced annihilation, so God would be faithful to me as I faced enormous odds that day. It was one of the most monumental meetings of my life. He was with me just as He had promised!

LaVon Fromm
North Valley Calvary Chapel
Yuba City, California

June 4

Remember

And when the people complained, it displeased the LORD.
Numbers 11:1 KJV

Our daughter Michelle went through a time in her life when she was very angry towards our family. "We have no family!" she would complain as she ran out of the door, wanting only to be with her teenage friends.

One day as I was looking at photos of birthday parties, holidays, pony rides, and prom dresses in our family album, I had an idea. I removed some of the photos and placed them in a box. I wrote a note to Michelle that said, "Remember," and placed the box of photos and the note on her pillow.

Even the Israelites had short memories, when it came to God's love and provision for them.

But our soul is dried away: there is nothing at all, beside this manna,
before our eyes.
Numbers 11:6 KJV

I started keeping a prayer journal where I stored memories of answered prayers, songs, and letters written to the Lord. It has also become my thankfulness journal. Each day, I write down what I am grateful for. It has changed my attitude. Rather than dwelling on what I don't have, I remember my many blessings and focus on what the Lord has given me.

My daughter's attitude changed also. After seeing the photos, she remembered that she was part of a very loving, caring, and supportive family.

Debbie Crawford
Calvary Chapel Somerset
Somerset, New Jersey

June 5

Those who are planted in the house of the LORD shall flourish in the
courts of our God.
Psalm 92:13

I love to garden. I love to plant because I love to see flowers blooming.
Maybe it's because I'm from England where so many people keep beautiful gardens. But what I love most is a flower with a sweet fragrance. To
walk up the path to my front door and smell the fragrance of flowers that
I have planted gives such satisfaction.

What does God see as He gazes at our lives? Does He see us flourishing in Him, giving off a pleasant fragrance? He will, if the soil of our
hearts is soft and fertile. In order to "flourish in the courts of our God,"
we must cultivate hearts of worship. True worship—for who God is, and
in thankfulness for all He has done for us—is like bringing Him a fragrant
blossom.

Enter into His gates with thanksgiving, and into His courts with
praise.
Psalm 100:4

So take some time today to be alone with the Lord. Come without a
list of requests. Gaze upon His beauty, His holiness, and worship Him,
for He is worthy!

Oh come, let us worship and bow down; let us kneel before the LORD
our Maker. For He is our God.
Psalm 95:6–7

Carol Wild
Calvary Chapel Merritt Island
Merritt Island, Florida

June 6

It's Your Move

The message of the cross is foolishness to those who are perishing,
but to us who are being saved it is the power of God.
1 Corinthians 1:18

I placed a small pewter cross among some family photos and travel memorabilia on my desk as a reminder of Christ's sacrifice. One day some unsaved friends walked through the house admiring the décor when suddenly they stopped at the tiny cross and said, "I thought you didn't do crosses." I immediately thought, "I don't have to 'do' crosses because Jesus did one for me."

Billy Graham said, "Calvary is the place of decision. It is the eternal sword, erected to divide men into two classes, the saved and the lost."[11] I realized my guests felt offended by the cross and didn't desire the forgiveness it offered. A cross is, indeed, a peculiar adornment since it is an instrument of capital punishment. It's like wearing an electric chair around your neck. Yet, it was there that the penalty for my sin—my death sentence—was paid.

On I-10 in Louisiana there is a large billboard standing high above the city near the Mississippi River Bridge. It displays a graphic picture of Jesus hanging on the cross of Calvary. The caption simply reads, "It's Your Move!" What will you do with the cross?

The wages of sin is death, but the gift of God is eternal life in Christ
Jesus our Lord.
Romans 6:23

Lenya Heitzig
Ocean Hills Community Church
San Juan Capistrano, California

June 7

God Is Our Counselor

Your statutes are my delight; they are my counselors.
Psalm 119:24 NIV

There are a lot of "counselors" in our world today trying to influence us, sell us things, and show us the way to live our lives. This can be very challenging and confusing, especially when we are struggling to know God's plan rather than the world's plan!

Our Lord is uniquely qualified to be absolutely the best counselor for a variety of reasons:

Isaiah 9:6—He is mighty and everlasting . . .
Isaiah 28:29—He is magnificent in wisdom . . .
John 14:16–17, 25–27—He lives with us and in us . . .
John 15:26—He always tells the truth . . .
John 16:13—He knows what our future holds . . .

What is your definition of a good counselor? I read somewhere that if all of us were better listeners, that is, if we listened more and advised less, the majority of psychiatrists would soon be out of work! God is the ultimate example of an excellent listener. He is acutely interested in every thought and worry that we have, and His advice is highly accessible in the form of the Scriptures, made alive by the inspiration of the Holy Spirit. Write to Him. Give Him your concerns—He is listening!

Donna Riley
Calvary Chapel La Mesa
La Mesa, California

June 8

Incense and Prayer

Let my prayer be set before You as incense, the lifting up of my hands
as the evening sacrifice.
Psalm 141:2

Have you ever wondered what happens to your prayers after you pray them? Did you know that your prayers are stored in heaven in golden bowls? Take a look at Revelation 5:8 and you'll see!

In the Bible, incense represents prayer. The fragrance of incense has a way of lingering with you. In the Old Testament, a priest who spent the day burning incense would carry that scent home with him. Due to his aroma, his entire family would immediately know where he had been and what he had done that day!

I know about incense from firsthand experience because I used to work in an incense factory. The scent from the incense was so strong it was almost impossible to wash off. I like how this illustration represents our prayer lives. If you and I are taking time daily to meet the Lord in prayer, others will know it, for our lives will show, and smell like it.

For we are to God the fragrance of Christ.
2 Corinthians 2:15

Karen Stangel
North Shore Christian Fellowship
Haleiwa, Hawaii

In the Crucible

In this you greatly rejoice, though now for a little while you may have had to suffer grief in all kinds of trials. These have come so that your faith—of greater worth than gold, which perishes even though refined by fire—may be proved genuine and may result in praise, glory and honor when Jesus Christ is revealed.
1 Peter 1:6–7 NIV

Whenever I read this Scripture, my mind is immediately taken back to the days when my husband Chuck made jewelry. He would take his piece of gold or silver and put it in a crucible and begin to skillfully torch it. As the metal became hot, it turned to liquid and the impurities would come to the surface. He would repeat this process over and over. Each time, it became more brilliant and more pure.

God promises here in 1 Peter that although the trials we go through can cause grief, they have purpose! They are actually refining who we are in Him!

Over the last twenty-eight years of my walk with my Lord, I can sincerely say that there has never been a trial, no matter how fiery, that didn't bring forth refinement in me when I surrendered myself totally to His plan. Each time my faith was put to the test. Would I continue to praise God and live a life that brought Him glory and honor? Will you?

Lynda Kelly
Calvary Chapel Bullhead City
Bullhead City, Arizona

June 10

Face to Face

For now we see in a mirror dimly, but then face to face . . .
1 Corinthians 13:12 NASB

Gabriella was visiting California from Peru when a couple she'd befriended decided to play matchmaker. Through their prayer group, they knew of a single father in Washington State who needed a wife. Introductions were made over the phone and Dale and Gabriella began a long-distance courtship. Though they came from different worlds—she'd been an engineer in Peru and he was a farmer—they had the Lord in common.

Weeks passed as they continued their phone relationship. They soon decided to meet. Gabriella felt both nervous and shy on the flight to Seattle. She had never seen a picture of Dale and worried that she wouldn't be able to find him in the crowd at the airport. But when she stepped off the plane, she found his eyes immediately. In the midst of a room full of strangers, she knew exactly who he was.

"I fell in love with his voice," she explained, "but I knew him the moment I saw him." They were married just weeks later.

We too have a Groom waiting for us. We have only His voice to cling to now, but the day is coming when we will put a face to the voice we've grown to love. We will look into His eyes, and we will know Him in an instant.

Shannon Woodward
Calvary Chapel Marysville
Marysville, Washington

June 11

A Gifted Fruit

~⌘~

Draw near to God and He will draw near to you.
James 4:8

When you think of the word *loneliness*, does it inspire negative feelings?

We can look at loneliness as a painful experience—something that causes hurt and depression, even thinking of it as an enemy. But as Christians, loneliness can be our friend. Loneliness can cause us to look to Jesus. Sometimes we forget how close at hand Jesus is; that He sticks closer than a brother or any sister!

When we are brought to the place of feeling abandoned by all, loneliness can remind us to call out to our Lord. It amazes me how much our heavenly Father loves us, that He patiently waits for us to come to Him, and then He lavishes us with His goodness.

Jesus said "He that abideth in me, and I in him, the same bringeth forth much fruit: for without me ye can do nothing" (John 15:5 KJV). Only when we are abiding in Jesus can we bear much fruit. Loneliness can be God's tool to draw us closer to Him so we can bear fruit. Jesus loves us enough to use opposing factors in our lives for His good purpose. The more intimate we are with Him, the more of His fruit we bear—not just fruit, but much fruit that ultimately brings glory to Him.

Angela Tomasso
Calvary Chapel Westside
Spencerport, New York

June 12

Tell Him Your Needs

∽

The mother of Jesus saith unto him, They have no wine.
John 2:3 KJV

When Jesus was at this wedding, the wine ran out, causing an obvious interruption in the flow of festivities. Mary, His mother, brought the problem to Him. She didn't tell Him how or when He should fix it. She simply told Him what was going on and said to the servants, "Whatsoever he saith unto you, do it" (John 2:5 KJV).

Our days are often filled with things that seem to put a wrench into the flow of things. We can go to the Lord in those moments and, like Mary, tell Him our needs. Then we need to be ready to hear what He says and we must be willing to do whatever He says.

Many times when we go to the Lord, we begin to suggest all the ways we think our Lord could solve a given problem. Let us learn from Mary, stating our needs and trusting that He is more than able to accomplish what concerns us today.

Maureen Schaffer
First Love Calvary Chapel
Whittier, California

June 13

No Greater Joy

I have no greater joy than this, to hear of my children walking in
the truth.
3 John 4 NASB

We have become "empty nesters," shedding tears as each of our four children moved away. Yet, this is the "independence day" we waited for and trained them up to attain (Proverbs 22:6). But passing an empty bedroom, I catch a whiff of one of their lingering scents. I hear their voices, their laughter, their chatter. The walls echo their presence. Resolutely brushing away another tear, I remind myself that I'm happy for their new lives. They prayed, took small, first steps of faith, moving to new places, beginning their journeys with God alone. He answered our prayers graciously, as they found new, fulfilling "loves" beyond us. They are productive workers, contributing to society and becoming taxpayers. They fill shoes we once wore as Sunday school teachers, Bible study leaders, and worship leaders; they are parents raising small children, professionals beginning careers, or college students finishing their degrees. They are imitators of us.

Don't you want to have it said of you, "I was very glad to find some of your children walking in truth, just as we have received commandment to do from the Father" (2 John 4 NASB)?

God assures me there are more who will hide in the shadow of His wing, in the shelter of our nest. Once your children leave the nest, rest assured that He has something else for you to do, for He says:

I know the plans that I have for you . . . to give you a future and a
hope.
Jeremiah 29:11 NASB

Jeneane Herrera
Calvary Chapel Las Vegas
Las Vegas, New Mexico

June 14

The Intervention

Behold the handmaid of the Lord; be it unto me according to thy word.
Luke 1:38 KJV

Mary, though a virgin, would give birth to the Messiah! As remarkable as the news was, Mary's full-of-faith response deserves our thoughtful attention. We have much to learn from her, God's highly favored one. How do we respond to the sometimes inexplicable revelations of God in our lives—full of faith, or fear?

Apart from faith, Mary's news would have seemed a death sentence. A young woman, pregnant before the final wedding vows, could face a public trial and stoning. But sweet Mary responded so full of faith, knowing that God would somehow intervene. In every Christian woman's life there will come a time, perhaps many times, when she will need to wait for the intervention of God. And even though friends and family may not understand it, she will believe the words of God and trust in Him.

What else can we do? Should we assume God has looked the other way in neglect or forgotten a fatal detail of our lives? Should we fight what God has brought upon us and challenge His infinite wisdom, calling Him inept? No, we go against our tangible fear, and yes, even at times our common sense, so that we may respond as Mary did: full of faith.

Gina Pimentel
Calvary Chapel Grants Pass
Grants Pass, Oregon

June 15

Sing to the Lord a New Song

He put a new song in my mouth, a hymn of praise to our God. Many will see and fear and put their trust in the LORD.
Psalm 40:3 NIV

Our Lord desires us to have fresh new things to sing about and praise Him for. Praise abounds from a heart that is experiencing His new mercies every day, like an overflowing cup, full to the brim and spilling over with joy.

There are times when I am in His Word and a certain passage blesses me so much that I have a new song of praise in my heart. My heart also begins to sing at a retreat or conference when a speaker shares about a treasured moment with the Lord. Often during worship I am so filled with adoration for the Lord that each word I sing is a new reflection on who He is and how worthy He is to be praised.

Remember Snow White and the seven dwarfs singing, "Whistle While You Work"? It's hard to be like Grumpy when you're singing. Singing changes our attitudes. It makes the ordinary extraordinary.

I'm convinced that if we are making music in our hearts to the Lord, melody will flow out to others who will put their trust in Him. Take time with God often and I promise that you'll have plenty to sing about!

Christy Michaels
Calvary Chapel of the Springs
San Marcos, Texas

June 16

What a Friend We Have in Jesus

There is a friend who sticks closer than a brother.
Proverbs 18:24

Whenever a trial or dramatic thing happens in our lives, we are quick to go to a friend for counsel and comfort. Often that friend is too busy or maybe we just cannot seem to locate her. Possibly, the one we wish to talk to is not our friend anymore.

There is a friend who is always available and never too busy. When we call upon Him, we will never get a busy signal or voice mail. He will never tire of us. He is not just a lifelong friend; He is a friend to the end of the ages. He is a friend for all eternity. That friend is Jesus.

He calls to us, "Come to Me, all you who labor and are heavy laden, and I will give you rest" (Matthew 11:28). "Call to Me, and I will answer you, and show you great and mighty things, which you do not know" (Jeremiah 33:3). Jesus longs for us to go to Him and let Him be our best friend. The old hymn states, "What a Friend we have in Jesus. All our sins and griefs to bear! What a privilege to carry everything to God in prayer!" He waits.

"The Son of Man, . . . 'a friend of tax collectors and sinners.'"
Matthew 11:19

Mary Grigsby
Calvary Chapel Golden Springs
Diamond Bar, California

June 17

Life on the Edge

⚞⚟

Do not love the world.
1 John 2:15

Bang! Bang! Bang! Where was Heber, Jael's husband, as she drove the tent peg through Sisera the Canaanite's skull?

Judges 4 says that Heber "had separated himself from the Kenites and pitched his tent near the terebinth tree . . . which is beside Kedesh. . . . [and] there was peace between Jabin king of Hazor [Canaan] and the house of Heber the Kenite" (verses 11 and 17).

Heber was nowhere around. He had separated himself from his brethren, moved his family close to the borders of Canaan, and made alliances with the enemy.

Do we find ourselves separating ourselves from fellowship—isolating ourselves? Are we living too close to the edge, flirting with the world, and making unhealthy alliances?

God has placed borders in our lives that are based on His holy character and for our protection.

Walk worthy of the Lord, fully pleasing Him, being fruitful in every good work and increasing in the knowledge of God.
Colossians 1:10

Julie Guglielmo
Calvary Chapel Manitowoc
Manitowoc, Wisconsin

June 18

A Loving Father

Moreover, we have all had human fathers who disciplined us and
we respected them for it. How much more should we submit to the
Father of our spirits and live! Our fathers disciplined us for a little
while as they thought best; but God disciplines us for our good, that
we may share in his holiness.
Hebrews 12:9–10 NIV

Now that my children are grown, I realize the importance of discipline in
their lives, even though it was hard to administer when they were little.
My fears that I would cause them to turn against me were actually the
opposite of the truth because respect develops and relationships deepen
when discipline is done with consistency and love. The same is true in our
relationship with God.

God disciplines us so that we may share in His holiness. He corrects
us that we may walk in a way that honors Him. Discipline by definition
means to instruct, correct, and mold moral character. As I have grown
in the Lord, I thank God for His faithful correction and molding of my
character.

Is there an area of your life today where you feel His correction?
Submit to the Father of your spirit and live! Remember, God's purpose
for discipline in our lives is that we would share in His holiness!

Let us purify ourselves from everything that contaminates body and
spirit, perfecting holiness out of reverence for God.
2 Corinthians 7:1 NIV

Lynda Kelly
Calvary Chapel Bullhead City
Bullhead City, Arizona

June 19

Abba

And because you are sons, God has sent forth the Spirit of His Son
into your hearts, crying out, "Abba, Father!"
Galatians 4:6

Have you ever seen amazing dads in action and thought, "Wow! I wish I
had a dad like that"? I had heard numerous stories, and had even exhorted
others to trust in our loving heavenly Father, but had never really seen
God as *my* Father.

I started to look around at all the loving things God had given me or
allowed me to observe. I saw how He had lovingly cared for me, directed
me, and even disciplined me. I began to realize that I do have an amazing Father—we all do! Not only is He like great earthly dads, He is far
better. Just look around and count your blessings! He has brought me so
many blessings, such as my husband and my home. He loves our children
and has taught them so much. For the first time, I really saw God as my
Father.

How about you? Galatians 4:6 says the Spirit was sent into our hearts,
"crying out, 'Abba, Father!'" By His Spirit we have the privilege of calling
the God of the universe, "Daddy."

Thank Him today for the everlasting benefits of being His child!

Roseann Amo
Calvary Chapel Macomb
Fraser, Michigan

June 20

There Is No Other Name

For if a law had been given that could impart life, then righteousness
would certainly have come by the law.
Galatians 3:21 NIV

There is no law that can impart life. Yet there are so many people who believe their righteousness comes through the law. Ask anyone to explain to you their understanding of the gospel and you'll be surprised at the variety of answers. They might mention baptism, church attendance, prayers, or rituals. They might bring up their good deeds or say they are a "good person." But none of this can impart life. If righteousness could come by any of these means, Jesus would not have had to die on the cross.

Jesus asked the Father in the garden if there was any way possible for the cup to be taken from Him. But there was no other way. Jesus had to go to the cross. He commanded Peter to put away his sword and asked, "Shall I not drink the cup the Father has given me?" (John 18:11 NIV) Take a moment to ponder what it meant for Jesus to drink of the cup. Then thank God for His wonderful provision in Christ and for Christ's willingness to do the will of His Father!

Salvation is found in no one else, for there is no other name under
heaven given to men by which we must be saved.
Acts 4:12 NIV

Susan Figgs
Calvary Chapel Greeley
Greeley, Colorado

Father, May I?

Show me Your ways, O Lord; teach me Your paths. Lead me in Your truth and teach me, for You are the God of my salvation; on You I wait all the day.

Psalm 25:4–5

Do you remember playing the game "Mother may I" when you were a kid? I can remember being so careful not to forget to give the required response to the command, "Take six giant steps." "Mother may I?" If you forgot to get permission you would have to go back to the starting line. Likewise, the Lord has a specific plan for us. He has set before us a way in which we should walk:

For you were once darkness, but now you are light in the Lord. Walk as children of light.

Ephesians 5:8

Ten baby steps, six giant steps, sometimes even a frog leap or two. But there is *a time* and His timing is PERFECT!

To everything there is a season, a time for every purpose under heaven.

Ecclesiastes 3:1

However, all too often we run ahead of His Spirit, and in a sense, we are sent back to the starting line. Has He given you a glimpse of His plans? Do you have a vision to do a work for the Lord? Is there an important decision you need to make? May I encourage you today to remember to ask first, "Father, may I?"

Dawn Restivo
Calvary Chapel Westchester
Yonkers, New York

Strengthened in Faith, Giving Glory to God

He did not waver at the promise of God through unbelief, but was
strengthened in faith, giving glory to God, and being fully convinced
that what He had promised He was able to perform.
Romans 4:20–21

Abraham had been given a promise that to the human heart would have
seemed impossible. If he had, even for a moment, dwelt on the things
that were against him physically, he certainly would have faltered. But, he
intimately knew the One who had given the promise. Their relationship
was deep. He knew that God was faithful, able, his everything and his all
in all (Job 42:2–5)! At times, we waver in unbelief, even falter in our faith
when we should be trusting Him.

So, how did Abraham become unwavering? How did he believe without faltering, even for a moment, at the promise of God? How do we
gain this kind of wholehearted trust in God? By sitting at His feet and
meditating on His Word (Psalm 1:2), by talking to Him in prayer (1
Thessalonians 5:17), and by worshiping Him at all times, in all things
(John 9:31). As you seek Him, He will make Himself known to you, even
the intimate things of His heart (Psalm 25:14). He is able, He is everything, He is our all in all!

. . . for I know whom I have believed . . .
2 Timothy 1:12

Lisa Stewart
Living in Christ Ministries
Dallas, Texas

June 23

Ready, Set, Jump!

He who testifies to these things says, "Surely I am coming quickly."
Amen. Even so, come, Lord Jesus!
Revelation 22:20

Satan does not want us to think, ponder, or get excited about the return of Christ or what we have to look forward to when He returns.

When I got saved, I was filled with excitement, zeal, and eagerness knowing Jesus was coming for me. I would look up into the heavens, point out the enormous white fluffy clouds to my children, and say, "This could be the day!" Then together we would say, "Ready, set, jump," and we would jump for joy, ready to be swept up into heaven.

That was many years ago and my five children have grown up. Now I am a grandmother of eleven. I can't jump as high with my grandchildren, but I can still tell them of His coming as we look into the sky with excitement on those absolutely beautiful days.

Don't get so busy that you miss the blessing He has set before you. And don't get so weighed down with anger, bitterness, ambition, or competition that you can't jump for joy.

Be eagerly waiting.

This is the day the LORD has made; let us rejoice and be glad in it.
Psalm 118:24 NIV

Marsha Johnson
Calvary Chapel Flagstaff
Flagstaff, Arizona

June 24

Delight in the One Who Delights in You

The LORD takes delight in his people. . . . Let the saints rejoice in this
honor and sing for joy.
Psalm 149:4 NIV

Think about the Lord: who He is and all He has done for you. He delights
in you and sings over you with great joy. Be close enough to the Lord to
hear His voice when He speaks or sings over you. The Father is near to
those who want to hear Him. He wants to reveal His presence to you
today. Don't be too busy or distracted to take the time to listen.

The Father delights in you, so delight in your Father. Pursue the things
of God. Pray that He would give you a zeal and a passion for His Word,
for worship, and for sitting at His feet.

Delight yourself in the LORD and he will give you the desires of your
heart.
Psalm 37:4 NIV

To "delight" is to be soft and pliable in the Lord's hands.

The LORD your God is with you, he is mighty to save. He will take
great delight in you, he will quiet you with his love, he will rejoice over
you with singing.
Zephaniah 3:17 NIV

Father, I want to delight in You as You delight in me.

Kathy Etheridge
Calvary Chapel Eastside
Colorado Springs, Colorado

June 25

Be Still and Wait

Rest in the LORD, and wait patiently for Him...
Psalm 37:7

We love to read the Psalms. They are so encouraging to us, particularly when we are struggling through challenging times. God is faithful to refresh our hearts and renew our faith through them. Such is the case with this glorious gem of a verse.

This verse, as with many others, was written by David not within the quiet comforts of the castle, but rather in the den of difficulty and caves of consternation. Saul was constantly after David. This was a time of unreasonable harassment for him. Yet it was there that he compiled his faith, devotion, and trust in God. He learned to rest, to be still, and to enjoy His peace. From those experiences and victories were produced powerful, heartfelt, anointed prayers, praise, and worship to God.

Psalm 37:7 reminds us what we are to do and where God desires us to be. To "rest" is to be silent, still, and quiet before Him. To "wait patiently" is to know with certainty that God will act, save, and deliver me from evil.

This process of resting and waiting is not easy, especially when God seems to be silent and we need God to help us "now." But, God will faithfully come through for those who wait upon Him and He will give us rest for our souls.

Carole Presley
Calvary Chapel of the Western Palm Beaches
Royal Palm Beach, Florida

June 26

In the Secret Place with Christ in the School of Prayer

"Pray to your Father who is in the secret place; and your Father who
sees in secret will reward you openly."
Matthew 6:6

"Lord, teach us to pray" (Luke 11:1). Prayer is something that I will continually learn, but I have found valuable lessons from Jesus' response to the demands of ministry.

And seeing the multitudes, He went up on a mountain and when He was
seated His disciples came to Him. Then He opened His mouth . . .
Matthew 5:1–2

For a higher experience with Jesus, we must pull away from the multitude of things that will crowd out our time alone with Him. When we come close to Jesus and sit still with Him, we have the promise that He will open His mouth and speak to us. And with that comes great reward!

What crowds Him out, oh restless soul? Do you desire the blessings of His voice, oh listening ear? Learn from the Master, oh disciple, the rewards of:

A secret place to meet with Jesus.
A set aside time to be with Jesus.

As a student ready to hear His voice, open your Bible. He has something to say to you.

Jesus opened His mouth and spoke to His disciples then, and when His disciples open His Word, He will speak to them today!

Candice Beckelman
Calvary Chapel Coastlands
Red Bank, New Jersey

June 27

Broken

"Father, if thou be willing, remove this cup from me: nevertheless not
my will, but thine, be done."
Luke 22:42 KJV

On a retreat, I heard a woman pray, "Lord, break me!" "But I don't want
to be broken," I thought to myself.

Then the Lord gave me an illustration. A man took a horse with a
stubborn spirit out of the wild. He gave the horse food and shelter. He
brushed the horse and whispered in its ear, "I love you; trust me."

The man wanted the horse to bear weight, so he would lie across the
horse's back, speaking softly to the horse, "I love you; trust me."

The day came when a bit was placed in the horse's mouth. The horse
now would turn to the right and left, guided by the reigns. "I love you;
trust me," the man said to the horse.

God is so gentle with us in His training process. Through trials and
time in the saddle we come to love, trust, and obey our Master. We need
to be broken, so our wills line up with God's will.

Soon the horse and rider ride off together, with one purpose, one goal,
one direction.

Our wills must line up with the Father's will so Jesus can be glorified
through our lives.

Debbie Crawford
Calvary Chapel Somerset
Somerset, New Jersey

June 28

I Am Hungry

〜

The disciples had forgotten to bring bread, except for one loaf that
they had with them in the boat.
Mark 8:14 NIV

The disciples were with Jesus when He had miraculously fed the five thousand and the four thousand. The disciples knew Jesus could multiply food to provide for them. Then why were they concerned?

"Maybe He would not want to do a miracle today . . . what if it is not His will?" they may have reasoned. Have you been at that point—wondering if God would provide for you? Have you limited God to your time schedule? Have you given Him a list of requests? Have you said, "I am hungry, now"?

We know intellectually that God can provide for us, but in all honesty, we would rather be in control ourselves. We would rather have our own fish that we can eat whenever we want. "Lord, help us to wait on You to provide. Help us to trust Your timing."

Holly Robinson
Calvary Chapel Oldsmar
Oldsmar, Florida

June 29

Do What You Can Do

"She has done what she could."
Mark 14:8

As Mary of Bethany brought the alabaster flask of precious oil to anoint Jesus she may have thought it was an insignificant act of worship. "What difference would it make?" "How could this possibly minister to Him?" Oh, but it wasn't insignificant to Him! It did minister to Him! Jesus called her act of worship "good" (Mark 14:6).

Too many times the Enemy or others tell us that what we are doing for the Lord is insignificant and isn't enough. Our own flesh can tell us it is not enough. But when our heart attitude is to pour our love on the Lord, serving Him in whatever way we can and in whatever capacity we can, He looks at it as "good"!

We may not be called to do what we think are great and mighty things for the Lord. But we must do what we can . . .

> the little things . . .
> the quiet things . . .
> the secret things . . .
> ALL that we can do . . .

And when we do what we can, Jesus is blessed, and He calls it "good."

Karin Kyle
Calvary Chapel Modesto
Modesto, California

June 30

You Are Not Alone

Let each of you look out not only for his own interests, but also for
the interests of others.
Philippians 2:4

Each time a woman comes to church for the first time, a few thoughts
come to mind. She thinks that everyone has known each other for years,
that all the women are good friends, and that she will not be welcomed
into their group. After some time she begins to identify certain faces and
begins to establish a friendship with a few who have a tendency to sit in
the same area. This may take some weeks or even months. Church is not
a place where someone should leave feeling lonely. Everyone needs to feel
that she belongs. After the wonderful worship service and the rich teaching, she needs to find at least one person who reaches out to her; someone
who will invest time in getting to know her, someone who will encourage
and pray for her.

Be kindly affectionate to one another with brotherly love, in honor
giving preference to one another.
Romans 12:10

Whenever there is an opportunity, enter church with the prayer that
the Holy Spirit will direct you to that person who needs to experience
God's loving kindness through you.

Carol Fitzgerald
Calvary Chapel of St. Louis County
Maryland Heights, Missouri

July 1

An Attitude of Contentment

I have learned to be content whatever the circumstances.
Philippians 4:11 NIV

Life is a series of circumstances, some more pleasant than others. How we respond to those circumstances determines our level of satisfaction in life. Paul's use of the word *learned* in his letter to the Christians at Philippi indicates that contentment is an attitude rather than an emotion. In other words, we can *choose* to be content.

Discontentment equals disappointment. Because of Paul's choice to be content, he was able to minister without complaints or disappointment—whether hungry or well fed, imprisoned or free. Discontentment stifles the work of the Holy Spirit in our lives and ministries. Because the circumstances in life are rarely what we would choose, it is difficult, if not impossible, to minister effectively without an attitude of contentment.

The psalmist David tells us that if we delight ourselves in the Lord, He will give us the desires of our hearts, and as we delight in Him, our desires begin to line up with His. When we focus on our ideas, goals, happiness, and comfort, we come across so many disappointments. On the other hand, when we are pursuing God and desiring to please *Him*, there is little that can disappoint us.

Once we have learned the attitude of contentment, our lives cease to be a series of disappointments; they become satisfying.

But godliness with contentment is great gain.
1 Timothy 6:6 NIV

Dea Gros
Calvary Chapel Silver City
Silver City, New Mexico

July 2

Get Back on the Horse

The steps of a good man are ordered by the LORD. . . . Though he fall,
he shall not be utterly cast down; for the LORD upholds him with His
hand.

Psalm 37:23–24

One of my favorite activities as a young girl was horseback riding. I especially loved jumping. It was such an exciting sport, but one that could be very dangerous as well. The higher the jump, the more likely I was to be injured. One day when I was attempting a jump that was very high, my horse froze and stopped dead in his tracks. Unfortunately, I kept going and was catapulted into the air and over the hurdle. Afterward, I lay on the ground stunned and in pain. As I slowly got up and started limping away, my trainer asked me, "Where do you think you're going?"

I thought that was a silly question. Obviously I was done there! But she said, "If you don't get back on that horse right now, you never will." She made me push through my pain and fear that day, and I'm glad she did.

I think of that lesson often in regard to the ministry. Being in the ministry can also be exciting and dangerous. As Paul said in 2 Corinthians 4:8–9, "We are hard-pressed on every side, yet not crushed, we are perplexed, but not in despair; persecuted, but not forsaken."

On those many dry, lonely, difficult, overwhelming, and painful days when we are tempted to limp off saying, "I am done here!" we need to listen to the encouragement we receive from the Lord to persevere. How many times I have wanted to stop, but He tenderly reminds me that the blessings are just ahead. The Scriptures promise us, "He who [began] a good work in you will complete it until the day of Jesus Christ" (Philippians 1:6).

So we need to dust ourselves off and get back on the horse, praying as one poet did:

> God harden me against myself,
> This coward with pathetic voice
> Who craves for ease and rest and joys
> Myself, arch-traitor to myself;
> My hollowest friend, my deadliest foe,
> My clog whatever road I go.[12]

Karen Pulley
Calvary Chapel Old Bridge
Old Bridge, New Jersey

July 3

Leaning on the Promises of God

For all the promises of God in Him are Yes, and in Him Amen, to the
glory of God through us.
2 Corinthians 1:20

What wonderful and precious promises our Lord Jesus has given to us.
God is good and He always keeps His promises. We can depend on that!
One of the action words that Jesus uses in speaking to us, and that is of
utmost importance, is the verb "to trust." Some Bible translations use the
original Hebrew word "to lean on." I pray that these verses will be planted
deep within your hearts this year.

He who heeds the word wisely will find good, and whoever [leans on]
the LORD, happy is he.
Proverbs 16:20

Whenever I am afraid, I will [lean on] You.
Psalm 56:3

Behold, God is my salvation, I will [lean] and not be afraid.
Isaiah 12:2

You will keep him in perfect peace, whose mind is stayed on You,
because he [leans on] You. [Lean on] the LORD forever, for in YAH,
the LORD, is everlasting strength.
Isaiah 26:3–4

Peggy Kravig
Calvary Chapel Downey
Downey, California

July 4

Shattered Frogs

∽

He heals the brokenhearted . . .
Psalm 147:3

"Mimi, I'm sorry I broke your frog."

It was Christmas day. All the kids and grandkids would soon be at my house. Everything was ready and I could smell warm cinnamon buns in the oven and fresh coffee.

My father had died in July and this would be my first Christmas without him. As we sat down to open our gifts, my daughter Christy gave me a big green frog. It was just like the one my dad had in his garden! I loved it!

I had many pictures and memories of Dad along with that big green garden frog. My granddaughter Leah picked up the frog to hand it to me and dropped it. It broke in a million pieces. She looked up at me in horror—fear was all over her face. I quickly picked her up to hug her and dry her tears. I said, "Leah, never, never be afraid of me! I love you and I can get another frog." She calmed right down and said, "Mimi, I thought you would be mad at me!"

I knew how Leah felt. I've messed up many things God has asked me to do. I, too, have cried holding broken pieces, afraid God would be mad at me.

Psalm 34:15 and 18 tell us, "The eyes of the LORD are on the righteous, and His eyes are open to their cry. . . . The LORD is near to those who have a broken heart."

Give Jesus the pieces of "your broken frogs." He can fix, replace, and renew any crushed or shattered issue in your life!

Karyn Johnson
Calvary Chapel Downey
Downey, California

July 5

Hope in Our Trials

Every good gift and every perfect gift is from above, and comes down
from the Father of lights, with whom there is no variation or shadow
of turning.
James 1:17

If we do not understand that because God alone is "good," only good can
come from Him, we won't experience His goodness as a shield between
us and the trials and temptations we regularly face. We must accept and
believe this truth in order to experience the power and presence of God
upholding us and strengthening us during those times. But if we doubt,
we will be drawn to the lies of our deceitful Enemy, the Devil.

If our focus is on the Lord and what He wants for our lives, then His
Word becomes a vehicle within us, aligning our thoughts and desires with
His thoughts and desires.

To know the Lord we must be in His Word. Only then will we be able
to confidently look at the trials we face and say, "What good can the Lord
bring about through this situation?" Once you've made this declaration,
wait with excitement to witness His faithfulness.

The LORD will guide you continually, and satisfy your soul in drought,
and strengthen your bones; you shall be like a watered garden, and
like a spring of water, whose waters do not fail.
Isaiah 58:11

Bonnie Botsford
Horizon North County
Rancho Santa Fe, California

July 6

Perfect Time to Pull

... that we through the patience and comfort of the Scriptures might
have hope.
Romans 15:4

I was weeding my garden where the ground was exceptionally hard when I came upon a weed with a particularly deep root. I wasn't sure how far down this root went, but I knew that if I didn't remove all of it, this wild plant would immediately grow back. After soaking the dirt, I carefully dug away, but I was expending a lot of time and effort on one weed. Resolving that I had sufficiently soaked the ground and spent more than enough time on this little plant, I pulled. Snap! Because of my impatience, part of the root remained deep in the ground.

Do you (or a person you know) have deep roots in hard soil? Does it seem like God isn't taking away a sin that you've been struggling with? Have you given something to the Lord that keeps sprouting back?

Victory takes perseverance. Soak yourself with His Word. Look into the face of the Master Gardener—Jesus. He knows the perfect time to pull.

... their souls shall be like a well-watered garden, and they shall
sorrow no more at all.
Jeremiah 31:12

Julie Moyer
Calvary Chapel Carlsbad
Carlsbad, California

July 7

Persnickety

To keep me from becoming conceited because of these surpassingly
great revelations, there was given me a thorn in my flesh, a messenger
of Satan, to torment me.
2 Corinthians 12:7 NIV

Thorns—who likes them? Have you ever pricked your finger on a rose
bush and wondered why God put thorns on something so beautiful?
Actually, the thorns are there to protect the delicate roses.

When my children were small, one of their favorite stories was
Persnickety, a *Serendipity* tale of a little dragon who decided to remove the
thorns from his rose bushes because he wanted to live in a perfect world.
Sound familiar? He soon discovered that his other dragon friends loved to
eat the petals, and they quickly destroyed his beautiful flowers. The lesson
Persnickety learned that day, as he taped the thorns back on the bushes,
was that without protection, the roses will be destroyed.

God will allow the thorns in our lives to keep our feet on the ground.
Paul declares this in 2 Corinthians.

Is there a "thorn" in your life that is ruining your perfect world? Accept
the thorns, His grace will be sufficient. And if you do, you will find that
you will bloom where God has planted you.

Remember, Christ accepted the thorns as He went to the cross for
you.

Lynda Kelly
Calvary Chapel Bullhead City
Bullhead City, Arizona

July 8

Don't Get Stung!

For the wages of sin is death, but the gift of God is eternal life in
Christ Jesus our Lord.
Romans 6:23

Ever notice people's reaction when they see a bee? Some approach curiously, realizing that it can sting. Others just ignore the bee and let it fly around, indifferent to the danger. Little boys will catch a bee to remove its stinger, believing it is a game. But there are those rare few who have been stung enough to have experienced the full brunt of the poison. Fear grips their heart because they know that just one bee sting can cost them their life.

Sin is much like the bee. The Bible says in 1 Corinthians 15:56, "The sting of death is sin." Sin can kill us, yet some see sin as no big deal. They curiously approach, indifferent to the danger, and believe they can win the game because they are impervious to the poison being deposited into their souls. But when their marriages fail, their lives fall apart, or their dreams are dashed, they finally understand the consequences of sin. It is in this raw recognition of the reality that the wages of sin is death that they gain the fear of the sting that will lead to life:

The fear of the LORD is a fountain of life, to turn one away from the
snares of death.
Proverbs 14:27

Diane Coy
Calvary Chapel Fort Lauderdale
Fort Lauderdale, Florida

July 9

Seek Him Today

Shew me thy ways, O LORD; teach me thy paths. Lead me in thy truth,
and teach me: for thou art the God of my salvation; on thee do I wait
all the day.
Psalm 25:4–5 KJV

In these last days there is but a short time before our Lord Jesus Christ calls for the body of Christ to come home. I want to make good use of my days. From early in the morning, all the day long, until evening.

"Teach us Your ways, oh Lord God Almighty. Teach us Your ways, oh Lord Emmanuel. We are nothing without You, Lord. Teach us to love, to give, to praise You, so that we can love, instruct, and encourage others in Your ways."

Oh, how God loves you and wants to have fellowship with you today so that He can use your life to make a difference in this world. "So teach us to number our days, that we may apply our hearts unto wisdom" (Psalm 90:12 KJV).

Jesus always sought to do His Father's will. Jesus did nothing before prayer. In the same manner, we shall follow Jesus and seek our heavenly Father in prayer and in His Word today.

And let the beauty of the LORD our God be upon us: and establish
thou the work of our hands upon us; yea, the work of our hands
establish thou it.
Psalm 90:17 KJV

Vickie Stahl
Deschutes Christian Fellowship
Bend, Oregon

July 10

Read Any Good Books Lately?

All Scripture is given by inspiration of God, and is profitable
for doctrine, for reproof, for correction, for instruction in
righteousness.
2 Timothy 3:16

Women are sometimes known for enjoying romance novels, historical fiction, and biographies—books that involve a hero saving the life of a heroine. Some of us love to read about the rich and famous, the dashing and
the daring. We enjoy reading about the tragedies in the heroine's life . . .
her accomplishments . . . the sacrifices she has made and hardships she has
endured. And we love reading about the hero—tall, dark, handsome, and
strong.

As believers, we often read Christian historical fiction, or Christian biographies. There's nothing wrong with a little diversionary reading. God
gave us rich imaginations and curious minds.

But when was the last time you stayed up half the night reading your
Bible because you couldn't put it down? And you couldn't wait to find out
what happened to Samuel? Or Paul? Or Jesus—a true hero? When was the
last time you chose to read the Word instead of watch a movie? There's
romance, heroism, tragedy, even comedy! Hardships are overcome. And
there is the ultimate sacrifice. Maybe we just haven't seen the Word as it
really is . . . a great book, full of life, and "able to make you wise for salvation through faith which is in Christ Jesus. . . . that the man [or woman]
of God may be complete, thoroughly equipped for every good work" (2
Timothy 3:15, 17).

Jayne Kier
Calvary Chapel Northwest
Kennesaw, Georgia

A Firm Foundation

The wise woman builds her house, but the foolish pulls it down with
her hands.
Proverbs 14:1

It's been said that women are the heart of their homes. We are the ones
who set the climate, keep things running smoothly, keep the kids fed and
clothed, and make our homes a place of refuge for our families. In order
for us to "build" our homes and not pull them down, we must have good
foundations.

First Corinthians 3:11 says, "For no other foundation can anyone lay
than that which is laid, which is Jesus Christ." We may build our homes on
good things: marriage, children, paychecks, even our ministry. However,
if we build them upon anything besides our Lord Jesus, they will eventually be pulled down because none of those things, however good, promise
to always be there.

Jesus does. He is the Rock immovable, and in Him, we have a solid
foundation. As we please the Lord, He will take care of those "good"
things. All of our needs and desires will be fulfilled, and we will be as trees
planted by streams of water, bearing the fruit that counts for eternity.

What are you building your house upon? Only Jesus is a foundation
that will not fail. Build your house on Him!

"Therefore whoever hears these sayings of Mine, and does them, I will
liken him to a wise man, who built his house on the rock."
Matthew 7:24

Lynn Fernandez
Calvary Chapel Twin Cities
Bloomington, Minnesota

July 12

Blessed Believer

Blessed is she who believed, for there will be a fulfillment of those
things which were told her from the Lord.
Luke 1:45

How sweet the concern of the Father for Mary, that He should also send
news that would give confirmation and comfort from her very own relative, Elizabeth. With Gabriel's morsel of information about Elizabeth,
Mary made haste to the hill country of Judea to speak for the first time of
her wondrous encounter and the promised hope of their nation Israel. I'm
sure she made haste for confirmation as well.

There were no telephones or e-mail. The journey would take several
days. What intense anticipation must she have felt on the way. Mary could
not afford to doubt Elizabeth's condition, for this would mean an uncertainty of her own. She must believe the word of the Lord. It is all she has.
Have you ever been in a situation that forces you to exercise your faith
in God's Word for you? In those days of hurried travel, there was a work
being done in Mary's heart. For where evidence is lacking, faith is growing
in the heart of a true believer. Until the time of sweet confirmation, she
must simply believe the word of the Lord.

Gina Pimentel
Calvary Chapel Grants Pass
Grants Pass, Oregon

July 13

What Shakes Your World?

I have set the LORD always before me. Because he is at my right hand,
I will not be shaken.
Psalm 16:8 NIV

Have you ever experienced an earthquake? I remember a strong quake that shook our home in Portland, Oregon, when I was seven years old. Dishes crashed off the kitchen shelves, and pictures swayed on the living room wall. It was a frightening experience I will never forget.

Even if you live where earthquakes are uncommon, it's still possible to face problems that shake your world: the death of a loved one, the miscarriage of a long-awaited child, relationship struggles with other Christians, serious illness, or financial hardships.

How do we deal with these life-shaking events? Our strength and stability come from the Lord. We can experience peace and a close connection with Him even in the midst of difficult times as He becomes our focus rather than allowing the fear to take control. Meditating on His awesome character and wonderful works will help keep Him in the forefront of our minds.

Joy, better health, security, and peace. Now that sounds like a great way to live!

My heart is glad and my tongue rejoices; my body also will rest secure.
. . . You have made known to me the path of life; you will fill me with
joy in your presence.
Psalm 16:9, 11 NIV

Carrie Turansky
Calvary Chapel Mercer County
Mercer County, New Jersey

July 14

The Housewife and the King

David replied to Abigail, "Praise the LORD, the God of Israel, who
has sent you to meet me today! Thank God for your good sense."
1 Samuel 25:32–33 NLT

Very often as wives, mothers, daughters, or career women, we are in the
middle. Beautiful Abigail was caught between two unreasonable men. Her
husband Nabal "was mean and dishonest in all his dealings" (1 Samuel
25:3 NLT). David, the future king who was usually wise and patient, had
told his men, "Get your swords!" He was angry—determined to kill her
and everyone in her household.

Two strong, powerful men out of control—one woman of great character. She could have run away, but instead she chose to stay and face the
battle. Courage and common sense are a beautiful combination. Be sure
that you are staying strong in the Word of God and prayer. When the
battle rages, you will be filled with God's wisdom. Abigail spoke boldly
to the great warrior and leader, David. Amazingly, he listened. More than
that, he took her advice. When we are speaking God's truth, even kings
and leaders will take note.

Arlene Schroer
Calvary Chapel Central Islip
Central Islip, New York

July 15

Ever, Only, All for Thee

❧

My eyes are ever toward the LORD.
Psalm 25:15

With all the busyness of life and all its trials, and with all the unrest in the world, *now* more than ever we need to become *passionate* about our Lord Jesus! *Webster's* defines *passion* as "a strong love and affection"; it implies a strong emotion that has an overpowering or compelling effect. We need to be passionate about His Word and about spending time in His presence. In these last days, we need to acquire a strong, overpowering love for Jesus that has a compelling effect on our lives, which in turn will affect all the lives around us.

Our passion grows as we spend time in His Word and in His presence. Our passion grows as we keep our eyes ever toward the Lord: focused, fixed, and firm. Dear precious one, are you in the Word daily? Are you seeking the Savior's heart in prayer? Where is your focus? What are you passionate about? May your life be one of passion for your Jesus! Lift up a heartfelt prayer unto Him!

> Take my love,
> My Lord, I pour
> At Thy feet its treasure store.
> Take myself, and I will be
> Ever, only, all for Thee.
> *Frances R. Havergal, 1836–1870*[13]

Cyndi Ballmaier
Calvary Chapel of Elk Grove Village
Elk Grove Village, Illinois

July 16

The Importance of Having a Testimony

And this is the testimony: that God has given us eternal life, and this
life is in His Son.
1 John 5:11

The Bible is full of instructions about what we are to remember and what we are to forget. The Israelites were told over and over again to remember where they had come from and the bondage they had once lived in. Why? Why did the Lord want them to remember? Wouldn't it just be better to forget the past?

What is a testimony? One dictionary defines it as that which confirms: evidence, proof, testament, confirmation, verification, authentication, substantiation, validation.

Deuteronomy 6:20–25 gives us some very important insights as to why having a testimony is so important. People everywhere are watching Christians and want to know why they follow the instructions of the Lord. Our testimony proclaims the mighty power and goodness of the almighty God. A changed life speaks louder than any words that we could say.

What evidence or proof can you point to in your own life of a true conversion to Jesus Christ?

The apostle Paul was a walking example of a true conversion. Paul said, "I consider my life worth nothing to me, if only I may finish the race and complete the task the Lord Jesus has given me—*the task of testifying to the gospel of God's grace*" (Acts 20:24 NIV, emphasis added).

What is your testimony? Have you ever taken the time to write out a one-to-three-minute testimony of how you came to Jesus Christ? Is your life living proof that God exists and has miraculous saving power?

Peggy Kravig
Calvary Chapel Downey
Downey, California

July 17

Is There Any Mail for Me?

❧

He who refreshes others will himself be refreshed.
Proverbs 11:25 NIV

In this day and age of faxes and e-mail, I still love to receive a card or a letter from one of my friends. I especially love to glance quickly through the letter for Scripture verses. Then I look them up and mark them in my Bible. So many times that verse or encouraging word comes just when I need to be uplifted.

Has the Lord laid on your heart a special word for a friend? Then take time today and send them a note or a letter. Proverbs 15:4 tells us, "The tongue that brings healing is a tree of life" (NIV). It is also "like cold water to a weary soul" (Proverbs 25:25 NIV).

When Mary went to visit her cousin, Elizabeth, she entered her home with a greeting. Elizabeth was filled with the Holy Spirit at that very moment. May the words we speak to others be so edifying that they are filled with God's joy and peace.

He who loves a pure heart and whose speech is gracious will have the
king for his friend.
Proverbs 22:11 NIV

Karyn Johnson
Calvary Chapel Downey
Downey, California

July 18

Look Out Ahead!

After the doings of the land of Egypt, wherein ye dwelt, shall ye not
do: and after the doings of the land of Canaan, whither I bring you,
shall ye not do: neither shall ye walk in their ordinances.
Leviticus 18:3 KJV

The Lord was giving His people a clear warning. They were not to walk in the ways of the Egyptians (the former ways), nor were they to walk in the ways of Canaanites (the ways of the world around them).

Many of us easily avoid the former things. Whether it was captivity to the approval of others, drugs, illicit sex, anger, or some other vice, most believers are so happy to be out of those traps. Leaving them is a joy.

It's those enticements in the land of promise that we more readily embrace, deceiving ourselves into thinking they are okay. These are those temptations that blend with the blessings He gives us and yet which can bring us into subtle compromises, causing us to blend in rather than to stand out.

Let us ask our God for discernment between the land He gives us and the practices of those He abhorred (Leviticus 20:23). We must be just as cautious walking into the land as we were when He first delivered us from Egypt.

Ye shall do my judgments, and keep mine ordinances, to walk therein:
I am the LORD your God.
Leviticus 18:4 KJV

Maureen Schaffer
First Love Calvary Chapel
Whittier, California

July 19

No Greater Blessing

❧

"It is more blessed to give than to receive."
Acts 20:35

Today, truly "give" this a try . . . put the needs of others before your own.

If we do this we will discover that our needs are being met and our desires are fulfilled. We will have an overflowing joy and a peace in our lives that passes all understanding.

The things we can obtain for ourselves cannot be compared to the blessings of the Lord. So do not lose heart; take every thought captive today to the obedience of Christ through your time in daily prayer and in His Word. Let Him set you free today by giving yourself to Him in service to others.

"For God so loved the world that He gave His only begotten Son, that whoever believes in Him should not perish but have everlasting life."
John 3:16

Bonnie Botsford
Horizon North County
Rancho Santa Fe, California

July 20

Morning Devotion

My voice You shall hear in the morning, O LORD; in the morning I
will direct it to You, and I will look up.
Psalm 5:3

It is clear from this verse that David had a devotional prayer time with the
Lord in the early part of the day. Morning devotions are such a blessing. In
the morning, our hearts and minds are more focused. God loves it when
we seek Him early in our day. He is always faithful to meet us with new
inspiration and direction each day.

God is concerned with those things that concern us, so He waits for
us to bring them to Him in prayer. David knew the benefit these special
encounters with the Lord would have and looked forward to them each
morning. I too have looked so forward to the special time the Lord has
given me in the mornings. Whenever I have missed time with the Lord, I
have felt the absence of His presence with me, even though I knew He was
there. I missed that special communion that comes from spending time
with Him each morning.

Start out each day with a devotional prayer time with the Lord. You
will feel His presence and have special communion with Him.

Terri Rodriguez
Calvary Chapel Corona
Corona, California

July 21

What's Today's Schedule?

My beloved spoke, and said to me: "Rise up, my love, my fair one, and come away. For lo, the winter is past, the rain is over and gone."
Song of Solomon 2:10–11

Have you ever missed an appointment and not remembered it until a day later? It's a dreadful feeling, realizing someone was expecting your arrival and they waited in vain. You apologize and pray they will understand and forgive your negligence.

Every day we have a special appointment to meet with Jesus. We don't even have to check our daily planner. Song of Solomon 2:14 calls to us, "O my dove, in the clefts of the rock, in the secret places of the cliff, let me see your face, let me hear your voice: for your voice is sweet, and your face is lovely."

The lover of our souls longs to meet with us every day to tell us how much He loves us, how much He longs to spend precious time speaking to our hearts. If you are like me, you are grieved when you miss those hair appointments, lunch appointments—any appointment. How much more should we ask the Lord to burden our hearts to keep that divine appointment with Him.

You who dwell in the gardens, the companions listen for your voice—
let me hear it!
Song of Solomon 8:13

Gay Nell Lazovich
Calvary Chapel on Hereford Road
Sierra Vista, Arizona

July 22

Caution: Wild Pigs!

By faith Noah, being divinely warned of things not yet seen, moved
with godly fear, prepared an ark for the saving of his household.
Hebrews 11:7

Years ago, my husband and I went camping at Big Sur, California. Upon
entering the campground we were met with a sign saying, "Caution: Wild
Pigs." The warning went on to say; "Do not leave anything unattended
in your campsite." We laughed at the warnings, even made fun of them.
In rebellion, we left our food and camping equipment unattended that
night. We were rudely awakened to the commotion of loud snorting. Not
willing to venture out of our tent, we watched helplessly as the wild pigs
destroyed our camp. The next morning, we were humbled at the destruction and at the dumbfounded gaze of our neighboring campers.

How often we bring calamity to our lives because we don't take to
heart the warnings God has given us. Colossians 1:28 tells us, "Him we
preach, warning every man and teaching every man in all wisdom, that we
may present every man perfect in Christ Jesus."

Give heed to the warnings that God has given in His Word that your
life may be filled with His blessings. Don't let the wild pigs destroy your
camp.

The judgments of the LORD are true and righteous altogether. . . .
Moreover by them Your servant is warned, and in keeping them there
is great reward.
Psalm 19:9, 11

Connie Gill
Calvary Chapel Running Springs
Running Springs, California

Spend Time with Jesus and Glow

Charm is deceitful and beauty is vain, but a woman who fears the
LORD, she shall be praised.

Proverbs 31:30 NASB

We buy cosmetics, fragrances, and creams that promise beauty and miracles. Our make-up bags are filled to overflowing with foundations, lipsticks, cover-ups, liners, eye shadows, blushes, etc. Don't get me wrong, there is nothing wrong with Christian women wearing make-up. Unfortunately, however, too often we spend time on the outside and forget about the inside.

Proverbs 31 tells us all about the characteristics of a wonderful woman of God: what a hard worker she is, how wise she is, and how her children rise up and call her blessed. Nowhere does it mention what she looked like. God counts external beauty of small value. He didn't come to earth looking like a movie star—He came looking average and ordinary—like us. Take comfort in 1 Samuel 16:7:

> For the LORD does not see as man sees; for man looks at the outward
> appearance, but the LORD looks at the heart.

After spending time in God's presence, Moses' face shone (Exodus 34:35). Women who love the Lord and spend time with Him have a joy and glow about them that cannot be purchased at the cosmetics counter.

Psalm 16:11 tells us,

> In Your presence is fullness of joy.

Spend time with Jesus.

Tonya Ruiz
Calvary Chapel Pacific Coast
Westminster, California

July 24

Thy Will Be Done

To obey is better than sacrifice.
1 Samuel 15:22 NIV

When we think of Christ, we think of patience, love, and compassion, but we need to think of how He obediently lived His life. You might ask, "Whom did He obey?" He is God after all! These Scriptures provide the answer.

"Truly, truly, I say to you, the Son can do nothing of Himself, unless it is something He sees the Father doing; for whatever the Father does, these things the Son also does in like manner."
John 5:19 NASB

"For I have come down from heaven, not to do My own will, but the will of Him who sent Me."
John 6:38 NASB

Jesus would do nothing apart from the Father. Total obedience! He was obedient in every move He made, even unto His death on the cross. This was not an easy command to obey. Jesus asked, "'Father, if you are willing, take this cup from me; yet not my will, but yours be done.' . . . And being in anguish, he prayed more earnestly, and his sweat was like drops of blood falling to the ground" (Luke 22:42, 44 NIV).

Was this painless for Christ? Obviously not, but He did it for love; He did it out of obedience to the Father. Obedience is not easy, but if you know the One you are obedient to, you can trust that He will work it out for your good.

Nancy Porter
Calvary Chapel Merced
Merced, California

July 25

The Lilac Tree

"He cuts off every branch in me that bears no fruit, while every branch
that does bear fruit he prunes so that it will be even more fruitful."
John 15:2 NIV

"He cuts off every branch." Often painful trials are the instruments our
Father uses to prune us. This past spring, my lilac tree was very beautiful;
the blossoms were bursting with joy. The lilacs perfumed the air, but one
of the smaller branches could not hold the weight of the blossoms and
began to break. I tried cutting off some of the lilacs to ease the weight, but
it still wasn't enough. It was time to cut off the branch.

Our heavenly Father is a loving gardener and He has a purpose for
every branch He prunes. Often the branches He desires to prune are the
ones we want to hold on to the most. Are we willing to let go, let the
branch break that He might do a greater, more fruitful work in us? The
fruit He desires for us to bear is fruit that will remain and cause lasting joy.
Are you in a place today where your branches are being broken? Rest in
the knowledge that He always completes the work He begins.

"This is to my Father's glory, that you bear much fruit, showing
yourselves to be my disciples."
John 15:8 NIV

Karen Gettemy
Calvary Chapel Vancouver
Vancouver, Washington

July 26

My Life as a Gymnast

❧

For do I now persuade men, or God?
Galatians 1:10

Here I sit at my daughter's gymnastic meet, anxiously waiting for her scores to come up. All the parents nervously watch the scoreboards, hoping their child's score meets with their approval. Judges watch for every unpointed toe, every bent knee, and every wobbly ending. The entire process is nerve-wracking!

As I watch her perform, I am amazed at how similar my life is to the gymnast. So often I live my life hoping to get a perfect score from others around me. I push myself to the limit, hoping and praying that this "thing" that I've done will meet with the approval of my peers. At times I feel like my every move is being evaluated, and I anxiously wait for the scorecard to come up telling me how I've done. What a tiring way to live!

It's easy to fall into the trap of trying to please man rather than God. The scores that others give me for my good works don't count. I'm saved by grace, not works, lest any man should boast (Ephesians 2:8–10). Why am I working so hard to please everybody with my fantastic flips and my awesome acrobatics? Forgive me, Lord, and thank You that I don't have to work for Your love. Thank You for loving me just as I am: clumsy and uncoordinated. I may not have stolen the hearts of the judges, but I am the apple of Your eye (Psalm 17:8).

Kelly Bell
Calvary Chapel Murrieta
Murrieta, California

July 27

God Calls His Own by Name

"And the sheep hear his voice; and he calls his own sheep by name and
leads them out."
John 10:3

While waiting anxiously for news updates on our son, I noticed something that horrified me. His chart had a different name written on it. The nurse explained to me that anyone coming to the trauma unit due to an accident is automatically called "John Doe." But my son had a name. He belonged to us. His friends and family were all present praying for him and rooting him on. His coach identified him on the street. So even before he was taken to the hospital, he had a name and belonged to our family.

Jesus calls you by name. He paid the ultimate price to make you a member of His family. Isaiah 49:1 says, "Listen to me, all of you in far-off lands! The LORD called me before my birth; from within the womb he called me by name" (NLT). Be careful not to live your life as a "John Doe." Know your Master's voice. He's calling you by name.

"The sheep follow him, for they know his voice."
John 10:4

A week later, no more coma, and no need for life support. My son was wearing a gift from his cousin, a baseball cap sporting a new name, "Miracle Man."

Terry Hoganson
Calvary Chapel Anaheim
Anaheim, California

July 28

Cracked Pot Beacons

"Let your light so shine before men, that they may see your good
works and glorify your Father in heaven."
Matthew 5:16

Examining Old Testament Scriptures for descriptions of the physical, tangible, presence of God, we discover that each possesses properties of a substance that doesn't stay in one place. These elements, if left unchecked, *spread*—like fire, smoke, sound, water, and light. By their very nature, they *disperse*.

Understand, the substances used as metaphors to describe the manifestations of God don't lose their original properties as they disperse. Undiluted water, at the end of its spreading, remains water (or hydrogen and oxygen). Similarly, God's character never changes, but remains the same—yesterday, today, and forever. God's Word, as it spreads throughout the earth, remains undiluted, undefiled, and unchanged. "The grass withers, the flower fades, but the word of our God stands forever" (Isaiah 40:8).

And, God's light, synonymous with God's love, cannot be contained. God has given each of us His light that spills out onto those lives we touch. We're all freight-damaged, leaky, earthen vessels. By virtue of our relationship with Jesus, His light and His Word spread through us to the outermost parts of the earth. Praise God, His perfect light shines through us to guide the lost out of darkness into His glory.

Helen Sacks
Calvary Christian Fellowship
Forest Grove, Oregon

July 29

At the Crossroads

Be not far from me, O God; come quickly, O my God, to help me.
Psalm 71:12 NIV

I entered the battlefield when my precious granddaughter Kylee was born with a congenital heart defect. She underwent two open-heart surgeries by the time she was two weeks old. I prayed for her daily, read her Scriptures, sang praise songs, and claimed God's promises. I was so sure that the Lord was going to heal her. After spending two-and-a-half months in the hospital, she was released to go home. What a glorious day that was!

However, when Kylee was four months old, my daughter woke up and discovered that she was having problems. When she reached the hospital, they performed CPR on her for one hour and then the doctor turned to us and said, "I'm so sorry, we did everything we could." It seemed that our world was turned upside down. What happened? Where was God? I was at the crossroads of either being angry with God and turning away from Him, or clinging to my Savior, leaning on my faith, and trusting Him. It was then that I was reminded of Psalm 71. It caused me to lean on the Lord's strength.

Who can separate us from Christ's love? Can trouble, distress, persecution, hunger, nakedness, danger or a sword?
Romans 8:35 ISV

Sandi Hostetler
Hosanna Christian Fellowship
Lakeside, California

It's a Walk of Faith, Isn't It?

Trust in the LORD with all your heart, and lean not on your own understanding; in all your ways acknowledge Him, and He shall direct your paths.

Proverbs 3:5–6

Why am I amazed when the Lord chooses to keep me "in the dark" on so many occasions, requiring me to trust in Him and not to lean on my own very limited comprehension? I see myself as a woman of faith until I am required to walk without the "sight" of my own understanding. How marvelous it is that the Lord only requires us to take one step at a time. My right foot does not need to worry about the destination of my left foot; *that* decision is in the Lord's capable hands.

Whenever I am afraid, because I cannot understand the circumstances the Lord has placed me in, I find myself running to this verse and clinging to it with both hands. No, I don't understand why things are happening most of the time. But this is when I have the opportunity to look, not at the swirling waters around me as Peter did, but to Jesus who is outside of time and space. He *can* and *will* direct, lead, and guide me as He promised He would.

For we walk by faith, not by sight.
2 Corinthians 5:7

Marcie Matsen
Calvary Chapel Portsmouth
Portsmouth, England

July 31

Come to Jesus and Obey

This day I call heaven and earth as witnesses against you that I have set before you life and death, blessings and curses. Now choose life, so that you and your children may live and that you may love the LORD your God, listen to his voice, and hold fast to him.
Deuteronomy 30:19–20 NIV

Dear, are our poor hearts troubled?
Did we fall and lose our way?
I can hear the master calling
Come to Jesus and obey.
Did Satan's lies deceive us?
Did we fail and fall to sin?
I can hear my Savior pleading
Children, stop and start again.
Did the guilt condemn and hurt you?
Did your prayers seem void and lost?
Is this sin so hard to turn from?
Jesus calls us—count the cost.
Is this wound too deep for healing?
Has your spirit cried in grief?
Yet, His blood has offered pardon,
He has purchased our relief.
Oh, I prayed for I was sorry,
Too sorry friend to tell,
But, in my penance He forgave me
For He loved me though I fell.
His sweet lips beckoned to me
And I listened to His Word

But, the purging burns within me now
To tell you what I've heard.
For though we fall, we are forgiven
If we'll only ask and pray
And hearken to that calling
Come to Jesus and obey.
Source unknown

Many times, we suffer under circumstances of our own choosing. Yet, see how merciful and patient our Savior is as He continues to call us back to His love. Fortunately, He gives us plenty of warning in His Word. He takes no joy in our pain. Like any parent, He would spare us, yet so often we choose poorly. Today, choose life, blessing, and the Father. Come to Jesus and don't forget to obey.

Susan G. Frisina
Calvary Chapel Northeast Columbia
Columbia, South Carolina

August 1

Rest

"Come aside by yourselves to a deserted place and rest awhile."
Mark 6:31

My husband and I are very fortunate to spend time alone with God and each other at a trailer in northern New Jersey. It is so important to take a break from our busy lives to be refreshed and refilled.

At the trailer we watch yellow finches and hummingbirds, chipmunks and squirrels as they look for food to be refreshed and refilled also. One day I even saw a bear plodding slowly through our campsite.

Nothing can compare to the spiritual refreshment we receive from the Lord. Spending time in His Word and in prayer, we sit at His feet and rest in peaceful surroundings that He created.

In the woods, we marvel at God's handiwork. What an artist God is! Look at the flowers, so brilliant in color. Look at the tall trees, their arms reach toward heaven as if to praise God.

Spending time alone with God strengthens and refills us. We need to stop often so we don't become dry and empty.

When we return home to see man's handiwork of concrete, steel, and blacktop, is it any wonder we long to steal away with the Lord, to that deserted place once again, to find that perfect rest in Him?

Debbie Crawford
Calvary Chapel Somerset
Somerset, New Jersey

August 2

Waiting Is Winning

Wait on the LORD; be of good courage, and He shall strengthen your
heart; wait, I say on the LORD!
Psalm 27:14

Alan Redpath, a famous Bible teacher from England, has been quoted as
saying, "Waiting is winning." As I have grown in the Lord over the years,
I have come to understand the deeper meaning of Mr. Redpath's quote.
We try to run ahead of God at times, only to find that we make foolish
decisions because of our impatience.

God's timing is always perfect. When we choose to wait, putting our
hope and expectations in the Lord, He opens up many awesome opportunities for us to learn and to know Him better. Are you in God's waiting
room? Are you waiting for God to move in a situation in your life? Be of
good courage and wait on the Lord. In doing so, He will strengthen your
heart. "Waiting is winning."

Terri Rodriguez
Calvary Chapel Corona
Corona, California

Never Run Dry

~✦~

The bin of flour was not used up, nor did the jar of oil run dry,
according to the word of the LORD which He spoke by Elijah.
1 Kings 17:16

Many years ago, I received this Scripture on a card at a retreat. When I came home, I cut it out and placed it near an old pitcher I had salvaged from my mother's estate. Since then, I have collected a few more pitchers, each representing the jar in today's Scripture. These pitchers are constant reminders of God's faithfulness to me: as a child of God, a wife of a pastor, and a mother of four. In my nearly seventeen years of knowing Jesus, I can say with certainty that the flour has not been used up and the oil has not run dry. God has always met my every need. He's always ready to fill me up and to satisfy.

[He] has given to us all things that pertain to life and godliness.
2 Peter 1:3

Oh, if we could continually lay hold of the limitless resources available to us through Him and dig deep into the bin of the Lord, we would truly experience the abundant life He has promised. Our struggles begin when we put our eyes on our circumstances and ourselves and somehow think we can fill ourselves or solve our dilemmas. If we do this, we will end up like the widow, saying, "[I] have . . . only a handful of flour in a bin, and a little oil in a jar, and see, and I am gathering a couple of sticks that I may go in and prepare it for myself and my son, that we may eat it, and die" (1 Kings 17:12). Don't give way to despair. Open your eyes! Look! Your bins and your jugs are full, "according to the word of the LORD."

"I am the bread of life. He who comes to Me shall never hunger, and
he who believes in Me shall never thirst."
John 6:35

Jennifer Buran
Calvary Chapel Costa Mesa
Santa Ana, California

Whom Can You Trust?

> . . . by which have been given to us exceedingly great and precious
> promises . . .
> *2 Peter 1:4*

God's promises are exceedingly great! This fleshly vessel cannot fully comprehend the vastness of that truth. We, in our humanity, break promises all the time; we are finite, frail, and imperfect. But God's promises relate to the very character of God Himself. He is holy; He is truth; He is infinite; He cannot lie; He is consistent, the same yesterday, today, and forever.

What He tells us in His Word is true and accurate. Everything He says will be done according to His good pleasure. He has promised and He will do it. He is awesome!

> . . . for it is God who works in you both to will and to do for His good
> pleasure.
> *Philippians 2:13*

How many promises from God's Word do you know? Do you know His character enough to believe that He will keep those promises? Can you trust Him in whatever situation you find yourself today? He is the only One who has proven Himself worthy.

Marcie Matsen
Calvary Chapel Portsmouth
Portsmouth, England

August 5

Spiritual Darvocet

Jesus said, "I am the way, the truth, and the life. No one comes to the
Father except through Me."
John 14:6

Recently after ankle surgery, I was given Darvocet to manage the pain.
Interesting drug, Darvocet. It made me imagine all kinds of silly things,
like creepy crawlers shimmying their way across my carpet. Once I even
thought a rat was speeding through my living room! Darvocet was not
welcomed in my home for long. I decided I would rather throb than hal-
lucinate.

It occurred to me that the Enemy of our souls works a little bit like
Darvocet. He wants us to see things that aren't really there. He wants us
to imagine that things are bigger than they are, to believe lies instead of
truth. It's easy to lose our perspective and allow problems to grow to an
overwhelming size. We then become frustrated, fearful, and sometimes
frantic.

How do we guard against the effects of "spiritual Darvocet," which
the Enemy encourages us to take? Simple. Search the Scriptures daily and
pray without ceasing. That will keep our hearts and our minds focused
on God, the problem solver. The Bible tells us that Satan is the Father of
Lies, but truth is found in Christ. Don't fall into the Enemy's trap. Don't
pop the "spiritual Darvocet" pill. Nourish yourself with the Bread of Life
and the Living Water; only then will you be able to discern what is true
from what is not. Then you will walk in faith rather than give in to fear
and frustration.

Kelly Bell
Calvary Chapel Murrieta
Murrieta, California

He Said

He did not waiver at the promise of God through unbelief, but was strengthened in faith, giving glory to God, and being fully convinced that what He had promised He was also able to perform.
Romans 4:20–21

Abraham didn't waiver at the promise of God with unbelief, but was strengthened in his faith because he knew God was able to do what He had promised.

God is still very much able to perform His promises in our lives. A few years back, we experienced the death of three family members within fifteen months: my husband's grandmother, his father, and our son.

He said He would be near to those with a broken heart and He was (Psalm 34:18).

He said He would be our comfort in all our tribulations and He was (2 Corinthians 1:3–4).

He said when we are weak, He would be our strength and He was (Psalm 73:26).

He said He would work all things out together for good and He did (Romans 8:28).

He said that those who believe on Him have eternal life and we do (John 3:15).

So if you're going through something difficult today, remember He said, "I AM" near, "I AM" your comfort, "I AM" your strength, "I AM" eternal life. He said "I AM" that "I AM." He is all we need.

Angela Halan
Calvary Chapel of Oakland County
Troy, Michigan

August 7

The Attitude of Gratitude

I will bring the blind by a way they did not know; I will lead them in
paths they have not known. I will make darkness light before them,
and crooked places straight. These things I will do for them, and not
forsake them.

Isaiah 42:16

The great hymn writer Fanny Crosby spent most of her ninety-five years
blind due to a doctor's mistake at birth. She wrote over eight thousand
hymns during her lifetime, among them "Blessed Assurance" and "To
God Be the Glory." Her very first poem at age eight read:

> Oh, what a happy soul I am,
> Although I cannot see!
> I am resolved that in this world
> Contented I will be.
> How many blessings I enjoy
> That other people don't,
> To weep and sigh because I'm blind
> I cannot, and I won't!

The "attitude of gratitude" is something that desperately needs to be
cultivated in our hearts and in our homes. As we celebrate each new day,
let us consider all that we have to be thankful for and encourage thankfulness in the hearts of our children. There are so many wonderful things to
think about and to thank God for.

Peggy Kravig
Calvary Chapel Downey
Downey, California

August 8

But my servant Caleb, because he had another spirit with him, and
hath followed me fully, him will I bring into the land.
Numbers 14:24 KJV

Even among God's people you sometimes meet those who stand out more
than others. They just seem to follow the Lord fully and enter into all that
the Lord has for them. Caleb did not just fit in with the group. He had
a different spirit than that of the majority of the people. They brought
back negative reports that resulted in murmurings against leadership and
against the Lord Himself. Caleb had a different spirit. He spoke up even
after the others declared their resignation to defeat.

And Caleb stilled the people before Moses, and said, Let us go up at
once, and possess it; for we are well able to overcome it.
Numbers 13:30 KJV

Caleb spoke up as a lone voice among the people and dared to have
another spirit.

He that hath knowledge spareth his words: and a man of understanding
is of an excellent spirit.
Proverbs 17:27 KJV

Caleb was a man of understanding. Caleb was a man with another
spirit, an excellent spirit.

May the Lord Jesus baptize us afresh with His Holy Spirit so that we
can be as Caleb before our God, following Him fully, and as a result, be
brought into the land He has for us.

Brethren, the grace of our Lord Jesus Christ be with your spirit.
Galatians 6:18 KJV

Maureen Schaffer
First Love Calvary Chapel
Whittier, California

I Prayed, He Heard, He Answered

For this child I prayed, and the LORD has granted me my petition
which I asked of Him.
1 Samuel 1:27

I desired a second child—not only did I, but so did my husband and my
thirteen-year-old daughter. We had waited seven years for our first daughter, and in His perfect timing we were blessed. Now we were praying and
waiting again. As time went by, I began to think maybe I should stop
praying because I was content and blessed with what God had already
done in our lives. I was getting older, but then I would remember Sarah.
I would be encouraged to know that nothing was impossible with God.
I began to pray more earnestly because my fear was that my daughter
would not understand a "No" answer from the Lord. I was afraid that her
faith would be hindered. Well, God heard and then He answered. After
ten years of prayer and waiting, I was pregnant again. What a testimony
to increase my daughter's faith! Then I miscarried. My daughter believed
that God had answered, but then why would He let the baby die? God is
sovereign and I trust Him even when I don't understand. You can always
find peace and comfort in the loving arms of our Lord Jesus.

For I know whom I have believed and am persuaded that He is able to
keep what I have committed to Him until that Day.
2 Timothy 1:12

So whether it's a baby, your salvation, your job, your schoolwork, your
friends, your husband, or your children, God is able to keep what you
commit to Him. God had given me Philippians 1:6,

Being confident of this very thing, that He who began a good work in
you will complete it until the day of Jesus Christ.

For three more years I held on to that promise, wondering if it was
my flesh or the Lord. Again, God heard and God answered—we adopted

a baby girl! With no intentions of adopting a child at the time, the Lord placed this little blessing in our laps. What a precious gift and what a praise to the Lord! What a faithful God!

If God has given you a promise to hold onto, don't give up—He is able. A day to the Lord is as a thousand and a thousand is as one day. God is doing a work that we don't understand—trust Him.

Patricia Maciel
Calvary Chapel Downey
Downey, California

August 10

Life Is Hard, But God Is Good

❧

"In this world you will have trouble. But take heart! I have overcome
the world."
John 16:33 NIV

We had just come home from a baseball game and were laughing when
the phone rang. I answered it . . . my brother was calling to tell me that
our sister had been killed. In a moment, our lives were turned upside
down. But, in the midst of the chaos, God spoke softly to my heart; "I am
sovereign and in control; trust Me."

Sometimes in the midst of crisis, we forget that God is on the throne.
It is during those times that we must cling to the Rock of our salvation.
When nothing seems to make sense, we hold fast to what we know. No
matter what the circumstances are, we know God is good; we know He
loves us and is in control. Nothing touches our lives without first going
through the Lord's hand of love. He is faithful and true; He is the only
constant when our worlds are falling apart. He alone can bring beauty
from ashes.

As we look back, we see that during times of great sorrow, we experience greater joy. In those times of sorrow, we are driven to the cross and
to the arms of Jesus. Embrace those difficult times. Trust the Lord with all
your heart, and know He loves you unconditionally.

I will turn their mourning into joy.
Jeremiah 31:13 KJV

Dottie Pratchard
Calvary Chapel Concord
Concord, California

August 11

A Transformed Life

Let this mind be in you, which was also in Christ Jesus.
Philippians 2:5 KJV

If you can change a woman's way of thinking, you can change her whole outlook on life! You can literally transform her into a new woman! How desperately we need the mind of Christ today so that we can think as He would think. *Mind* in this verse speaks of your attitude, morals, and way of thinking. To have the mind of Christ means that we must set aside worldly thinking and think according to the Word of God.

True joy comes with right thinking. That was Paul's secret to maintaining his joy. He refused to allow himself to turn the doorknob of discouragement! He kept the truth on his mind, and any thought that was contrary to truth, he cast aside. When confusion comes into your life, go to the Word and ask the Lord for right thinking. Pray for His mind and heart in the matter troubling you. Remember, like Paul, nothing can touch you unless God allows it, and if God allows it, then it's going to work for your good.

Give the Lord permission to search your life. Ask yourself if there's an area of your thinking that needs to be transformed. If so, surrender that area to Him and pray for the Lord to begin that transforming work on your mind today.

Gail Mays
Calvary Chapel South Bay
Gardena, California

August 12

Fingers in the Pudding

"Blessed are the peacemakers; for they shall be called the children of
God."
Matthew 5:9 KJV

Abby was seated at the table in the order of her birth, between her two
brothers. They had finished their pudding first and were dipping their fingers into hers with many justified protests from her. As the mother of four
boys, and now as a grandmother, I was the veteran of many such disputes,
and felt more than qualified to mediate a quick end to this one. The roles
of villains and victim were clearly defined, after all! "Boys, get your hands
out of your sister's pudding. Abby, take your pudding and sit on the other
side of the table so they won't be tempted." Well, she stood up to move,
but couldn't resist waving her pudding in their faces, so a chase around
the room ensued. The victim had become a vixen and every peacemaker's
nightmare was realized!

Similar scenarios are reenacted every day in our homes, churches,
workplaces, and on the world stage—wherever people interact. As matur-
ing Christians, our goal in all of our relationships must be to "seek peace
and pursue it" (Psalm 34:14; 1 Peter 3:11). How much we desperately
need to call upon the Prince of Peace, Jesus Christ, to empower us for this
difficult role in our places of influence!

If it be possible, as much as lieth in you, live peaceably with all men.
Romans 12:18 KJV

Shary Bove
Calvary Chapel Anaheim
Anaheim, California

August 13

Jesus Knows and Cares

We do not have a high priest who is unable to sympathize with our
weaknesses, but we have one who has been tempted in every way, just
as we are—yet was without sin.
Hebrews 4:15 NIV

This past year the flare up of a chronic illness kept me in bed for several months. Unable to do even the simplest tasks for myself and my family, I was tempted to give in to despair. My battle to overcome discouragement became even more important to me than my physical healing. I discovered I can live with illness, boredom, and weakness, but I can't live without hope and God's comfort.

Poring over Scripture, I found this verse in Hebrews 4. What a relief to know Jesus understands my weakness and cares about me. He sympathizes with me in my pain and troubles, and He longs to pour out His mercy and grace on me.

Whether I'm sick or well, I can choose to pour out the burdens of my heart to God and expect to receive His mercy and grace to help me through even my most difficult days.

Let us then approach the throne of grace with confidence, so that we
may receive mercy and find grace to help us in our time of need.
Hebrews 4:16 NIV

Carrie Turansky
Calvary Chapel Mercer County
Mercer County, New Jersey

August 14

The Secret of Prayer

So He Himself often withdrew into the wilderness and prayed.
Luke 5:16

The Creator of the universe who gave you life invites you into the very heartbeat of heaven, the Holy of Holies, to pour out to you the depth of His heart, the riches of His glory beyond which nothing can compare. Prayer fills our emptiness with God's riches, lifting us out of the earth and into the heavenlies.

If anyone could have lived a life without prayer, it would have been Jesus Himself. But prayer was as natural to Him as breathing. He knew its magnificence. It was His habit, His love, and His life. He was a master at the fine art of prayer. He had an intense desire to be with His Father, and He prayed often through the night. Jesus' prayers weighed heavily with the Father because of the holy and obedient life He led.

William James Willis, saved during the Welsh Revival of the 1900s, said, "Prayer sets the hand of God in motion to ignite a mighty upheaval in hearts."[15] If every real Christian in the world would start praying, you'd have the mightiest upheaval you've ever seen, and the Welsh Revival would fade into insignificance.

The secret of prayer? Do it. Do it. Do it.

Vi Goodrich
Horizon Christian Fellowship
Indianapolis, Indiana

Fighting the Battle

～≈～

For the word of God is living and powerful, and sharper than any
two-edged sword, piercing even to the division of soul and spirit, and
of joints and marrow, and is a discerner of the thoughts and intents
of the heart.

Hebrews 4:12

Let's face it, we're in a battle here on earth. Situations arise constantly that
we must combat, like fear or some hidden sin. The Lord of Hosts, the
Creator of the universe, has provided an effective weapon for us to fight
through these battles—the Word of God. I don't know about you, but I'm
not going to just stand by and watch; I'm going to fight and I'm going to
pick up this wonderful, powerful weapon God has given to me.

Your word I have hidden in my heart, that I might not sin against You.
. . . I will meditate on Your precepts, and contemplate Your ways. I will
delight myself in Your statutes; I will not forget Your word.

Psalm 119:11, 15–16

During battle, a soldier must be able to quickly draw his weapon, and
that's why it's important to know the Word and have it hidden in your
heart. Mark those Scriptures that you have found useful and memorize
them, whatever it takes. You can do it! Just start today, and before you
know it, you'll have an entire arsenal ready for use!

CeeCee Greenroyd
Calvary Chapel Los Alamitos
Los Alamitos, California

August 16

God Is at Work!

❧

I'm convinced: You can do anything and everything. Nothing and no
one can upset Your plans.
Job 42:2 MSG

It was an all-too-close look at the circumstances of my life (and a not-close-enough focus on the promises of our faithful God!) that caused me to be discouraged one beautiful spring day. The sun was shining outside, but I couldn't seem to shake the heaviness that clouded my heart. "Lord, I've been praying and waiting so long for You to accomplish a miracle in these difficult things! Why aren't You working?" I pleaded with Him.

Oh, the love of God, which encircles us every moment of the day and has the ability to cut through the fog of our limited human perceptions! There in His Word, like a soothing balm for my emotion-wracked heart, was the promise of Job 42:2. Overcome with gratitude, I was again reminded that our loving God is, indeed, the sovereign controller of all! He is busy behind the scenes, orchestrating the events and circumstances of all that I have entrusted to Him, whether I can detect it or not!

Are you feeling overwhelmed by *your* circumstances today? Remember this: Your God is mighty, and He is working with loving detail behind the scenes of every situation you have committed into His care. Let's walk in the confidence that indeed, He can do anything and everything! Nothing or no one can upset His plans!

Robin Milhouse
Calvary Chapel Moreno Valley
Moreno Valley, California

August 17

Clear Minded-"I Can See Clearly Now"

The end of all things is near. Therefore be clear minded and self-controlled so that you can pray. Above all, love each other deeply, because love covers over a multitude of sins. Offer hospitality to one another without grumbling. Each one should use whatever gift he has received to serve others, faithfully administering God's grace in its various forms. If anyone speaks, he should do it as one speaking the very words of God. If anyone serves, he should do it with the strength God provides, so that in all things God may be praised through Jesus Christ. To him be the glory and the power for ever and ever. Amen.

1 Peter 4:7–11 NIV

We live in a time of urgency, making it imperative that we be clear minded—having the mind of Christ—and that we walk in obedience to the Lord so that nothing can separate us from the Father's heart. Knowing the Father's still, small voice as you surrender your all in all ensures the victory. These are choices we all must make. Are you making right choices? Do everything to please Him. Then you can sing, "I can see clearly now!" because He has opened your eyes!

I pray also that the eyes of your heart may be enlightened in order
that you may know the hope to which he has called you.
Ephesians 1:18 NIV

Kathy Etheridge
Calvary Chapel Eastside
Colorado Springs, Colorado

August 18

Love in Action

❧

And now abide faith, hope, love, these three; but the greatest of these
is love.
1 Corinthians 13:13

God's Word tells us that the evidence of being born again is *love*. Never really taking the time to consider what that love might entail, I just assumed it would produce itself and flow freely from my life. It came as a shock one day while reading 1 Corinthians 13:13 and 14:1 that I am called to pursue love. To *pursue* means "to follow or press hard after, to pursue with earnestness and diligence in order to obtain." What kind of love are we to pursue with earnestness and diligence?

> Love suffers long and is kind; love does not envy; love does not parade itself, is not puffed up; does not behave rudely, does not seek its own, is not provoked, thinks no evil; does not rejoice in iniquity, but rejoices in the truth; bears all things, believes all things, hopes all things, endures all things. Love never fails.
> *1 Corinthians 13:4–8*

Sandi Prudhomme
Calvary Chapel Solano
Fairfield, California

August 19

What Is Your Favorite Scent?

But thanks be to God, who always leads us in triumphal procession
in Christ and through us spreads everywhere the fragrance of the
knowledge of him.
2 Corinthians 2:14 NIV

Walking through the airport to catch a connecting flight, I detected the delicious aroma of freshly baked cinnamon rolls. I'm sure shop owners blow the scent out into the concourse hoping to attract hungry travelers like me. My eyes scanned the row of shops and soon spotted the familiar sign. I cringed and took a sip from my water bottle, then I reminded myself those gooey treats definitely weren't good for my diet.

As I passed the shop and made my way to the gate, my mind drifted to other favorite scents . . . freshly cut Christmas trees, apple spice candles, warm chocolate chip cookies, and lilacs in spring. Each scent brought pleasure and special memories.

Did you know that our lives can give off a sweet smelling fragrance? As we share the gospel and live out the powerful, life-changing truths in His Word, we can attract others to Him . . . just like an irresistible scent. And there are no calories to regret!

Lord, help me to spread the fragrance of Christ wherever I go today!

Christ loved us and gave himself up for us as a fragrant offering and
sacrifice to God.
Ephesians 5:2 NIV

Carrie Turansky
Calvary Chapel Mercer County
Mercer County, New Jersey

August 20

Overwhelmed Once Again!

Hear my cry, O God; attend unto my prayer. From the end of the
earth will I cry unto thee, when my heart is overwhelmed: lead me to
the rock that is higher than I.
Psalm 61:1–2 KJV

Once again I awake and remember all the demands of the day. This life is
so busy. I have groceries to buy, food to make, and the house has yet to be
cleaned. Then there are the events that need to be attended to. I am overwhelmed with all the needs. As I am making coffee, I remember whom I
serve and say, "Lord, I know You will help me make it through the day,"
and He reminds me of this verse: "when my heart is overwhelmed: lead
me to the rock that is higher than I." Yes! I cry out to God about the day
and let Him know I am overwhelmed. He brings me into fellowship with
Him through time in the Word. I obtain the peace that passes all understanding (Philippians 4:7).

The Creator of the universe is on my side. He is walking through the
day with me. He has heard my cry. No need to be overwhelmed. Take time
to seek His face and be in the Word, and you will not be overwhelmed.

Denise Johnson
Calvary Chapel Mesa
Mesa, Arizona

August 21

A Fork in the Road

For the ways of the LORD are right; the righteous walk in them.
Hosea 14:9

We live in a world of sound bytes, microwaves, and instant messaging. It seems the whole world is in a rush. The road we travel is a high-speed superhighway.

The New Testament calls us to walk, and in Colossians 1:9–10, we are told why.

> For this reason we also, since the day we heard it, do not cease to pray for you, and to ask that you may be filled with the knowledge of His will in all wisdom and spiritual understanding; that you may walk worthy of the Lord, fully pleasing Him, being fruitful in every good work and increasing in the knowledge of God.

Every day we come to a fork in the road: we choose to walk on God's righteous path or on the world's superhighway. On God's path we are filled with the knowledge of His will when we spend time daily with the Lord through His Word. When we spend time with Him in His Word and know His will, we have spiritual understanding and are fully pleasing to Him. When we are fully pleasing Him, we are fruitful in every good work and we increase in our knowledge of God. You have come to the fork in the road. Which way will you choose?

Terry Urciuoli
Calvary Chapel Ontario
Ontario, California

August 22

The Light of Life

❧

"I am the light of the world. He who follows Me shall not walk in
darkness, but have the light of life."
John 8:12

I very much enjoy lighthouses. When looking at a lighthouse, it isn't just
the outward building that is so amazing, but the responsibility that it represents. These lighthouses are interesting and some are pretty to look at,
but without the light shining from it, it becomes just that—a pretty building. Add the dimension of light and now it has purpose—to save lives.

We are our Lord's lighthouses. We can put on a pretty paint job, but
add the dimension of His light shining forth from us and we then have a
purpose—to help save lives. Ephesians 5:8 exhorts us to walk as children
of light.

Lighthouses are placed on the edge of a rocky shore or sometimes
right in the midst of a tumultuous sea. They are made of stone to withstand the pounding storms that come along. So we are to shine for the
Lord right where He has placed us. He encourages us in Psalm 27:1 not to
fear, for He is our strength. So today, stand strong in our Lord and shine
His light of life.

"Let your light so shine before men, that they may see your good
works and glorify your Father in heaven."
Matthew 5:16

Tami Hall
Calvary Chapel Fortuna
Fortuna, California

August 23

The Power of Words

My purpose is that they be encouraged in heart and united in love.
Colossians 2:2 NIV

We would all like to believe that we are fighters. We see movies and read about great men and women who, despite the criticism around them, pressed on toward their goals and achieved the seemingly impossible.

I want to be that kind of person, don't you? A fighter working for the Lord and not seeking the approval of man, but pressing on toward the goal no matter what. That's what God wants from us right?

Yes, God does want us to "press on," but He also knows how hard that is at times. Feelings of doubt come our way often. That's why in Hebrews we are told to encourage each one another *daily*.

I wonder how often we have contributed to the downfall and destruction of our own Christian brothers and sisters with our silence, our lack of support, or our active criticism. Then again, how many people have gone on to achieve great things for the Lord through a simple encouraging word we've given?

Encourage one another daily, as long as it is called Today, so that
none of you may be hardened by sin's deceitfulness.
Hebrews 3:13 NIV

Cindy Tipton
Calvary Chapel Molokai
Kaunakakai, Hawaii

August 24

Who Is My Friend?

*A man that hath friends must shew himself friendly: and there is a
friend that sticketh closer than a brother.*
Proverbs 18:24 KJV

In this day and age there are many that will align themselves as friends
with us. I have seen and felt the hurt and sorrow that is wrought upon us
at the hands of friends. Harsh words, gossip, backbiting, and suchlike—
damage that can be hard to heal and that remains long in the memory. But
I have a friend indeed in Christ our King.

*He that loveth pureness of heart, for the grace of his lips the king
shall be his friend.*
Proverbs 22:11 KJV

Have you been hurt? Have you scars that need healing? Reach out to
the best friend that we have—Christ our Lord. Our King is a friend who
does truly stick closer than any brother. He is a friend to us, so let us show
that we are His friend. Look to Him and you will find no hurts. Find in
Jesus a true and constant friend who will not let you down nor fail you in
any way. He has been your eternal friend; show yourself to be His.

*And the scripture was fulfilled which saith, Abraham believed God,
and it was imputed unto him for righteousness: and he was called the
Friend of God.*
James 2:23 KJV

Christina Stead
Calvary Christian Fellowship Glasgow
Glasgow, Scotland

August 25

Keep Smiling

Strength and dignity are her clothing, and she smiles at the future
[latter days].
Proverbs 31:25 NASB

Amidst all the turmoil and uncertainty of these days in which we live, His Word exhorts us to smile at the future. What a blessing!

This is God's Word, especially for women. Remember the old saying, "The hand that rocks the cradle rules the world"? To be able to smile at these latter days, knowing that God, in His providence, placed you in this time, should encourage your heart. Your purpose in Him is now!

What an opportunity we as women have to demonstrate the utmost confidence in our heavenly Father to our husbands, children, family, friends, and to the world that needs Jesus. We should inspire faith instead of uncertainty and fear. Instead of worrying about things that haven't happened, let's smile at these latter days together, knowing that our Father, the Creator of all things, is in perfect and total control. Keep smiling!

Treon Goossen
Mountain Area Calvary Chapel
Florissant, Colorado

August 26

The Perfect Blood of Jesus

Fire came out from the presence of the LORD and consumed the burnt
offering and the fat portions on the altar. And when all the people
saw it, they shouted for joy and fell facedown.
Leviticus 9:24 NIV

A hush fell over the people. Would the offering be accepted? They waited
anxiously to see. Yes! There it is! Fire came down from the Lord and consumed the offering. A cheer broke out and they fell facedown in worship.

I wonder if this was the way it was when Jesus entered the heavenly
sanctuary to sprinkle His blood on the altar (Hebrews 9:24). Was there
great anticipation in the heavenly realm? Did a hush fall over heaven
when Jesus entered the Most Holy Place "once for all by his own blood"
(Hebrews 9:12 NIV) in order to "cleanse our consciences from acts that
lead to death" (Hebrews 9:14 NIV)? Can you imagine the cheers and the
worship that broke out in heaven when Jesus' blood was accepted on our
behalf?

Had Jesus' sacrifice been anything short of perfect, had Jesus not completely fulfilled the Father's will, His blood would have been rejected in
that Holy Sanctuary, and we would have no hope of salvation. Take time
to praise Jesus today for His perfect sacrifice!

Without the shedding of blood there is no forgiveness.
Hebrews 9:22 NIV

Susan Figgs
Calvary Chapel Greeley
Greeley, Colorado

August 27

Fly Away

Oh that I had wings like a dove! for then would I fly away, and be at
rest.

Psalm 55:6 KJV

Heartache. Depression. Anxiety. King David prayed this prayer to fly
away in a moment of hopelessness and discouragement. You and I can
relate to feelings of frustration and desperation. I like David's honesty in
expressing that he wanted to escape the conflict in order to find rest. I too,
at times, would like to make a run for it. But, we know that we can't run
away from life's conflicts and problems. When we do, our problems seem
to find us at our new location! Remember what happened to Jonah? He
didn't get very far, did he?

God wants to cause growth and maturity in our character, and He
uses the difficult times we encounter to do so. Not only that, but He desires for us to realize and experience that He will sustain us in the midst
of the difficulty.

Next time you're in a trial, rather than praying, "Lord, get me out of
here," realize God is using the trial. Pray as David did in verse 22 of this
Psalm: "Cast your burden on the LORD, and He shall sustain you; He will
never permit the righteous to be moved." Once you have gone through
the trial, you will be able to comfort others with the same comfort you
have experienced from the Lord.

Karen Stangel
North Shore Christian Fellowship
Haleiwa, Hawaii

August 28

God Is Not Late

For He says: "In an acceptable time I have heard you, and in the day
of salvation I have helped you."

2 Corinthians 6:2

Every believer in the Lord Jesus serves Him in the ministry one way or another. Your calling could be to serve the Lord as a housewife, a business-woman, or a missionary. Whatever we do, we have a calling, a ministry to obediently fulfill.

Without a doubt, we have all experienced, will experience, or are currently experiencing times of discomfort and trials (2 Corinthians 6:4–10). But we must not forget what God Himself is saying to us. He promises to hear and help us in His perfect time!

Consider the promises of God found in this verse. As you reflect on past trials, you can rejoice in the faithfulness of God who always hears and saves in the acceptable time. If you are currently being refined through trials and hardships, take heart knowing that the promise of God's perfectly timed deliverance is at hand. And as you look ahead, be at peace no matter what the future holds, and rest your hope in the Lord who hears and saves you. What He has said He will surely do!

Blessed be the LORD, who has given rest to His people, . . . according
to all that He promised. There has not failed one word of all His
good promise.

1 Kings 8:56

Karen Nikiforos
Calvary Chapel Cape Town
Cape Town, South Africa

August 29

Grace to the Hearers

. . . good for necessary edification, that it may impart grace to the hearers.
Ephesians 4:29

We were sitting at the dining room table putting together every puzzle we owned at the request of our two little girls. Praise music played softly in the background, inspiring conversation about our Lord. My husband told the girls, "I sure do love Jesus, but sometimes I do things wrong, and when I decide to do things my way instead of His way, it makes Jesus sad and disappointed in me."

Thinking he had done a good job of imparting the knowledge that Jesus is hurt and sad when we disobey Him, my husband was interrupted by our five-year-old daughter, who said, "Daddy, I think I hear Jesus saying, 'I love you, Bill.'"

Oh, Lord Jesus, thank You for a little girl who can hear Your voice and speak Your Word.

What has the Lord been speaking to you lately? Are you investing your time in listening for His voice?

Joy Welsh
Calvary Chapel Huntington Beach
Huntington Beach, California

August 30

Not My Agenda, but Yours

"Your kingdom come. Your will be done on earth as it is in heaven."
Matthew 6:10

Sometimes I get up in the morning and my mind starts racing with all the things I have to do. Knowing how easy it is for me to forget important items, I start making a list, and then I am tempted to get going! But the Holy Spirit is faithful to draw me into fellowship, and by experience I've learned that it's not worth it to proceed without submitting myself and every single thing on that list to my omniscient, loving Shepherd, so that I can be led each day by Him. So, gratefully I say, "Not my agenda, but Yours."

After all, Jesus has told us that His *sheep* will hear His voice (John 10:4); and what are the chief characteristics of sheep? They are stupid, helpless, defenseless, prone to wander, and totally dependent on their wise and powerful shepherd. What folly to rely on ourselves! After all, nothing good dwells in *me* (Romans 7:18); and apart from Him I can do *nothing* good (John 15:5). My adequacy for this day *must* be from Him (2 Corinthians 3:5–6).

So today, if you want to walk with inward rest and outward victory over sin, be determined not to be self-willed. The good things on your list might be from the Lord, but are they for today? And in what order are they to be done? "Father, not my agenda, but Yours."

Juanita Hall
Calvary Chapel Rio Rancho
Rio Rancho, New Mexico

August 31

Forgiveness!

But God demonstrates His own love toward us, in that while we were
still sinners, Christ died for us.
Romans 5:8

The greatest joy that we can ever experience is God's forgiveness! Only God can give us hope and set us free from our past ways of life. God gives this free gift to all of us the moment we accept Jesus Christ as our Lord and Savior. It is only by the blood of Jesus that we can be made clean.

Another great joy in life is learning to follow Jesus in forgiving others. Many times the hardest thing for us to do as Christians is to forgive those who have hurt us. Our greatest example is Jesus; as He hung on the cross, He cried out:

"Father, forgive them, for they do not know what they do."
Luke 23:34

A third great joy in life as we mature in the Lord is asking others to forgive us. We often look at what others have done to us, but we need to recognize the hurt that we have caused others and ask their forgiveness. All three aspects of forgiveness will bring great joy!

Brethren, I do not count myself to have apprehended; but one thing I do, forgetting those things which are behind and reaching forward to those things which are ahead, I press toward the goal for the prize of the upward call of God in Christ Jesus.
Philippians 3:13–14

Peggy Brown
"U" Turn for Christ
Perris, California

September 1

September Blues

~⬧~

Rejoice always.
1 Thessalonians 5:16

"September Blues." Do you ever experience them? It's the feeling you get when you suddenly realize that "everything" will be starting up again very soon. School schedules, homework, back- to-school nights, PTA meetings, bed times. The list goes on. When I even *start* to think about September, I get flustered. I love the break of routine that the summer season brings.

This year I have decided to fight the "September Blues." I am going to think positively about September. I will look forward to the excitement that a new year of school can bring. I will believe that God has some exciting "new beginnings" for me and for my family. The Lord has a plan just waiting to unfold.

Psalm 118:24 says, "This is the day which the LORD has made; we will rejoice and be glad in it." I can substitute the word "month" for "day" and welcome whatever God has in store. What about you? Are you with me? Are you ready to fight the "September Blues"? Let's all make the choice to rejoice this month and celebrate God's plan for the coming year.

Kelly Bell
Calvary Chapel Murrieta
Murrieta, California

September 2

Run to the Well

Therefore with joy you will draw water from the wells of salvation.
Isaiah 12:3

The sorrow was too great. The loss was so painful. My mind screamed why—why—why? How can this be? My heart ached and my spirit was crushed. I couldn't cry one more tear!

As I lowered my head to pray again, I heard the Lord say, "Run to the well, my daughter, run to the well." I felt so empty—bone dry. But I knew the Lord meant for me to run to His well—a well filled with His hope, grace, mercy and love for me. I so needed a drink of "living water." Without water there is no life. All living things need water to survive. I needed to hear from a source that had nothing to do with self.

In Deuteronomy 6:11, God tells Abraham to drink from wells he did not dig, to eat from vineyards he did not plant. God wants to be the sole provider of our strength, not mingled with any self-effort.

So I ran to His deep well of refreshment and was filled. The Holy Spirit comforted me and I found rest.

And the Spirit and the bride say, "Come!" And let him who hears say, "Come!" And let him who thirsts come. Whoever desires, let him take the water of life freely.
Revelation 22:17

Karyn Johnson
Calvary Chapel Downey
Downey, California

September 3

The Hands of God

. . . guided them by the skillfulness of his hands.
Psalm 78:72

"All I have needed Thy hand hath provided; great is Thy faithfulness, Lord, unto me."[16] These powerful words from a famous hymn, framed by my bed, remind me every morning and night of the awesomeness of God's faithfulness and the provision of His hands. When I get to heaven, I want to see His beautiful hands!

Hands of a carpenter. A teacher. A physician. A shepherd. A servant. Tiny hands of a baby in a manger. Hands that made the stars and sculptured mountains. Hands that span the universe and measure the waters. Hands that formed us in His own image. Hands from which no one can pluck us out. Hands that reach out still. They are not shortened that He cannot save. Beautiful, precious, nail-scarred hands of a God who "so loved . . . that He gave . . ." (John 3:16).

His hands pick you up when you fall, wipe your tears, and send you on your way again. At this moment, He is interceding for you—at the right hand of the Father.

As those in the world use their hands to tear down and destroy, consider the unfailing faithfulness of a covenant-keeping God and the work of His hands on your behalf, and lift your hands to Him in thankfulness.

Thou changest not,
Thy compassions, they fail not;
As Thou hast been,
Thou forever will be.[17]

Vi Goodrich
Horizon Christian Fellowship
Indianapolis, Indiana

September 4

God Is Our Deliverer

In you our fathers put their trust; they trusted and you delivered
them. They cried to you and were saved; in you they trusted and were
not disappointed.

Psalm 22:4–5 NIV

They were not disappointed! When you want a job done right, you hire a
professional! It is God's business to deliver. No one else even comes close
to His credentials.

2 Samuel 22:17–20—When we feel as if we are drowning.
Psalm 34:1–7, 15–20—When we are poor, fearful, and brokenhearted.
Psalm 91:9–16—When we are surrounded by dangers.
Isaiah 46:3–4—From the time we are conceived to when we are old and
gray.
2 Corinthians 1:8–10—When (and because) there is no other deliverer.

A deliverer is defined as one who sets free or rescues and as one who
assists in birth. I love the second part of that definition: we are reborn
because of Jesus' redemptive work! He brought us from darkness into
the light. He did not leave us in a place where we would surely die, but
brought us out to experience His kingdom eternally. Do you know someone who needs to be delivered? Maybe even now they are being suffocated
by the darkness of this corrupt world. Make a list, pray without ceasing,
and ask the Holy Spirit what your part can be in helping them to meet
the Deliverer!

Donna Riley
Calvary Chapel La Mesa
La Mesa, California

September 5

Passion for God

O God, You are my God; early will I seek You; my soul thirsts for You; my flesh longs for You in a dry and thirsty land where there is no water.

Psalm 63:1

Have you ever been at the movies when they flash pictures of popcorn and soda on the screen? You can smell the popcorn and all of a sudden you are hungry and thirsty. You've gotta have it! Why? Because the concession stand is calling out to you, saying "You want popcorn! You're thirsty! Come to me!"

Jesus says the same thing, "If anyone thirsts, let him come to Me and drink" (John 7:37). Are you drinking from the well of Jesus and thirsting for more? Let's be honest: Wouldn't you love to have more passion for God and increase your desire for Him?—the kind of passion and longing that David was speaking about in Psalm 63? How do you increase your desire for God?

I think it's a lot like eating chocolate! I love chocolate, but I've gone for weeks and even months without eating it. What happens when you eat chocolate? You want more. You feed your desire by tasting it, and it makes you want more!

Take time to seek the Lord by feeding on His Word. Taste and see that the Lord is good! May you increase your desire and passion for God by tasting of Him early each morning.

Karen Stangel
North Shore Christian Fellowship
Haleiwa, Hawaii

September 6

The Sacrifice of Praise

Through Jesus, therefore, let us continually offer to God a sacrifice
of praise—the fruit of lips that confess his name. And do not forget
to do good and to share with others, for with such sacrifices God is
pleased.

Hebrews 13:15–16 NIV

Praise is precious to God, and we are exhorted here to continually offer
this sacrifice to God. But it's not just what I say—the praise of my entire
life is precious to God. It is how I act and what I do. It's not just a song or
saying, "Praise the Lord," but it is an attitude of my heart and life.

Many times this is where the sacrifice comes in, dying to myself in
each situation and choosing to submit to His lordship over my life, crisis by crisis, moment by moment, turning my focus, my attention, my
gratitude, my hopes, and my needs to Jesus. Through Jesus, I refocus the
attitudes of my heart and I find myself able to give to others the love of
Jesus.

It is giving up my right to be in control.

What are you struggling with in your life today? A situation, a fear, a
need, a sin? Learn to offer up to Him the sacrifice of praise—and things
will start to change within you! And with such sacrifices, God is pleased.

Lynda Kelly
Calvary Chapel Bullhead City
Bullhead City, Arizona

September 7

Is It Me That Is Seen?

Wash me, and I shall be whiter than snow.
Psalm 51:7 KJV

Originally from upstate New York, I grew up with snow. I always loved the first "real" snowfall of the year. It was a beautiful white—pristine, unspoiled, and glistening—as it fell to the ground covering all surfaces.

One winter day while gazing out the window to my yard, I saw a space that had the potential to become a garden next summer but was in desperate need of weeding and tending. The areas of bare exposed ground where grass no longer grew had been traveled on by too many feet. Inches thick of fallen leaves that had not been raked since the fall were scattered throughout the yard. Yet with the snowfall, it was all beneath a glimmering white covering. Unlovely things had become lovely.

I see my life this way. There were so many unkempt places in my heart: overgrown gardens full of weeds, unsightly worn and beaten paths caused by sin, things dwelling in comfort that should have been removed. With Jesus in my heart and life, He clothes my ugliness in His beauty. My dirt is made clean through His purity. Thus, as God gazes at me, the glorious covering of Jesus is what He sees.

No matter how deep the stain of your sins, I can remove it. I can make you as clean as freshly fallen snow.
Isaiah 1:18 NLT

Lynda Crespo
Calvary Chapel Puerto Rico
Guaynabo, Puerto Rico

September 8

What Hinders Our Prayers?

"When thou prayest, enter into thy [inner chamber] . . ."
Matthew 6:6 KJV

Andrew Murray said, "As the Lord Jesus has given us the promise of His presence and shows us the way to the inner chamber, He will assuredly be with us to teach us to pray. It is through Him that we have access to the Father."[18]

So, what hinders our prayers? "If I had cherished sin in my heart, the Lord would not have listened" (Psalm 66:18 NIV).

Most likely, none of us would say that we love sin, but when we are not willing to repent and walk away, we are cherishing sin in our hearts. The word *cherish* means: to hold dear, to protect, treat tenderly, foster, nurture, care for, encourage, or favor. If we cover up and protect sin in our lives, God will not hear our prayers.

Isaiah 59:2 "But your iniquities have separated you from your God; your sins have hidden his face from you, so *that he will not hear*" (NIV, emphasis added). We know that God does not listen to sinners (John 9:31). He listens to the godly man who does His will.

> Then I acknowledged my sin to you and did not cover up my iniquity. I said, "I will confess my transgressions to the LORD"—and you forgave the guilt of my sin. Selah. *Therefore* let everyone who is godly *pray* to you while you may be found; surely when the mighty waters rise, they will not reach him. You are my hiding place; you will protect me from trouble and surround me with songs of deliverance. Selah
> *Psalm 32:5–7 NIV, emphasis added*

In these last days, unheard and unheeded prayers are not an option! Repent and be heard!

Peggy Kravig
Calvary Chapel Downey
Downey, California

September 9

First

I will go before you and make the crooked places straight.
Isaiah 45:2

"You first." My two-year-old wasn't being gallant. This was not a buffet line or first crack at a plate of cookies. He wasn't holding a door open for me. We were walking in the woods, and he had just confronted an enormous spider web.

"You first, Mama." I obliged. Where the brush was thick, I stepped and smooshed, clearing a path for him. Where spider webs crisscrossed between bushes and trees, I swung my mighty stick and made the path safe for little spider web-fearers.

He followed, carefree, like the young prince that he is. When he grew hungry, I pulled a granola bar from the mysterious depths of my pocket. I even took off the wrapper for him. When he thirsted, I gave him a swig from my water bottle. And when he yawned and slowed his steps, I picked him up and turned us both for home—despite all his crabby protestations.

How comforting to know that our Father has gone before us to clear the cobwebs, to straighten the path, to make a way for us in the wilderness. How good to know that He is there to satisfy our hunger, quench our thirst, and carry us when our strength is gone. Though we are tempted sometimes to run ahead, it's so much better to follow.

You first, Lord.

Shannon Woodward
Calvary Chapel Marysville
Marysville, Washington

September 10

The Fragrance That Lasts

And the house was filled with the fragrance of the oil.
John 12:3

It was one of those days. You've had them. I had missed my quiet time and felt out of sorts. As I sat on the stairs waiting for Christian and Caitlyn to come down, I heard my son exclaim, "Mommy, what is that beautiful smell?" And then, as if to an audience, he continued, "It must be my mommy. No one smells as good as my mommy." I began to suspect that something was up when his next sentence struck an arrow right in my spirit, "Mom, when you smell good, the whole house smells good!"

My mind immediately went to Mary as she broke that alabaster jar in an act of worship at the feet of Jesus, representing her own broken and humble heart. My little six-year-old son had spoken a timeless truth about the place of women in the home. Our attitudes and demeanor can make our home one that exudes the fragrance of Christ or the foul stench of the flesh. The difference is determined by whether we spend our time worshiping the things of the world, or remaining at the feet of Jesus.

For we are to God the fragrance of Christ among those who are being
saved and among those who are perishing.
2 Corinthians 2:15

Diane Coy
Calvary Chapel Fort Lauderdale
Fort Lauderdale, Florida

September 11

9/11 Emergency

And who knoweth whether thou art come to the kingdom for such a
time as this?
Esther 4:14 KJV

September 11, 2001, changed America's history. We no longer feel entirely secure in a country that prided itself on freedom. Our sense of physical safety has been diminished as we realize we have become vulnerable to barbaric, demonized acts of terrorism. It's a time for every Christian to take the challenge Mordecai gave to Esther. Like Esther, we need to be bold, willing to do whatever God calls us to, coming out of our comfort zones, risking our own lives to bring the message of salvation to a devastated, lost, and dying world—for such a time is this.

Today, sanctify your heart to the Lord God and be ready always to give an answer to every man that asks you a reason for the hope that is in you (1 Peter 3:15). God loves this world so much that He's given us this time to minister salvation in a way never known before. Be bold for Jesus.

We are in God's kingdom and are living at this present time for a purpose. We have a voice, feet, and arms for a reason. If you want to exalt Jesus, ask Him to fill you with passion and equip you for His good purpose. Today is the day for each of us to be effective in His kingdom.

Angela Tomasso
Calvary Chapel Westside
Spencerport, New York

September 12

Following the Leader

❧

And the LORD spake unto Moses face to face, as a man speaketh unto
his friend . . . but his servant Joshua . . . a young man, departed not
out of the tabernacle.
Exodus 33:11 KJV

Joshua followed Moses out to the tabernacle when Moses went to be alone
with the Lord. After Moses returned to the camp, Joshua stayed in the
tabernacle. He desired to follow his mentor's example and hear from the
Lord as well. He stayed after Moses had finished.

Our pastors and teachers have spent time with the Lord preparing
the Bible studies we receive. When they close their Bibles and end their
studies, do we close ours as well and go back to our lives? Maybe we, like
Joshua, should take time to remain in the tabernacle. We ought to go
home and review our notes or that section of Scripture and wait on the
Lord to speak to us face to face.

As a result, we may become more like our teachers and those whom
God has put over us. Joshua became the one whom the Lord used to take
His people into the Promised Land. If we remain in the tabernacle, we
should grow up into all things.

And Joshua . . . was full of the spirit of wisdom; for Moses had laid
his hands upon him: and the children of Israel hearkened unto him,
and did as the LORD commanded Moses.
Deuteronomy 34:9 KJV

Maureen Schaffer
First Love Calvary Chapel
Whittier, California

September 13

The Value of a Deposit

How sweet are Thy words to my taste! Yes, sweeter than honey to my
mouth!
Psalm 119:103 NASB

God's Words are to be like honey to us. Honey is made over a period of
time. It is not the immediate result of the work that the "forager bees"
conduct. One bee can visit up to ten thousand flowers a day, and it takes
over a million flowers to make one pound of honey.

After a bee collects the nectar, he returns it to the hive where it is deposited into a cell. With time and through the process of evaporation, it
thickens and ripens.

As we read and hear God's Word, we do not always have the time to
reflect on it. The Word must be deposited in a cell where it can ripen. This
process takes time. Sometimes it takes suffering and trials. Sometimes it
takes repeated exposure to the same Scriptures.

But we know God's Word is powerful and active. He will cause what
we deposit to ripen and mature if we are diligent to deposit it on a regular
basis and take care of it.

This passage says the value of God's Word is as far above the satisfaction and pleasure that comes from fine honey. If we are careful to deposit
God's Word into our hearts and then live it, each of us will yield a wonderful bounty.

Jolene Jones
Calvary Chapel of Skagit Valley
Mount Vernon, Washington

September 14

Our God Reigns

❧

Being confident of this very thing, that he which hath begun a good work in you will perform it until the day of Jesus Christ.
Philippians 1:6 KJV

As women, we are so full of questions. We spend time wondering about our children, our finances, our careers, our health, and our future. When we don't get our questions answered, we begin to worry. It isn't long before we lose our confidence and find ourselves emotional messes. Settle it in your heart today that our God reigns! This powerful truth will instantly calm your heart and bring peace, even in the fiercest of storms. To say "our God reigns" is to accept the fact that everything that touches your life first comes through the loving hands of your good and perfect heavenly Father, and He knows what is best for you. He reigns in heaven, on earth, and in all things of a woman's life. When this truth is confidently received, you won't question your future; instead you'll rest assured that your life is in God's hands.

The Lord clearly promises that He will complete the good work that He has begun in you. No circumstance of your life will keep Him from fulfilling that promise. Your part is simply to let go and let God do it. Give Him permission to change whatever is necessary to do this good work in you.

Gail Mays
Calvary Chapel South Bay
Gardena, California

September 15

The Salesman-Sin

"Satan has asked for you, that he may sift you as wheat."
Luke 22:31

An accurate picture of sin is rarely seen when faced with temptation. So sinister, in fact, is this salesman—sin—that he makes his full introductions only when the deed has already been done. By then, it is too late to decide on what should never have taken place, and my private sin comes back to haunt me in full public view. That once-dismissed old fact invades—welcomed by me or not—and with powers almost entirely forgotten, sin engages me in the very things I wish I didn't know about. How did I get here so fast? The ungodly desires that make themselves at home in my mind always overstay their welcome. How can I avoid sin's trap?

This relentless and persuasive salesman should be on wanted posters in every home—particularly in the homes of those who must hate him. I must call him what he truly is—he that diverts me from fellowship with God. How do I turn this salesman away? Only God's Spirit within can empower me to have victory over this intruder. So I resist my ancient foe, with God's Word uncovering his tactics. In faith, I draw near to God in repentance, believing God's promise that He will draw near to me.

Gina Pimentel
Calvary Chapel Grants Pass
Grants Pass, Oregon

September 16

Familiar Friend and Faithful Forewarning

Be steadfast, immovable, always abounding in the work of the Lord,
knowing that your labor is not in vain in the Lord.
1 Corinthians 15:58

My Bible had seen years of wear and tear, so my daughter gave me a new one before I attended a recent conference. It seemed odd to read whole sections of Scripture without seeing any underlined areas or marks in the margins. But there is one verse that is so deeply ingrained in my mind that it needed no highlighting; and unbeknownst to me, it was the conference theme.

Many years ago, I was given the opportunity to write the words "Be steadfast and immovable" in calligraphy for a backdrop at a retreat. With limited time, a three-inch trim brush, and bright blue house paint, I painted those words on a banner made of dot matrix printer paper. The quiet time that was scheduled to be a special getaway with Jesus was spent carefully painting each individual stroke that formed the ten-inch tall letters. As it turned out, my time alone was indeed a very sweet time of fellowship and divine instruction.

The Lord has continually used this verse as a familiar friend to bring faithful forewarnings of difficulties on the road ahead. Has our heavenly Father given you a verse that has become a familiar friend? May we seize those opportunities and allow the Holy Spirit to vibrantly paint His Word into our hearts.

Isel Vázquez
Calvary Chapel Miami
Miami, Florida

September 17

You Are a Star

*...that you may be innocent and pure as God's perfect children, who
live in a world of corrupt and sinful people. You must shine among
them like stars lighting up the sky.*
Philippians 2:15 GNB

I remember as a little girl going upstairs into my father's home office, pretending to be the host of my very own television show. Later in my teens, I learned to sing and play the guitar with dreams of performing before thousands—my name in lights. But after coming to Christ in my early twenties, I soon discovered that Jesus had different plans for my life.

For twenty-two years now, I have been an elementary teacher in Christian schools. I help lead worship in church, and do a lot of one-on-one singing in hospitals. As a pastor's wife, I spend hours counseling and praying with people.

Recently, one of my first grade students drew me a picture and captioned it, "I love you, Mrs. Mello. You are a star!" Tears came down my cheeks as I realized how thankful I am that God's plan all along was to make me into the kind of star mentioned in Daniel:

*And those who are wise—the people of God—shall shine as brightly
as the sun's brilliance, and those who turn many to righteousness will
glitter like stars forever.*
Daniel 12:3 TLB

Hallelujah!

Lynette Mello
Calvary Chapel Livermore
Livermore, California

September 18

Remain in Him

You have given us your laws to obey—oh, how I want to follow them
consistently.
Psalm 119:4–5 TLB

How can we remain faithful in our walk with God? He has given us the
answer in Psalm 119:9: "How can a young man stay pure? By reading
your Word and following its rules." Verse 11 says, "I have thought much
about your words and stored them in my heart so that they would hold
me back from sin" (TLB).

Take time to meditate on what you are reading in the Bible. God's
Word is powerful and able to keep you from stumbling. Hide His Word
in your heart, and keep it fresh in your mind.

I will delight myself in Your statutes; I will not forget Your word.
Psalm 119:16

Jolene J. Cesmat
Calvary Chapel North Bend
North Bend, Washington

September 19

No Lord, Not This

Trust in the LORD with all thine heart; and lean not unto thine own
understanding.
Proverbs 3:5 KJV

It was Mother's Day weekend; I was calling my mom to check on my dad
who has cancer. Call home first, then the hospital; so goes the routine. "Oh
wait, your dad wants to talk to you." Some man got on the phone . . . none
of the words went together . . . he dropped the phone. . . . Mom's back,
"Honey, your dad just can't talk right now." We hang up.

The tears come, sadness follows, then fear. "I sought the LORD, and he
heard me, and delivered me from all my fears" (Psalm 34:4 KJV). My parents are hundreds of miles away, tomorrow is Mother's Day, and I should
be at church. There are so many things going on. My husband comes
downstairs to find me a mess on the sofa. "Make your reservations," he
decided, "you're going home."

By the week's end, my *precious* dad would be home with my *perfect*
dad. An amazing thing in this whole experience is that my sister-in-law,
who is a nurse, provided my dad's care until the end. My husband, who is
a pastor, provided the care after that. What an amazing God we serve. He
will meet all our needs, even those we've not yet thought about.

Let us therefore come boldly unto the throne of grace, that we may
obtain mercy, and find grace to help in time of need.
Hebrews 4:16 KJV

Kim Yannuzzi
Dayspring Christian Fellowship
Quakertown, Pennsylvania

September 20

F.O.C.U.S.[19]

Let us fix our eyes on Jesus.
Hebrews 12:2 NIV

There are many distractions in this world. Every day is filled with all sorts of challenges that rock our walk with the Lord. These things can trigger frustration, anger, hate, disappointment, et cetera, and cause us to lose focus. Take a closer look at F.O.C.U.S. and keep your eyes on Jesus.

F. *Free . . .*

Being then made free from sin, ye became the servants of righteousness.
Romans 6:18 KJV

O. *Obedience . . .*

Know ye not, that to whom ye yield yourselves servants to obey, his servants ye are . . . whether of sin unto death, or of obedience unto righteousness?
Romans 6:16 KJV

C. *Continue and Commit . . .*

If ye continue in the faith grounded and settled, and be not moved away from the hope of the gospel . . .
Colossians 1:23 KJV

Commit thy way unto the LORD.
Psalm 37:5 KJV

U. *Undefiled . . .*

BLESSED are the undefiled in the way, who walk in the law of the LORD.
Psalm 119:1 KJV

S. *Stand . . .*

Wherefore take unto you the whole armour of God, that ye may be able to withstand in the evil day, and having done all, to stand.
Ephesians 6:13 KJV

Patricia Maciel
Calvary Chapel Downey
Downey, California

September 21

Where Are You, Lord?

❧

Speak, LORD, for Your servant hears.
1 Samuel 3:9

One day, my five children and I were at a petting zoo. It was bustling with activity, children darting here and there in excitement as animals wandered about. As I looked around, I could not find one of my boys. I called out, "Anthony! Anthony! Where are you?" His small soft voice answered, "Here I am, Mom. Look!" There he was, right between the stroller and me. I began to think, how often we cry out to God, "Where are You, Lord? Speak to me!" Have you ever done that?

The Lord said, "I will never leave you nor forsake you" (Hebrews 13:5). God is always present and actively working in our lives. He is always speaking to our hearts, but He often goes unheard because of the many distractions that surround us. It is amazing how God will use simple things in everyday life to reveal His truths.

Throughout the day: Stop, look around, and listen. What is the Lord saying or revealing to you? What is He trying to teach you? Whatever it is will always line up with His Word.

Call to me and I will answer you and tell you great and unsearchable
things you do not know.
Jeremiah 33:3 NIV

Johnelle Goalstone
Calvary Chapel Lone Mountain
Las Vegas, Nevada

September 22

God's Love Never Fails

I pray that you, being rooted and established in love, may have power,
together with all the saints, to grasp how wide and long and high and
deep is the love of Christ.
Ephesians 3:17–18 NIV

There is a great contrast between human love and divine love. Man's love is trapped inside the confines of the unregenerate human heart, in misunderstandings, emotions, expectations, and personal desires. This self-serving kind of love only works for a season, but when tested by adversity, it always fails.

God's love is forgiving, restorative, instructive, corrective, and sanctifying. His immeasurable love is deeper than the grave, higher than the heavens, wider than the world, and extends into eternity. We need to extend God's love towards one another, especially in difficult times.

God has drawn us to Himself in a love relationship with Jesus Christ. His Spirit indwelling us has brought God's love to be in us and expressed through us! Jesus prayed, ". . . that the love with which You loved Me may be in them, and I in them" (John 17:26).

As the tree must get its roots deep into the soil if it is to have both nourishment and stability, we must have our spiritual roots deep into the love of God. And as we are rooted and established in Christ, His love surrounds, directs, strengthens, and keeps us—even in adversity. God's love never fails!

Teri Mathison
Calvary Chapel Hendersonville
Hendersonville, North Carolina

September 23

Fill My Soul Today, Lord!

The LORD is my portion, saith my soul . . .
Lamentations 3:24 KJV

Why is it some Christians do not heed the call of self and the world to compromise and sin, while other Christians find themselves easily distracted and enticed by it? Why do some believers struggle so? Perhaps today you are asking that question of yourself. Proverbs 27:7 reveals one answer, "The full soul loatheth an honeycomb; but to the hungry soul every bitter thing is sweet." Let's view this Scripture as an analogy about sin, noting two things: First, sin is bitter, yet it masquerades as something sweet. What could be sweeter than honeycomb? Second, we each have a soul (comprised of the heart and mind). The soul craves to be filled, to be full. With what?

When a Christian chooses daily to be filled up with the love of Christ (Ephesians 3:19), the Holy Spirit (Ephesians 5:18), and the Word (Psalm 119:11), their soul experiences a blessed fullness. The result? They loathe even the sweetest enticement of sin. In contrast, a believer who neglects the Word, doubts the effectiveness of prayer, and doesn't completely surrender, that soul experiences hunger. The hungry souls tempted by sin's promise to fulfill often succumb, eating some bitter thing, thinking it will be sweet; yet later discovering they've been deceived, always to their harm!

Only the Lord can satisfy the hunger of your soul. So, to whom will you look to find fulfillment today?

Mary Jo Stevens
Calvary Chapel Cypress
Cypress, California

The Necessary Meeting

*And in the morning, rising up a great while before day, he went out,
and departed into a solitary place, and there prayed.*
Mark 1:35 KJV

Within a two-day period described in Mark chapter 1, Jesus traveled around Galilee preaching the gospel, enlisted four disciples, walked to Capernaum, taught in the synagogue, healed Simon's mother-in-law, then, with the needy throng gathered at the door, proceeded to cast out devils and heal many sicknesses long past sundown. Even though those two days were demanding and draining, and the hours long, Jesus got up early and purposed to have a quiet meeting with His Father. But, Mark tells us that Simon and the others sought Him out, "Everyone's looking for You!" With more urgent needs to meet in Capernaum, Jesus responded by telling them they must attend meetings in the next towns.

Jesus showed us something profound: there is one necessary meeting in any given day concerning any work, and that meeting is with the Father. Even though it seemed His quiet time was interrupted much too soon, because Jesus purposed to attend that one necessary meeting, His Father made sure He got exactly what He needed to continue doing His will.

You too should have an early morning meeting with your heavenly Father before anyone's looking for you. Don't miss that meeting!

Commit thy works unto the LORD, and thy thoughts shall be established.
Proverbs 16:3 KJV

Jeanie Matranga
Calvary Chapel Downey
Downey, California

September 25

Who Is the Fairest?

Favour is deceitful, and beauty is vain: but a woman that feareth the
LORD, she shall be praised.
Proverbs 31:30 KJV

Today there is so much pressure to conform to a particular body image.
The world places great emphasis on the outward appearance, and often
we get caught up pursuing a largely unattainable goal. Even as Christian
women, we become prey. In Psalm 39:11, we are informed that beauty
is an empty pursuit. When Samuel was searching for Israel's king, God
clearly expressed His viewpoint, "Man looks at the outward appearance,
but the LORD looks at the heart" (1 Samuel 16:7).

What is God's perspective? Song of Solomon portrays us as having:

Eyes like doves (4:1). Jesus was baptized and the dove came upon Him.
We can see life through the discernment of the Holy Spirit.

Teeth white and clean (4:2). Ephesians says we are washed by the water
of the Word.

Lips like scarlet (4:3). Our mouths speak rivers of life to those in
need.

Temples like pomegranates (4:3). Our thoughts are fruitful and sweet.

A strong *Neck* (4:4). In King David's time, shields signified protection
against harm.

Breasts that satisfy (4:5). In 1 Peter 2:2 we are exhorted to "desire the
sincere milk of the word" (KJV).

What a beautiful image! This is how God sees you. Next time you
struggle with those "I'm ugly; I'm useless" thoughts, agree with your
Maker who says:

You are all fair, my love.
Song of Solomon 4:7

Helen Carmody
Calvary Chapel Secret Harbor
Secret Harbor, Australia

September 26

Back, with a Vengeance of Grace

My grace is sufficient for you, for power is perfected in weakness.
2 Corinthians 12:9 NASB

In December, 2000, the Lord allowed me to go into a deep coma for two weeks with brainstem encephalitis. My family was told I would not live. During that time, the Lord gave me the most unhindered fellowship with Him. He spoke clearly and I was finally still enough to listen. Losing control over my body, and having my brain shut down so severely that I could not distinguish between dreams and reality or remember what my children looked like, caused such grief to my mother heart. My spirit, however, was totally unaffected. Prayer was my only option. I could hear my family talking and praying. Our Lord told me He would heal me one hundred percent and He did. The Lord did not have to heal me. But, in His grace, He allowed me to return to my wonderful husband, three young children, and our extended family, and friends.

During that time, the Lord struck my heart about the lack of grace pouring out of our lives. As Christians, we have opportunities every day to show grace. Let us be quick to forgive as we have been forgiven, offer soft answers to those who speak harshly, continue to teach the Word even when it is rejected, and demonstrate love to the most unloving. God will give us the grace.

Debbie Haworth
Calvary Chapel of the Raccoon River Valley
Panora, Iowa

September 27

That Your Joy May Be Made Full

*"Whenever a woman is in travail she has sorrow, because her hour
has come; but when she gives birth to the child, she remembers the
anguish no more, for joy that a child has been born into the world."*
John 16:21 NASB

I cried at age forty-two when I found out I was pregnant again. I already
had a handful of beautiful boys (that would be five). Since I was over forty,
I thought I couldn't handle another pregnancy. God knew what I could
handle, and months later, He blessed us with the desire of our hearts—a
precious daughter. We named her Joy because He says in John 16:24,
"Ask, and you will receive, that your joy may be made full" (NASB).

Six months later our family of eight was heading to Laramie, Wyoming,
to plant a church. Just starting a church seemed difficult to me, but moving to Wyoming was frightening, especially coming from warm Southern
California.

The move was made easier for me knowing that if I could trust God
for a daughter, then I could trust God to provide for us in a land far from
home. I can now truly say that Wyoming is my home. God not only gives
us the desires of our heart, but God also changes our desires!

*Delight yourself in the LORD; and He will give you the desires of your
heart.*
Psalm 37:4 NASB

Julie Sanderlin
Horizon Christian Fellowship of Laramie
Laramie, Wyoming

September 28

There Is No Other Way

How shall we escape, if we neglect so great a salvation?
Hebrews 2:3 KJV

When we think of our salvation, so often we limit it to the future. True, salvation is eternal, but it is also a very present salvation.

He that spared not his own Son . . . how shall he not with him also
freely give us all things?
Romans 8:32 KJV

I need no other argument,
I need no other plea;
It is enough that Jesus died,
And that He died for me.
Lidie H. Edmunds, "No Other Plea," 19ᵗʰ century

His salvation is enough for every moment, every circumstance, and every situation because Jesus is enough! He does not give salvation, He is salvation and He gives Himself, the all-in-all.

"He has become my salvation; He is my God" (Exodus 15:2). He wants to become your complete salvation. You have a choice today. Will you "neglect so great a salvation," or will you invite Him to receive great glory in your needs, your failures, your lacks, your days, your life? He never expected you to succeed alone; in fact, He knew that you couldn't. This is why He has given you Himself: "So great a salvation." "Behold, now is the day of salvation" (2 Corinthians 6:2 KJV).

Dear Lord, "Say to my soul, 'I am your salvation'" (Psalm 35:3). "You are the God of my salvation; on You I wait all the day" (Psalm 25:5).

Nancy Sylvester
Calvary Chapel York
York, England

September 29

My Neighbors

"You shall love your neighbor as yourself."
Matthew 19:19

We really do not know how unloving we can be until we are put in a situation where we must love the "un-loveable." I was tested on this a few years ago when a new couple moved in next door to us. Outwardly, they were really hard to love. He had long hair and drank beer all day, she was not much better; and, of course, they were not married. They were just not the kind of people that you would have picked as neighbors.

As a young mom, I felt it was my duty to protect my two children from evil outside influences—but how do you protect them from the neighbors? As it turned out, God really did know what He was doing when He moved them in next door—He was doing a work in my heart. He wanted to teach me what He really meant when He said that we should love our neighbors as ourselves.

I have to admit that as I got to know them, they began to grow on me. But when my very impressionable thirteen-year-old son wanted to hang out with them on Sunday mornings instead of going to church, that is when I started to panic. I wanted to ask my neighbor (in the name of the Lord, of course) to stay away from my son who was already not too thrilled about being a pastor's son. But instead, God kept nudging me to invite them over for dinner, so that is what I did, and I am so glad I obeyed.

Not too long afterwards, while visiting at our house, my neighbor sat with my husband in tears. He told him that he was a backslidden Christian and that his father was a pastor. My husband asked him why he had walked away from God and he said it was because of his father's example—he was one way in the pulpit, and another way in private. He told my son Jeremy, "You have the best dad; I see him come home and play baseball with you every day. If I had a dad like yours, I'd still be walking with the Lord."

He and his girlfriend eventually came back to the Lord and my husband was able to marry them. My son learned a lesson through all this, and obviously so did I. I realized that I would have missed out on one of the biggest blessings of my life if I had refused to love my neighbor. Isn't it amazing how God works?

Karen Pulley
Calvary Chapel Old Bridge
Old Bridge, New Jersey

Treasure Beyond the Stars

Do not be afraid, Abram. I am your shield, your exceedingly great reward.
Genesis 15:1

Abraham went on to ask the Lord what He would give to him. The word of the Lord came to him, saying, "Look now toward heaven, and count the stars if you are able to number them. . . . So shall your descendants be" (Genesis 15:5).

From the seed of Abraham and Sarah would the "exceedingly great reward" be revealed. Jesus is that exceedingly great reward, the great gift of God—the reward Moses saw afar off, "esteeming the reproach of Christ greater riches than the treasures in Egypt; for he looked to the reward" (Hebrews 11:26).

Let us like Moses and Abraham look to the shield, the great reward, rather than to the riches and treasures of this world.

Patricia Ayub
Calvary Chapel Costa Mesa
Santa Ana, California

October 1

No Way Out?

Do not be afraid. Stand still, and see the salvation of the LORD, which
He will accomplish for you today.
Exodus 14:13

As Moses led the children of Israel out of Egypt, they came to a place
where there seemed to be no way out. The Egyptian army was behind
them and the Red Sea was before them. They were afraid. With their
natural eyes they had every reason to be afraid. God spoke to Moses and
told him to lift up his rod over the sea and it would be divided.

Faith enabled Moses to stretch out his hand over the sea, and in doing
so, he could see the Lord holding back the waters on each side, making a
way out for them. Faith brought Moses and the children of Israel safely
through on dry ground.

When we face impossible situations where there seems to be no way
out, we must look to the Lord and have faith to believe that God can and
will bring us safely through. The Lord fights for us . . . if we "stand still,"
trusting Him, we *will* see His salvation!

Karin Kyle
Calvary Chapel Modesto
Modesto, California

October 2

Who Put Flies in My Ointment?

Dead flies putrefy the perfumer's ointment, and cause it to give off a foul odor; so does a little folly to one respected for wisdom and honor.

Ecclesiastes 10:1

Can you imagine receiving a bottle of your favorite perfume only to find a fly stuck inside! Not an appealing thought, is it? Flies can be nasty, bothersome little creatures that often appear at the most unwanted times. They can ruin a glass of water in one stroke, and can be unrelenting when they try to land on your face.

Flies torment sheep in the summertime. Nasal flies buzz about the sheep's head and try to deposit their eggs on the sheep's nose. If they are successful, the eggs will hatch to form small, slender, worm-like larvae that burrow into the flesh of the sheep's head, causing terrible irritation.

The shepherd applies an oil mixture to the head and nose that will give relief and must be applied throughout the summer for continuous protection.

We can have the little "flies" of sin that, if left to hatch, can ruin our witness for Christ. To protect us, we must have the oil of God's Holy Spirit applied continuously to keep those little "flies" of worry, contention, and irritability at bay.

Allow the Good Shepherd to anoint you and:

Let not oil be lacking on your head.
Ecclesiastes 9:8 NASB

Sally Lee
Calvary Chapel Kingman
Kingman, Arizona

October 3

The Body

⤜❧⤏

But now God has set the members, each one of them, in the body just
as He pleased.
1 Corinthians 12:18

Over and over again the metaphor of the body is used in Scripture. In order to fully appreciate this metaphor, we need to think about how our physical bodies function and how unity within our bodies is necessary to maintain good health.

My son was recently diagnosed with a heart condition, but before the diagnosis could be confirmed, he needed to get an echocardiogram. As I sat in the room watching his heart beat on the monitor, I realized if it did not function, he would die.

As I became overwhelmed, the Lord spoke to my heart, saying, "I sustain his every breath, and his heart is in My hands."

My son did not strive to maintain his heartbeat. God caused it to function. So it is with the body of Christ. We do not have to strive to maintain our service for others. It flows from a heart sustained by Jesus.

I pray that you will function in the capacity that edifies the rest of the body today. Rest in His grace—there will be health in the body of Christ, and your service will be acceptable to God!

Let us have grace, by which we may serve God acceptably with
reverence and godly fear.
Hebrews 12:28

Sally Van Wick
Calvary Chapel Bible Fellowship
Temecula, California

October 4

Traveling Light

Therefore, since we are surrounded by such a great cloud of witnesses, let us throw off everything that hinders and the sin that so easily entangles, and let us run with perseverance the race marked out for us.

Hebrews 12:1 NIV

If you have ever traveled or taken a long hike, you know that the secret to success in persevering through the journey is traveling light! Spiritually, that is true as well.

In my excursions, I have had to learn this the hard way, as I lugged around (that's why they call it luggage) clothes and things that I didn't need. I have actually left some of my belongings behind on trips because I was tired of hauling them around! One year, as I came home from our women's retreat where I had challenged the ladies with this Scripture, I could only laugh that my garment bag had been put on top of the van with the zipper open. I arrived home with much lighter luggage!

Today, take an inventory of your spiritual luggage. What is weighing you down in the race marked out for you? What sin is entangling your feet, making it hard to run? Remember this isn't a fifty-yard dash we are on—it's not who gets there first. It is simply who gets there! Your path has been set; you will finish the race and even enjoy it if you travel light!

Lynda Kelly
Calvary Chapel Bullhead City
Bullhead City, Arizona

October 5

Worldly Wisdom or Simple Faith

For the wisdom of this world is foolishness with God.
1 Corinthians 3:19

Jonah had convinced himself it was illogical for God to love his enemies, the people of Nineveh. Leaning on his own understanding got Jonah in a world of trouble and separated him from experiencing the perfect will of God . . . until he surrendered. There is complete grace in God, but that doesn't give us the freedom to sin. Just like Jonah, God had to send a message to the people in the church of Corinth. They were in a horrible mess simply because of their knowledge of the truth and their decision to go another way.

When people allow worldly wisdom to rule their lives, their enthusiasm for the Lord will eventually die out. How often do we limit the Lord's ability to work in our lives by leaning on our own understanding? Do we have the same thinking as Jonah and the church in Corinth who both believed in God but failed to trust Him as Lord for their everyday decisions? They didn't stop believing in God, they just lost the passion and the simple purity of faith. The challenge is not only to receive God's knowledge and wisdom for our lives, but also to apply it in complete surrender and childlike faith.

Let today be a day in which our faith in God is not system of belief but a way of life.

Bonnie Botsford
Horizon North County
Rancho Santa Fe, California

October 6

What Drives Me?

But none of these things move me; nor do I count my life dear to myself, so that I may finish my race with joy.
Acts 20:24

I was watching a show the other day about a secular pop star and her drive to get to the top of the music industry. She is willing to do whatever it takes to get there. Money and fame are hers.

Then I started to think about my walk with the Lord. Am I working as hard as she is, but for the Lord? Her goal is passing away—mine is eternal! I want to be serving Jesus every day, whatever the cost.

In Mark 2, there is a story about some men who were willing to take apart a home to get their friend to Jesus.

And when they could not come near Him because of the crowd, they uncovered the roof where He was. So when they had broken through, they let down the bed on which the paralytic was lying. When Jesus saw their faith, He said to the paralytic, "Son, your sins are forgiven you."
Mark 2:4–5

What drives the pop star? Fame and fortune.

What drove the men? A chance to see Jesus.

What drives me? Eternity with my Lord!

"And if I go and prepare a place for you, I will come again and receive you to Myself . . ."
John 14:3

Beth Gagliardi
Calvary Chapel Norman
Norman, Oklahoma

October 7

Women of Influence

"Lord, show us the Father, and it is sufficient for us." Jesus said to
him, "Have I been with you so long, and yet you have not known Me?
. . . He who has seen Me has seen the Father."

John 14:8–9

Aunt Bessie was an infectious older woman who came to our house every
week to teach the Good News Club. Her energetic and genuine love for
the Lord held us kids spellbound as she brought the stories of the Bible to
life. The beautiful bright flannelgraphs that she used to illustrate biblical
scenes certainly helped, but it was her life that was the real inspiration.

Mrs. Vaughan was another godly woman who influenced my life
greatly. She was my Sunday school teacher, and although you could not
help noticing her saggy nylons each week, she was beautiful. Her sparkling blue eyes were full of the love of Lord; she glowed for Jesus.

Today, as a pastor's wife, I have to say that there is no one who is a
greater inspiration to me than Kay Smith. Her steadfast love and devotion
to the Lord has been a tremendous example to me over the years. She has
truly "shown me the Father" by the way in which she has willingly allowed
Him to use her in the ministry.

It is my desire that my life would be a reflection of the Lord to others
as well. I want to be a godly influence. To be an influence means "to have
sway" and the ability to affect the way another thinks and lives. An in-
fluential person sets the pace and compels others to follow. To be a godly
influence means that your *life* is an inspiration—the way you live spurs
others on in their faith.

There really is no greater blessing than to meet a woman who at one time
had been in your "sphere of influence" (whether in a Sunday school class or
a women's Bible study) and to hear her say that she saw Jesus in you.

Karen Pulley
Calvary Chapel Old Bridge
Old Bridge, New Jersey

Leaving an Inheritance

Surely the land whereon thy feet have trodden shall be thine
inheritance, and thy children's for ever, because thou hast wholly
followed the LORD my God.
Joshua 14:9 KJV

Many times we, as mothers, plan out the future for our families. Most
likely we are the ones responsible for milk in the refrigerator and clean
underwear in the dressers.

There is a danger, though, of thinking that food in the refrigerator,
money in the college account, and well-scheduled academics and extra-
curricular activities will give our children the best hope for a great future.
We can so easily begin in the Spirit only to frustrate the grace of God by
attempting to parent in the flesh, according to man-made precepts and
priorities.

Caleb reminded Joshua:

Nevertheless my brethren that went up with me made the heart of the
people melt: but I wholly followed the LORD my God.
Joshua 14:8 KJV

It was because Caleb followed the Lord with his whole heart that his
children would forever benefit from his loyalty. Are you following the
Lord with your whole heart today? Do you see the correlation between
your walk with Jesus and your children's future? Could you possibly be
distracted from your devotion to the Lord and His kingdom even by the
very children He so graciously gave you? Remember what our Lord said
in Matthew 10:37 (KJV):

"He that loveth son or daughter more than me is not worthy of me."

Maureen Schaffer
First Love Calvary Chapel
Whittier, California

October 9

What I Don't Have, I Don't Need

He has made everything beautiful in its time.
Ecclesiastes 3:11 NIV

I'm a child of God, a pastor's wife, and a quadriplegic. I have a beautiful home, good food on my table, three teenagers that love our Lord, a loving husband, and I have Grace (my attendant). I have God's precious Word, and most important, Jesus, my Lord. Am I boasting? Certainly not! I'm counting my *many* of blessings. Do I need anything else or am I lacking? Nope! Second Peter 1:3 says that He has given me everything I need: "His divine power has given to us all things that pertain to life and godliness, through the knowledge of Him who called us by glory and virtue."

Are you lacking something? Maybe you think it's health, money, affection, respect, or even romance. Maybe you need more spiritual blessings or more godliness. Look around you and count all your blessings. What you have right now is what you need! It is beautiful for its time.

Now, look unto Jesus! In Him everything is good and perfect. We must make the best of what we have, and we must accept and adapt to everything as beautiful for this time. Let's be content with the beauty of His time. "I know that there is nothing better for men than to be happy and do good while they live" (Ecclesiastes 3:12 NIV).

But godliness with contentment is great gain.
1 Timothy 6:6 NIV

Sylvia Rosales
Calvary Chapel El Paso
El Paso, Texas

October 10

Lord, Shine Through Me

Search me, O God, and know my heart; test me and know my anxious
thoughts.
Psalm 139:23 NIV

I try to set a good example at work, especially since everyone knows that
my husband is a pastor. People are always watching me. One day someone
asked if I was all right, with a very serious look on their face. I said I was,
and went on with my work. If this had happened once, I might have been
able to ignore it. God is so good. After the fourth person asked the same
question, I stopped and asked the Lord if there was something wrong in
my countenance. He spoke to my heart. "Cherylee, they are looking at
you today, not Jesus in you." Then I remembered: "Let your light so shine
before men . . ." (Matthew 5:16).

   I had been hiding my light under the proverbial bushel. All the people
who had been watching from the dark that morning were ministry opportunities. I don't know what they saw in my look, or heard in my responses,
but I knew I needed to brighten my outlook. Thankfully the Lord is graciously bright and ever-ready, even when I have allowed my light to dim.

For God, who said, "Let light shine out of darkness," made his light
shine in our hearts to give us the light of the knowledge of the glory
of God in the face of Christ.
2 Corinthians 4:6 NIV

Cherylee Dawson
Countryside Christian Fellowship
Eugene, Oregon

October 11

Worthy to Be Praised

Therefore David blessed the LORD before all the assembly; and David said: "Blessed are You, LORD God of Israel, our Father, forever and ever."

1 Chronicles 29:10

O LORD, our Lord,
How excellent is Your name in all the earth,
who have set Your glory above the heavens!

Psalm 8:1

The undying sun goes day to day
As our Creator's power display;
And announces to every land,
The work of His almighty hand!

Read 1 Chronicles 29:10–20 and Psalm 8.

A prayer of adoration:

In your own words, write a prayer of adoration and praise to your God.

Patti Bottger
Calvary Chapel Lakeside
Lakeside, California

October 12

Not the Shirt Off His Back

"Assuredly, I say to you, inasmuch as you did it to one of the least of
these My brethren, you did it to Me."
Matthew 25:40

One winter day, as my husband drove our family home, he suddenly
pulled the car over to the side of the road, jumped out, and ran back
down the street. I watched as he sat down on the curb next to a homeless
man, removed his shoes and socks, and handed them to him. They spoke
for a few moments, then he ran barefoot back to the car. I asked why
he did that. He said, "Didn't you see him? He didn't have any shoes." I
pointed out that now *he* didn't have any shoes. He replied, "Yeah, but I
have more at home." He didn't say anything else, but as we drove home,
I thought about how my husband lives his faith. I never even noticed the
homeless man. He not only noticed the man's need, but he did something about it.

We've all heard the expression, "He'll give you the shirt off his back."
This wasn't a shirt, but the principle is the same. My husband often says,
"I'd rather see a sermon than hear one." As we go through our days, may
we remember that our service to others is really service unto the Lord.

Rose Beal
First Love Calvary Chapel
Whittier, California

October 13

God Is Our Comforter

Even though I walk through the valley of the shadow of death, I
will fear no evil, for you are with me; your rod and your staff, they
comfort me.

Psalm 23:4 NIV

Isn't it fantastic to know that God wants to comfort us? He tells us this
repeatedly in His Word:

Psalm 71:17–22—Young or old . . .
Psalm 94:17–19—When we feel anxious and shaky . . .
Isaiah 66:13—Like a mother comforts a child . . .
Matthew 5:4—When we are mourning . . .
2 Corinthians 1:3–5—In all our troubles, so we can comfort others!
. . . and the list goes on and on! (Check your concordance.)

I love the picture of a "covering" that accompanies the word "comforter" in the dictionary. It made me think of a "security blanket" that
keeps out the cold, makes the world less scary, and helps us feel better
when we are sick. Of course, Jesus is so much more than that, because
He actually understands our hurts, worries, and fears. He came to earth
as a man and experienced all that we do. What better qualification than
becoming one of us to be the ultimate "Comforter!" List those things
that make you want to hide under the covers, then give them to Him. He
knows!

Donna Riley
Calvary Chapel La Mesa
La Mesa, California

October 14

Micaiah? Who's That?

I saw the LORD sitting on his throne . . .
1 Kings 22:19 NIV

Sound familiar? It seems we ought to recognize the name of the first man recorded in Scripture to have received a heavenly vision of God sitting on His throne. Usually we think of Isaiah, or maybe Ezekiel or Daniel. But Micaiah, son of Imlah? We scarcely know the name and vaguely recall this little known prophet who was hated by King Ahab "because he never prophesies anything good about me" (1 Kings 22:8 NIV). His distinction among the prophets is far exceeded by the extraordinary vision itself.

Undaunted by Ahab's contempt, Micaiah boldly declared the word of the Lord for the first time, "I saw the LORD sitting on his throne with all the host of heaven standing around him on his right and on his left" (verse 19 NIV). *I saw.* That simple fact attests to Micaiah's godliness, as few were granted this singular privilege. Doesn't Amos explain that God reveals His secret to His servants, the prophets?

Micaiah detailed the remarkable scene of a heavenly council meeting, during which the Lord recruited a volunteer to persuade Ahab to go into battle. Isn't it astonishing that the sovereign, omnipotent God would even consult the heavenly host, hear suggestions, and ask questions? Certainly this glimpse of glory must have sustained the prophet's subsequent suffering. Even so, may we seek and proclaim His glory.

The LORD confides in those who fear him.
Psalm 25:14 NIV

Wendy Hodges
Calvary Chapel St. Petersburg
Pinellas Park, Florida

October 15

My "All" in Ministry

She does him good and not evil all the days of her life.
Proverbs 31:12

One day, the Lord reminded me of a time in my life when I was challenged to give my husband Joe my "all." At the time, my behavior and attitude three or four days per month made this verse nearly impossible.

This womanly condition, to which Rachel referred in Genesis 31:35, consistently resurrected my ugly flesh. A close friend challenged me to implement three biblical steps: *see*, *search*, and if necessary, *seek*. She pointed to Rachel's sin and helped me *see* how Rachel used her womanly condition not only to hide her father's idol, but also her sin.

Was I sinning by forgetting to abstain from "fleshly lusts" which war within me? (1 Peter 2:11). She then challenged me to *search* my heart. Perhaps I had used my feminine ailment as an excuse not to love; love is supposed to "bear all things" (1 Corinthians 13:7).

Finally, she encouraged me to bring closure to this monthly dilemma by *seeking* necessary medical attention. Like Nahum, I recognized, "The LORD is good, a stronghold in the day of trouble" (Nahum 1:7). Now, by doing my husband good *all* the days of his life, I have the Lord as my stronghold—whatever physical challenges may exist!

Terri Carroll
Calvary Chapel Cedar City
Cedar City, Utah

October 16

Is It Real or an Illusion?[20]

A deluded heart misleads him; he cannot save himself, or say, "Is not this thing in my right hand a lie?"
Isaiah 44:20 NIV

A few years ago our married couples' group had a Christian illusionist as the entertainment before our study time. I was so excited. I wanted to sit right in front so that I could "catch" the slight of hand. The illusionist came out with a pan full of fire. He put out the fire with a domed lid, then removed it, and out came a beautiful white dove flapping its wings to fly. As we were all clapping, the illusionist grabbed the dove's skinny feet and began to beat the dove on the side of the table. The room went quiet. He held up the limp bird; it was made of rubber. The illusionist said to our group, "Did I deceive you?" Yes, he had indeed. Then he asked, "But did I lie to you?" No, we saw what he wanted us to see. We had been deceived.

What is an illusion? It is something that looks, feels, and seems so real, but in truth it is only an erroneous perception of reality. God doesn't want us to be deceived. He sent His Holy Spirit to give us discernment. Look at that relationship, that desire, or whatever it is that you have in your hand. Is it a dove or a rubber bird? Is it really from the Lord? Stay in God's Word, in fellowship, and in prayer. Ask God for discernment. He alone can reveal truth.

Karyn Johnson
Calvary Chapel Downey
Downey, California

October 17

Do You Believe?

Lord, if You had been here, my brother would not have died.
John 11:21

I have often used this text to teach to women in jail—women who have felt that if only God had been there, or if only He had heard, they wouldn't be in jail. I have sought to comfort them by explaining that God heard them. He just did not answer the way they wanted Him to. Martha felt the same way. She had often been with Jesus and had seen Him heal many times. Why hadn't He come sooner?

Never before had I, like Martha, wanted the Lord to turn back time. Never had I wanted Him to have acted sooner. Never before had I understood Martha's pain at knowing His loving grace and His power to heal, and yet feeling as though He had purposely withheld it. Jesus, being all-knowing, had another plan—a more perfect plan—a purpose Martha could not yet understand. He hadn't come to heal. He didn't want to heal. He wanted a resurrection! He needed to know one thing first: in verses 25 and 26, Jesus said to Martha, "I am the resurrection and the life. He who believes in Me, though he may die, he shall live. And whoever lives and believes in Me shall never die. *Do you believe this?*"

I thought I believed that. Then He asked *me*, "Do you believe it when it comes to those you love? Do you trust Me to be their salvation? Do you trust Me when I ask death from them?" I have always known that the flesh hates death, but God demands death of self before life can begin in Him. Yet, could I watch flesh of my flesh die and believe? That was His new question for me. Like Martha, the only answer I can give is: "Yes, Lord, I believe that You are the Christ, the Son of God, who is to come into the world" (verse 27). I will fall at Your feet; I will trust in Your work, through Your Word, to accomplish Your perfect will. Not only in my life but also in the life of those whom I love.

Patricia Ayub
Calvary Chapel Costa Mesa
Santa Ana, California

Made-Servant

Here is your maidservant, a servant to wash the feet of the servants
of my lord.
1 Samuel 25:41

This response to David's proposal of marriage was more than Abigail's acceptance, it was her predetermined commitment to be David's helpmate. Her approach to marriage may not seem romantic, it may even offend some women in today's society; brides dream of being swept off their feet, not of washing feet. Yet, it is in having this biblical perspective of the wife's role that fulfillment and romance in marriage find fertile ground in which to blossom. Abigail would enter into marriage with a man she hardly knew, but what she did know was her role as helpmate—this she had learned as the wife of a very ungodly man, Nabal, the fool.

You can be the wife and helpmate God has called you to be whether your husband is a David, a Nabal, or somebody in between. Abigail understood that she was a maidservant to her husband. Have you understood that in Christ you are a "made-servant" as well? The Lord just might have you wash some feet today, quite possibly your husband's. It may not seem glamorous, but it will be glorious—maybe even romantic.

"If I then, your Lord and Teacher, have washed your feet, you also
ought to wash one another's feet. . . . If you know these things, happy
are you if you do them."
John 13:14, 17

Laurie Barillaro
Capilla Calvario Mexicali
Mexicali, Mexico

October 19

We Need a Hero

I will put enmity between you and the woman, between your seed and her Seed; He shall bruise your head, and you shall bruise His heel.
Genesis 3:15

Are you overwhelmed by the daily pressures of life? The world tells us to be tough and efficient. "You can do it *all*, you are *woman*." Striving for the independence and efficiency that perspective requires of us makes me . . . *tired!*

Our hearts' desires are to be protected, fought for, wanted, noticed, pursued, and cherished. We want to be "number one" in our husbands' lives, their first priority. We want to be rescued from the daily pressures of life. After all, didn't God give them to us to *fix* things? Eve went to Adam to *fix* her situation, and his best effort was getting her to sew fig leaves! God provided her a covering and it wasn't the man He gave her.

I find much freedom in submitting to the strength and comfort of my husband. But, we need to remember who our true Hero is:

"For your Maker is your husband—the LORD Almighty is his name—
the Holy One of Israel is your Redeemer; he is called the God of all
the earth. The LORD will call you back as if you were a wife deserted
and distressed in spirit—a wife who married young, only to be
rejected," says your God.
Isaiah 54:5–6 NIV

HE IS OUR HERO.

Jeanette Graves
Calvary Chapel Bangor
Orrington, Maine

His Healing Touch

❧

And when Jesus was come into Peter's house, he saw his wife's mother
laid, and sick of a fever. And he touched her hand, and the fever left
her: and she arose, and ministered unto them.
Matthew 8:14–15 KJV

One of the ways our bodies let us know there is something wrong is
through fevers. We are weakened until weariness forces us to lie down;
there is just no strength left for our tasks. At the very touch of Jesus, the
fever left Peter's mother-in-law, and she got up and began to serve.

"For thy pleasure they are and were created" (Revelation 4:11 KJV).
Jesus' healing touch had purpose. Lord, give me eyes to see clearly how
and where I am to serve, and help me to remember the reason I was made
whole.

Alejandrina DeChristopher
Calvary Chapel Redmond
Redmond, Oregon

Could God Use Me?

For we are His workmanship, created in Christ Jesus for good works.
Ephesians 2:10 NASB

As Christians, our hearts' cry is to serve our Creator. We desire to be used by Him in a special way. However, oftentimes when presented with an area of service, we begin to doubt if God could ever really use us. We see all of our inadequacies and wonder if God knew what He was doing in choosing us.

Do you struggle with these thoughts? Be encouraged! God makes no mistakes. He knows the end from the beginning and He chose you with all your unique characteristics to serve Him as no one else can.

Not that we are adequate in ourselves to consider anything as coming
from ourselves, but our adequacy is from God.
2 Corinthians 3:5 NASB

Remember David when he fought Goliath? He was the most unexpected person in Israel to take on the challenge. But the Lord laid the burden on his heart and David proceeded in faith. He used his shepherding skills to defeat the giant. David was not adequate in and of himself, but the Lord chose to use him. He used a shepherd boy, with shepherd boy skills, and called him to do a giant-size job! Why? So that God would get the glory!

Take heart! If the Lord chose you, He'll use you. Just keep your eyes on Him and your heart in tune with His.

Emille Johannes
Calvary Chapel Phoenix
Phoenix, Arizona

October 22

If the Lord Permits

For I know the thoughts I have toward you, says the LORD, thoughts
of peace and not of evil, to give you a future and a hope.
Jeremiah 29:11

So many times we make plans and set out to do them, thinking that
nobody and nothing is going to stop us. We need to always stop in every
situation and ask, "Is this my plan that I *will* do or is this a plan that I
would like to do, if the Lord permits?"

God loves us, He has a plan; it is a perfect plan, and it leads us to His
best, not only for us but for everyone around us. We will never experience
this plan and the blessings it will bring if we are not praying for, diligently
seeking, and joyfully committed to walking the path that He sets out
before us.

If we don't completely surrender everything, we won't get God's best
for our lives.

Fear not, for I am with you; be not dismayed, for I am your God. I
will strengthen you, yes, I will help you, I will uphold you with My
righteous right hand.
Isaiah 41:10

For you did not receive the spirit of bondage again to fear, but you
received the Spirit of adoption by whom we cry out, "Abba, Father."
Romans 8:15

Bonnie Botsford
Horizon North County
Rancho Santa Fe, California

Little Bunny Go Along

❧

"He will separate them one from another, as a shepherd divides his
sheep from the goats."
Matthew 25:32

As my daughter, Monique, hurried to milk her goat, Bunny, she prayed
Bunny would cooperate. Bunny would "go along" for a while, then suddenly stomp her legs, toss her haughty head, and jolt from the milking
stand. Off she would go, dashing to the haystacks or racing to the horses'
gate. Dragging her back to the milking stand left Monique exasperated.

But observing Bunny's antics caused Monique to examine her own
behavior.

She knew that goats resist authority, while sheep yield to authority.
She would "go along" with the Lord to a certain point, then demand to be
the leader and protest obedience.

Matthew 25:32–33 says that at the judgment time Jesus will set the
sheep on the right hand, but the goats on the left. The goats' selective
service and obedience was based on reward and self-interest.

Does your willful behavior blind you from God's best? Then pray, as
Monique did, for the Lord to clothe you in humility and obedience so
that you may be like the faithful sheep on the "right" side of Jesus.

Georgia Babb
Calvary Chapel Bible Fellowship
Temecula, California

October 24

"I Am the Light of the World"

～✦～

"He who follows Me shall not walk in darkness, but have the light of life."
John 8:12

As children, my brothers, sisters, cousins, and I would gather in a corner of the huge basement in our house. We'd turn off all the lights and shut the door tight. The darkness was heavy; you could feel it all around you. One by one we would begin to share visions of what we imagined coming towards us from the far corner of the room. Various ghosts, monsters, and evil beings would crawl, limp, or glide across the darkness to our corner. We'd stay for as long as we could bear the tension, then run screaming for the door and fling it open. A bright rectangle of light would flood in, dissolving our apparitions; our fears and imaginings fading, we would laugh in great relief.

How often do you find yourself in a corner, darkness surrounding you, vain imaginations going round and round your mind, fears and anxieties piling up by the second? Old ghosts from the past taunting you, evil visions of the future looming in front of your face?

Our Father has delivered us from the power of darkness and set us in the kingdom of the Son of His love (Colossians 1:13)! No longer do we walk in darkness, not knowing what makes us stumble; now we walk on the path of the just, which is as bright as the shining sun (Proverbs 4:18–19). Now when fears and doubts want to cast darkness over our minds, we simply remember that we are children of light. We've been called out of darkness and into His marvelous light!

Christina Fadness
Calvary Chapel Pocatello
Pocatello, Idaho

October 25

As Wives Accountable before the Lord

Fulfill my joy by being like-minded, having the same love, being of
one accord, of one mind.
Philippians 2:2

Our purpose is to glorify God whether we have a good marriage, a bad marriage, or have never been married at all. The point is this, to glorify God today in whatever situations we find ourselves.

Sometimes, especially as wives, we want to behave in response to the type of husband we have. If he is being nice, we will be nice. If he is being a jerk, well, we can be jerks too. Responding like this is not what God and His Word calls us to do. We are accountable to the Lord in how we are as a wife, and we are to respond to who God is and not our husband.

If you are a wife as unto the Lord, the Lord will bless you for it. Without the eternal perspective you'll just think about what you need, what you think is good for you today.

We need to remember that eternity is ahead of us. Are we glorifying the Lord today?

And whatever you do, do it heartily, as to the Lord.
Colossians 3:23

Bonnie Botsford
Horizon North County
Rancho Santa Fe, California

October 26

Love and Obey

❧

This is love for God: to obey his commands. And his commands are
not burdensome.
1 John 5:3 NIV

When I first read this, I found it to be very harsh. I didn't understand why
God would say that I didn't love Him if I wasn't obedient. In my heart, I
really believed that I loved Him more than anything.

As time went on, and I drew closer to the Lord, God was dealing with
me on the deeper levels about the issue of obedience to Him. He specifically showed me that at my times of disobedience, the points in which I
chose to sin, I was saying to Him that I loved that sin more than Him.

Aha! It clicked! I finally understood that my obedience reflects my
love for Him. That broke my heart; I wanted it to be said that I loved Him
more than any sin!

When faced with the choice of following your desires or obeying His
commands, do you choose Him?

We know that we have come to know him if we obey his commands.
1 John 2:3 NIV

Kimberly Chikeles
Calvary Chapel Saint Paul
Saint Paul, Minnesota

October 27

Your Will, Not Mine

"My Father! If it is possible, let this cup of suffering be taken away
from me. Yet I want Your will, not mine."
Matthew 26:39 NLT

Several years ago, my husband and I made arrangements for a private
adoption. The birth mother was a divorced, backslidden believer with a
six-year-old daughter. I had prayed for years for a child, and I always included in my prayer, "I want Your will, Lord, not mine." The mother lost
the baby one month before it was due.

She became estranged from her family and overwhelmed with guilt.
During our time of mutual suffering, we became good friends. I was able
to counsel her, comfort her, and pray with her. A year later, she became
very ill and required surgery. She recovered in our home for three weeks. I
took care of her and drove her daughter to and from school every day. To
this day, we have a special bond. It is a great blessing to be in God's will.

God has kept me childless for His purposes. Are you asking for God's
will regardless of the suffering? Are you willing to suffer that God's good
purposes may be accomplished? May God comfort you when you suffer,
and may He continue to use you for His good purposes as you remain
yielded to His will.

For you have been given not only the privilege of trusting in Christ
but also the privilege of suffering for him.
Philippians 1:29 NLT

Ceci Flores
Calvary Chapel El Paso
El Paso, Texas

Knight in Shining Armor

Wives, likewise, be submissive to your own husbands, that even if some do not obey the word, they, without a word, may be won by the conduct of their wives, when they observe your chaste conduct accompanied by fear. Do not let your adornment be merely outward—arranging the hair, wearing gold, or putting on fine apparel—rather let it be the hidden person of the heart, with the incorruptible beauty of a gentle and quiet spirit, which is very precious in the sight of God.

1 Peter 3:1–4

We want our husbands to be our knights in shining armor. But, that armor can become weak and tarnished if they're not obeying the Word of God. When his armor is down, no one can make him more vulnerable to the attacks of the Enemy than you, his wife. Instead of questioning and complaining, we need to submit to the Lord, and win him, with a gentle and quiet spirit. His number one need is to know you trust and believe in him. Verse 5 says, "For in this manner, in former times, the holy women who trusted in God also adorned themselves, being submissive to their own husbands."

We tend to trust our feelings and follow our hearts, which we carry around on our sleeves, causing us to rebel instead of submit. Our rewards come from our submitting to the Word of God and His commands.

Trust God, not your heart.

The human heart is most deceitful and desperately wicked. Who really knows how bad it is? But I know! I, the LORD, search all hearts and examine secret motives. I give all people their due rewards, according to what their actions deserve.

Jeremiah 17:9–10 NLT

He will reward us when we submit and trust Him.

Jeanette Graves
Calvary Chapel Bangor
Orrington, Maine

October 29

Are You Tired and Heavy Laden?

"Lay up for yourselves treasure in heaven, where neither moth nor rust destroys."

Matthew 6:20

Talking with a weary pastor friend about the ministry, he abruptly stated, "I think I am going to quit preaching. I have been doing this for twenty-five years; maybe that's enough." Looking into his tired, weary eyes, I agreed that a rest would do him good. But, to my surprise, I replied, "When you look into the eyes of Jesus and see His nail-scarred hands, and when His glory is all around, you will wish you would have done more, tried harder, stayed longer, ran faster, invested yourself more fully."

Are you tired of your race? Do you find yourself wanting to give up, retire, or walk away from the calling of God? "I therefore so run, not as uncertainty; so I fight, not as one that beateth the air" (1 Corinthians 9:26 KJV).

As my pastor friend got into his car, he looked up at me with a renewed expression, a spark of Spirit-filled fire rekindled, and a new determination to stay in the race divinely designed for him. I was reminded of an old poem my mom used to quote when I was growing up, "Only one life, 'twill soon be past, only what's done for Christ will last."

I have fought a good fight, I have finished my course; I have kept the faith.

2 Timothy 4:7

Merrily Huether
Calvary Chapel Buhl
Buhl, Idaho

October 30

I Am Scared

And there arose a great storm of wind, and the waves beat into the ship, so that it was now full. . . . And they feared exceedingly, and said one to another, "What manner of man is this, that even the wind and the sea obey him?"
Mark 4:37, 41 KJV

After seeing Jesus perform many miracles, the disciples are in a crisis of their own. They had seen Him do so much for others, but now they feared for their lives. Did they believe for themselves? Up to this point they had been spectators to His awesome power. Now they were personally experiencing it.

We can be so involved in ministry that we become mere spectators of what the Lord is doing in other people's lives. We can believe for others, but worry in regard to our own situations. We can overlook the fact that He is interested in us. He wants to show Himself daily to us.

Lord, soften our hearts to Your presence in our lives; daily reveal Yourself to us.

Holly Robinson
Calvary Chapel Oldsmar
Oldsmar, Florida

October 31

Ready . . . Go!

❧

Let them give glory unto the LORD, and declare his praise in the
islands.
Isaiah 42:12 KJV

The green flag was up and we had a great start. In fact, it was perfect. We
jumped into an early lead. We were set to win the race.

You see, when I moved to Maui, I decided to get involved in some of
the local activities. I love the water, so paddling with an outrigger canoe
club seemed like a natural choice.

This was to be our race. I was the steersman and captain. My eyes were
fixed on the flag at the finish line. We were almost there when—to my
horror—I realized we had veered off the path. My eyes had been fixed on
the wrong flag. I made a sharp right turn, startling my teammates in the
canoe. They stopped paddling, and we finished the race in a disappointing
fourth place.

Life can be like that race. It is so easy to get distracted by the things of
this world, to take our eyes off the finish line (Jesus Christ), and to find
ourselves in the wrong place.

The lesson is that we must stay focused, pressing toward the goal,
which is the prize of the upward call of God in Christ Jesus.

I press toward the mark for the prize of the high calling of God in
Christ Jesus.
Philippians 3:14

Deana Vestnys
Calvary Chapel South Maui
Kihei, Hawaii

November 1

Becoming One

And Isaac went out to meditate in the field in the evening; and he
lifted his eyes. . . . Then Rebecca lifted her eyes . . .
Genesis 24:63–64

Marriage is wonderful, and I must say that I am incredibly blessed in my
marriage, but it can be difficult at times. Some people say, "If I give up
a little of me and he gives up a little of him, with what's left over we will
become one." But this is not the case. When you give up all of you and he
gives up all of him, only then can you become one together in Christ.

We must sacrifice all and not say, "Well, I could do without a little
of this and I will give in a little on that." That plan doesn't work. It is a
complete giving up of everything and replacing it with the character of
Christ.

Our marriages are an earthly expression of our heavenly position with
Jesus Christ. In this world, we are on a wilderness journey, blessed to have
a helper by our side to travel with us until we see our Savior face to face,
our true groom—Jesus Christ. May our thoughts and actions today prepare us to be the bride God has called us to be.

Let nothing be done through selfish ambition or conceit, but in
lowliness of mind let each esteem others better than himself. Let
each of you look out not only for his own interests, but also for the
interests of others.
Philippians 2:3–4

Bonnie Botsford
Horizon North County
Rancho Santa Fe, California

November 2

Wonderful Counselor

Unto us a Son is given; and the government will be upon His shoulder. And His name will be called Wonderful, Counselor, . . . Prince of Peace. Of the increase of His government and peace there will be no end.

Isaiah 9:6–7

Several years ago when my Christian marriage was falling apart, I felt alone in my shame and heartache. Nobody could know that we had serious problems, because Christians just don't have serious marriage problems! We attended church smiling, praising the Lord, and looking outwardly *fit*, while internally we were screaming in agony for help. Well, guess who heard our screams while everyone else was oblivious? Jesus, the Wonderful Counselor, the Prince of Peace.

This world may have counselors who can temporarily help you or advise you how to obtain peace in your life. They may give you rules to govern your home that may help. But there is absolutely no one like Jesus. When Jesus governs the affairs of your life, He takes your burdens and carries them on His shoulders. He takes your shameful sins and washes them in His blood that saves. If you let Him, He gives you life: love, peace, joy, and healing that can *fix* (i.e. adhere) themselves to your life!

Now when the woman saw that she was not hidden, she came trembling; and falling down before Him . . .

Luke 8:47

Kathy Salaiz
Calvary Chapel West Covina
West Covina, California

November 3

God Is Our Fortress

He who fears the LORD has a secure fortress, and for his children it
will be a refuge.
Proverbs 14:26 NIV

My favorite hymn is "A Mighty Fortress Is Our God," particularly the
verse that says "The Prince of Darkness grim, we tremble not for him; his
rage we can endure, for lo, his doom is sure, one little word shall fell him."
Amen! When worries about children, jobs, and life in general overcome
us, we need to remember that we live in the fortress of God, surrounded
by His unfailing love:

Psalm 18:1–3—He is our strength . . .
Psalm 59:16–17—In times of trouble . . .
Psalm 91:1–8—Despite flying arrows and deadly pestilence . . .
Psalm 144:1–2—He prepares us for battle . . .
Jeremiah 10:10—Because He is the only true God.

What comes to mind when you think of a fortress? A castle? A fort?
Whichever picture appears, the same feeling should prevail—one of abso-
lute safety. Nothing in this world is as sure as God's love for us. It is bigger
and more secure than any fortified building that man could create. It does
not change; we can trust it. Even though we cannot always understand
our circumstances, He does. And He surrounds us, as a secure fortress,
because of His love for us. Is there something that you are afraid of today?
Give it to God, and let Him take control of it for you.

Donna Riley
Calvary Chapel La Mesa
La Mesa, California

November 4

Let us then approach the throne of grace with confidence, so that we
may receive mercy and find grace to help us in our time of need.
Hebrews 4:16 NIV

When we went to Disneyland last year, and we were given "special passes"
to go on their new roller coaster ride. As we walked through the gate and
passed by all the people waiting in line, not only did we feel special, but
we were so thankful we didn't have to wait—we just walked right in!

It crossed my mind recently—what a privilege you and I have to pray!
There's no waiting; there's no standing in line. God, through Jesus Christ,
has issued you a personal invitation to call on Him at any time. Now that
is a privilege!

Don't take for granted the "special pass" and privilege that you have to
pray. May you realize that you are special to God and that He is waiting
for you to call out to Him. He desires you to come into His presence, talk,
and share your concerns with Him.

Call to Me, and I will answer you, and show you great and mighty
things, which you do not know.
Jeremiah 33:3

Karen Stangel
North Shore Christian Fellowship
Haleiwa, Hawaii

Following Our Gentle Shepherd

Trust in the LORD with all your heart, and lean not on your own understanding; in all your ways acknowledge Him, and He shall direct your paths.
Proverbs 3:5–6

Experiencing motherhood for the first time, I faced myriad new things—a new love, a new joy, a new sense of responsibility, a new lifestyle. There were many questions as well. I had dozens of books on the "how-tos" of caring for a newborn, but nothing on how to balance motherhood and ministry.

After being inseparably involved in ministry for ten years with my husband, I found myself torn between the desire to meet the needs of the body and my new passion of meeting the needs of my baby. Not wanting to be led by emotion, I began to seek the Lord for His wisdom. In a moment of tender compassion, God directed my path to Isaiah 40:11 and hand delivered, by the inspiration of God's Spirit, a word of encouragement to me for my dilemma as a new mommy. God assured me that if I simply followed Him daily, like a Good Shepherd, He would lead me and bring the balance that would glorify Him.

He will feed His flock like a shepherd; He will gather the lambs with His arm, and carry them in His bosom, and gently lead those who are with young.
Isaiah 40:11

Diane Coy
Calvary Chapel Fort Lauderdale
Fort Lauderdale, Florida

November 6

Come and See

. . . (Master,) where dwellest thou?
John 1:38 KJV

Jesus asked two disciples who were following Him, "What seek ye?" They asked to see where He lived. He answered simply, "Come and see" (verse 39). So began their journey of learning about Jesus and discovering that who He is—is where He lives.

Jesus did amazing things as He consistently lived in the center of His Father's will. He lived in constant companionship with the Father. "And He who sent Me is with Me. The Father has not left Me alone; for I always do those things that please Him" (John 8:29). That was what He invited the disciples to come and see.

"Come and see;" it's recorded in the Word for you and me so that we might be able to live there, too. Jesus has beckoned, "Come and see." Come and see where He lives. Come and see who He is. Come and see the One who knows all about you and can do something about your life. It's all unfolded in His Word. Come and see.

"If ye keep my commandments, ye shall abide in my love; even as I
have kept my Father's commandments, and abide in his love."
John 15:10 KJV

Jeanie Matranga
Calvary Chapel Downey
Downey, California

November 7

Ultimate Challenge

❦

Sit still, my daughter . . .
Ruth 3:18 KJV

At times in our Christian walks, it seems difficult to know God's will for our lives. One thing for certain, God is always with us. He doesn't have a difficult time communicating with us, but we are so busy struggling that we can't settle ourselves to communicate with Him. He is a perfect Father who knows all of our needs and delights in ministering to them.

When I find it most difficult to hear Jesus' voice, or to know His direction, I realize it's time for me to be still, to quiet my thoughts, and to settle my anxious heart. The only way I can do this is to rest in the only One in whom I find true comfort—Jesus.

Throughout the book of Ruth, we read promises like: do not fear, for I will do for you all that you request; I will bless you, grant you rest, and deal kindly with you. These words of constancy were given to Ruth to settle her and establish her. They are also encouraging words to us, our heavenly Father's daughters.

Hide yourself under the wings of almighty God, and you will find comfort, rest, and peace. There you will be so secure from the distractions of this world (including worry, fear, and confusion) that you will be still and know your God.

Angela Tomasso
Calvary Chapel Westside
Spencerport, New York

November 8

Tell of the Judge

He commanded us to preach to the people and to testify that he is the
one whom God appointed as judge of the living and the dead.
Acts 10:42 NIV

When we preach Jesus to people, we often tell them about His incredible sacrifice on Calvary or His powerful resurrection from the dead. We are commanded to declare both of these. Yet this verse instructs us to let people know that Jesus has been appointed as judge of the living and the dead.

He determines right from wrong. He determines good from best. He judges the hearts of men, and He establishes truth in every matter. Jesus sets the consequences and extends mercy.

Do you try to take the seat of judge in your life? Have you told someone lately that their judgments on a matter are not the final authority, but that Jesus' judgments are? Have you committed that complicated situation to the One who judges the living? Let us testify that Jesus judges perfectly by keeping our opinions to ourselves and, instead, keeping our matters in prayer.

Maureen Schaffer
First Love Calvary Chapel
Whittier, California

November 9

Mmmm . . . What's That Smell?

Now thanks be to God who, . . . through us diffuses the fragrance
of His knowledge in every place. For we are to God the fragrance
of Christ among those who are being saved and among those who
are perishing.
2 Corinthians 2:14–15

We all have preferences on what types of smells appeal to us: woodsy, floral, citrus, musky. We fragrance our homes with candles, electric outlet plug-ins, lamp rings, incense, potpourri, and sprays. We fragrance our bodies with scented oils, creams, lotions, hair products, soaps, salts, gels, and perfumes.

Did you know as a believer your life has a spiritual signature scent, "the fragrance of Christ"? "This little light of mine, I'm gonna let it shine." Remember that familiar children's song? Well I would like to propose that we are aromatherapy-scented candles!

As we go through our day-to-day walk here on earth, let's burn for the Father of lights until we are with Him. Are we willing to let Him use us to diffuse the fragrance of Christ to draw others to the knowledge of Himself?

Use me, diffuse me, Lord, to scent the world for You.

For God, who said, "Let light shine out of darkness," made his light
shine in our hearts to give us the light of the knowledge of the glory
of God in the face of Christ.
2 Corinthians 4:6 NIV

Carla Lawson
Calvary Chapel of the Sandhills
Aberdeen, North Carolina

November 10

The Wisdom of God

But God chose the foolish things of the world to shame the wise; God chose the weak things of the world to shame the strong.
1 Corinthians 1:27 NIV

The day that I realized my little newborn son did indeed have Down syndrome was very disheartening. After a very difficult pregnancy, it just didn't seem fair. I asked myself difficult questions. Why me? I was serving the Lord, not involved in any gross sin, and besides, I was a pastor's wife! What did I do to deserve this trial?

The disciples thought a lot like I did. One time they were walking with Jesus when they observed a man who was blind from birth. They asked Jesus, "'Rabbi, who sinned, this man or his parents, that he was born blind?' 'Neither this man nor his parents sinned,' said Jesus, 'but this happened so that the work of God might be displayed in his life'" (John 9:1–2 NIV).

God desires to display His work in my little boy's life, and that's good enough for me!

What about you? Maybe you don't have any physical or mental handicaps, but do you ever feel somewhat foolish in the eyes of the world? Take heart in knowing that your heavenly Father desires to display His works in your life as well. Then He will get the glory!

Carla Brown
Calvary Chapel Columbus
Columbus, Ohio

November 11

Prayer or Paralysis

Be careful for nothing; but in every thing by prayer and supplication
. . . let your requests be made known unto God.
Philippians 4:6 KJV

Are you facing a problem or a situation in your life that seems to have a paralyzing effect on you? You're stopped in your tracks; you can't seem to move forward; you can't think right. In fact, you're making yourself sick over the whole thing. You've tried to work it out; you've gotten advice from people; you're desperate. You fret; you worry; you bite your nails and lose sleep, and still nothing changes!

In this verse, we are told to worry about nothing, not one thing, and to commit everything to God in prayer. Instead, too often we worry about everything and pray about nothing! Soon we realize we are spiritually paralyzed. Prayer is so powerful it can set captives free. It can demolish strongholds. But first, it has to be utilized.

Have you forgotten what prayer can accomplish? Sometimes it seems like we will do anything rather than pray, and yet prayer is the most powerful force in the universe. Make a resolution right now to commit everything to the Lord in prayer. Not just the big things, the major problems or worries in your life, but *everything*. Tell the Lord about all your cares and concerns. Exchange those heartaches, those things that paralyze you, for His incredible peace.

Gail Mays
Calvary Chapel South Bay
Gardena, California

November 12

He Calls His Sheep by Name

He guides me in paths of righteousness for his name's sake.
Psalm 23:3 NIV

In Bible days, the grain fields were rarely fenced. The shepherd led his sheep down narrow paths between fields of forbidden grain belonging to others. If his sheep became disobedient and partook of food in the forbidden field, the shepherd was required to pay damages to the owner of the field.

Unfortunately, Isaiah tells us "All we like sheep have gone astray; we have turned, every one, to his own way, and the LORD has laid on Him the iniquity of us all" (53:6). Every one of us has turned from the right path to nibble the forbidden grain. And who has paid the damages for our wandering off the path and eating in forbidden grain fields? Our gracious Shepherd—Jesus Christ.

Jesus is such a gentle and faithful shepherd. We would never have the means to pay for our transgressions, but Jesus is willing to keep leading us in paths of righteousness every day, helping us to learn to obey by the power of His Holy Spirit. My desire is to be an obedient sheep, to listen to His voice, to watch what path He takes, and follow Him intently.

He calls his own sheep by name and leads them out. When he has brought out all his own, he goes on ahead of them, and his sheep follow him because they know his voice.
John 10:3 NIV

Sue LeBoutillier
Calvary Chapel Ontario
Ontario, Oregon

November 13

Our Plans—God's Best

I know the plans I have for you . . .
Jeremiah 29:11 NIV

As a new Christian I knew that God had special plans for me and that He would give me the desires of my heart. I knew I would marry a blond-headed, blue-eyed, 6'4" football player, and we would live in Colorado in a little house with a white picket fence where we would serve God. Never did I desire to live outside the United States. But God began working on my heart and asking me to give Him my all. "Will you trust Me to give you My best?" Isaiah 55:8–9 tells us that His ways are not our ways.

As I did trust God, He gave me the desires of *His* heart. He took me to a faraway land where I served Him for seventeen years. My husband has black hair, beautiful black eyes, is the same height as me (5'7"), does play *futbol* (a.k.a. soccer), and loves God. My house has a wrought-iron fence (it lasts longer than wood), and the Lord took me to . . . COLOmbia. Well at least I got the four first letters right! May we trust our heavenly Father to give us His best, because He knows the true desires of our hearts.

May he give you the desires of your heart and make all your plans
succeed.
Psalm 20:4 NIV

Hallie Martinez
Calvary Chapel Golden Springs
Diamond Bar, California

November 14

God Our Provider

Abraham called that place The LORD Will Provide. And to this day it
is said, "On the mountain of the LORD, it will be provided."
Genesis 22:14 NIV

Before moving to Texas to plant Calvary Chapel of the Springs, our family
served the Lord in Siegen, Germany. Among the many stories we share
about the Lord's faithfulness during that time, our favorite is the "Cake
Story."

I had invited a small group of German ladies to an afternoon coffee
time at our apartment. However, we were nearing the end of the month,
and when the time came to host the group, our cupboards were bare,
and our support wouldn't arrive for another week or so. "Lord, should I
cancel?" I prayed, "Or would that be rude? I could serve baking powder
biscuits instead of the traditional cakes! Help, Lord!"

Later that morning the phone rang. A dear lady on the other end of
the line said, "Yesterday we had a birthday party for my father. Many cakes
were prepared and we have several left over that haven't been touched.
Would you like one?" She said that she was embarrassed to call, but felt
prompted anyway. Rejoicing, I accepted her glorious offer.

In the years since then we have recounted many ways that the Lord
has met our needs, both big and small—especially in the simplicity of a
cake. Take heart: on *your* mountain He will provide!

Christy Michaels
Calvary Chapel of the Springs
San Marcos, Texas

November 15

Oh, How I Love Your Law!

Oh, how I love Your law! It is my meditation all the day.
Psalm 119:97

Don't you just love the Word? It is given to us by God—a treasure chest filled with precious gems: the gems of God's wisdom, knowledge, guidance, correction, love, and truth. It has all the answers to life's questions.

The Word purifies and sanctifies. It is "living and powerful, and sharper than any two-edged sword;" it is "a discerner of the thoughts and intents of the heart" (Hebrews 4:12). It is a healing balm to our souls!

Where do you run for counsel? Run to the Word! Oh, that you would make His Word your delight and counselor (Psalm 119:24).

Dear precious one, are you in the Word daily? Read it, meditate on it, memorize it, journal Scriptures by topic and pray it! Make it your priority! May God's Word be your very life source! May Psalm 119:38 become your heart's cry:

Establish Your word to Your servant, who is devoted to fearing You.

Cyndi Ballmaier
Calvary Chapel of Elk Grove Village
Elk Grove Village, Illinois

November 16

A City on a Hill

"You are the light of the world. A city that is set on a hill cannot be hidden."
Matthew 5:14

The road between Bogota, Colombia (at the top of the Andes mountain range), and Villavicencio (at the foot of the range), is life threatening! I learned to love the adventure of traveling on that treacherous road with its one-thousand-and-one curves. Rock slides, avalanches, and steep ravines threaten one's life as they fall unannounced into the furious black river ripping and winding its way between the mountains.

Traveling this unlit road one night, and terrified of its hazards, my eyes were lifted up to the tops of the mountains where little village lights flickered in the faraway distance. Who on earth would live there? What were they like? They must be courageous, strong, unafraid, and very happy! Where was the road up to the village? I wanted to go up to the villages, visit them one by one, stay in their little houses, share their table, and experience the view: mountaintops, plains, roads, rivers, clouds, rainbows, the stars in the heavens, the presence of God!

As mountaintop villages, we are bright shining lights, sparkling in the night, beckoning and challenging those who are lost to see Jesus—our indwelling Savior, the Light of the World—to sit at His table and experience His salvation in this dark and dying world.

Sharon Faith Ries
Calvary Chapel Golden Springs
Diamond Bar, California

November 17

Stand Firm

Always give yourselves fully to the work of the Lord, because you
know that your labor in the Lord is not in vain.
1 Corinthians 15:58 NIV

Two years ago my family moved to Stockport, England. Having spent six
years in America living in a small community amongst many Christians,
this move was a big adjustment. As I encountered people, I discovered an
incredible disregard for their need to have a personal relationship with
Jesus. They saw church as a place for Christmas, Easter, and christening,
all of which ended not in prayer, but in pubs! They seemed quite content
with their lives the way they were.

My desire to share the gospel with them began to spiral downward
as I met with their apathy! "This is all in vain," I thought. "These people
don't want to hear that they will spend an eternity in hell unless they turn
to Him."

I knew *my attitude* was not right. I recognized that my heart needed
to soften once again to the Great Commission. I asked God to show me
specifically that my work was "for real" and not "for nothing." He gave me
Isaiah 45:19: "I have not said to Jacob's descendants, 'Seek me in vain.' I,
the LORD, speak the truth; I declare what is right." What a confirmation!
Serving Jesus and sharing His life with others is not in vain; actually, it is
all that will remain!

Yvonne Murray
Calvary Chapel Stockport
Edgeley, England

November 18

For His Eyes Only!

᷂

"Do good to them . . . without expecting to get anything back. Then
your reward will be great, and you will be sons of the Most High."
Luke 6:35 NIV

When she left us for a more exciting church, I found myself counting the
hours of prayer and counseling I had invested in her. Being with her was a
joy, but finding the time was a sacrifice; and as I felt the sting of rejection,
I also felt our Father's gentle rebuke. "Did you take care of her for you
or for Me? What did you expect in return? Her loyalty and devotion are
Mine alone, and I alone will reward you."

Ouch! Busted! I had indeed begun to feel entitled to something in
return. Living through a very painful time in our little church's history,
I had fallen into the trap of hoping for human loyalty. Not that I didn't
know better! The theme of my personal devotions and my teachings had
long been, "Fear of man will prove to be a snare, but whoever trusts in the
LORD is kept safe" (Proverbs 29:25 NIV).

But my Father didn't hit me over the head. Instead, He lovingly dem-
onstrated the beauty of this Scripture in action. He kept me safe, even
from my own mistake, and He wooed me into that place in His love
where wayward longings hush and bow in adoration, "so that what is
mortal may be swallowed up by life" (2 Corinthians 5:4 NIV).

Let's live there!

Elisabet Fountain
Calvary Chapel Miami Beach
Miami Beach, Florida

November 19

Tuned Lives

I urge Euodia and I urge Syntyche to live in harmony in the Lord.
Philippians 4:2 NASB

Euodia and Syntyche had shared Paul's struggle in the cause of Christ and enjoyed sweet service together in the church at Philippi. Now, they were at odds with each other and their lives had become dissonant. Paul pled with them, "I urge Euodia and I urge Syntyche to live in harmony." Their discord and disunity needed immediate resolution. How were they to live and serve together harmoniously once again? Their lives needed to be tuned.

Have you ever been to the symphony? The anticipation mounts, as moments before the concert, the orchestra members are in their places, warming up their instruments or practicing an especially difficult measure. This cacophony fills the hall, but when the concertmaster stands, everyone is silent. The signal is given and the oboist plays a pure, clear "concert A." Every instrumentalist tunes his or her instrument to the oboe's note. Then the conductor enters the stage, raises his baton, and the hall is flooded with the sweetness of harmony.

How can we maintain the unity of the Spirit, living in harmony as we serve the Lord? Just as the orchestra plays harmoniously because each instrument is tuned to one source, the oboe, our lives will be united in harmony as we tune them to one source, Jesus Christ.

Come, Thou Fount of every blessing, tune my heart to sing Thy grace.[21]

Leslie Martin
Calvary Community Church
Phoenix, Arizona

November 20

Time Alone with God—Just Do It!

He who keeps you will not slumber. Behold, He who keeps Israel will
neither slumber nor sleep.
Psalm 121:3–4 NASB

As a pastor's wife and home schooling mom of five boys, this verse is very reassuring to me. Until age thirty-six, as a single adult, and then as a wife and career woman, I had my devotions when I got up every morning. The year I turned forty, my husband Kevin started a Bible study in south Seattle, we had our first son, and my well-ordered world began slipping out of control.

During the past twelve years, we had our second son, adopted three more boys, moved our family four times, our church three times, and my parents came to live with us. My devotion time has gone through many changes—during morning naps, afternoon naps, the middle of the night—and currently it's when Kevin puts the boys to bed. Whatever the time, God is there to meet me.

Please don't let Satan condemn you if your schedule isn't consistent enough to have a fixed devotion time. Go to God when you can and as often as you can. He is always there, desiring to encourage you through your fellowship with Him.

Blessed are the flexible, for they shall not be broken.
Pastor Chuck Smith

Charlotte Day
Calvary Chapel South
Kent, Washington

November 21

Yes, Jesus Loves Me

We then that are strong ought to bear the infirmities of the weak,
and not to please ourselves. . . . For even Christ pleased not himself;
but, as it is written, The reproaches of them that reproached thee
fell on me.
Romans 15:1, 3 KJV

Jesus loves us and bears with our weaknesses. So, we ought to bear the infirmities of the weak. Sometimes we think that someone is less strong in conviction, less robust in faith, less sincere, or less mature, etc., than we are. We get impatient when we should be strong in love.

God is merciful to us, and through the mercy of Jesus we are saved. His Holy Spirit comforts us. His thoughts toward us are good—thoughts of peace (Jeremiah 29:11). In love, Jesus gently washed the disciples' feet.

In humility, patience, encouragement, goodness and joy, we can edify and welcome each other as Jesus Christ our Lord welcomes us. Knowing all our weaknesses, He still loves us. What amazing grace—what incredible, unmerited favor!

Jesus loves me! This I know, for the Bible tells me so.
Little ones to Him belong; they are weak, but He is strong.
Yes, Jesus loves me! Yes, Jesus loves me! Yes, Jesus loves me!
The Bible tells me so.[22]

Shauna Higgins
Calvary Chapel Tri City
Tempe, Arizona

November 22

Anchor-Strong Hope

This hope we have as an anchor of the soul, both sure and steadfast.
Hebrews 6:19

The picture we get from this metaphor is that of an ancient ship finding its way through the narrow entrance to a harbor. To keep from crashing onto a reef, a wise and experienced captain would lower the anchor into a smaller boat, which would then be rowed through the narrow entrance into the harbor. The anchor would then be dropped and the ship would be pulled past all obstacles, through the narrow opening and into the safety of the harbor.

Hebrews 2:10 calls Jesus the captain of our salvation. As our captain, He is capable of navigating our lives, and He will safely bring us through all of life's experiences.

As Christians, we are not immune from the struggles and hardships that life brings our way, but take heart—our captain has gone through life, and He has experienced all of life's hardships. He has gone before us and is pulling us towards Himself.

In the meantime, we have hope—anchor-strength hope—because He has promised to be with us, to guide us, and to see us through to the end, when we will spend eternity with Him.

In hope of eternal life which God, who cannot lie, promised before time began.
Titus 1:2

Sista Antelo
Calvary Chapel Alhambra
Alhambra, California

November 23

When Storms Come

Teacher, do You not care that we are perishing?
Mark 4:38

How many times have you expressed these words as you deal with a situation that appears overwhelming? Jesus said to His disciples, "Let *us* cross over to the other side" (Mark 4:35). After being obedient to His will, the disciples found themselves in a severe storm.

We all have misconceptions about how God's plans should be accomplished in our lives. This story reveals three misconceptions and three lessons to learn concerning God's will.

Misconceptions:

First, do you think that when you're in God's will life should be smooth sailing with calm seas? Second, in the midst of the storm, do you question God's care? And third, do you think that you will "perish" in the storm?

Lessons:

First, recognize His plan. He was the one directing His disciples *across the lake*. They were in His perfect will. Second, recognize His presence with you in the storm. Jesus did not jump ship when the storm came. His disciples made the mistake of forgetting who was traveling with them. Third, recognize His power. Where God's presence is, there His power will be. He still speaks to the sea, "Peace, be still" (Mark 4:39).

Today, if you find yourself in a storm, ask God first to remind you of His plan, second, to allow you to experience His presence, and third, to behold His power.

Susie Carr
Calvary Chapel Arroyo Grande
Arroyo Grande, California

Instant Confession–Instant Forgiveness

I acknowledged my sin to You and my iniquity I have not hidden. I said, "I will confess my transgressions to the LORD," and You forgave the iniquity of my sin.
Psalm 32:5

A while ago I was by the kitchen sink washing up two- or three-day-old dirty dishes. The Lord spoke very clearly to me regarding the way we should deal with sin in our lives. Washing up plates that have just been used is a lot easier than washing three-day-old dirty dishes. All our husbands know that! So too when we go to Jesus, asking for His forgiveness—the quicker we do it, the easier it is.

The Lord Jesus offers us instant forgiveness that should inspire us to go to Him immediately. Satan loves to make us feel unworthy and condemned—to keep us away from the Lord for as long as possible. We often confuse this feeling with the conviction of the Holy Spirit. No—the same Holy Spirit who convicts us of our failures also woos us to repentance and confession. We need to train ourselves to confess immediately that we might be healed, and by so doing, enjoy the freedom this offers to us on a daily basis.

He who covers his sins will not prosper, but whoever confesses and forsakes them will have mercy.
Proverbs 28:13

Rebekah Olphert
Calvary Chapel Belfast
Belfast, Northern Ireland

November 25

A Precious Possession

The soul of a lazy man desires, and has nothing; but the soul of the
diligent shall be made rich.
Proverbs 13:4

Webster's Dictionary defines *diligence* as "constant and earnest effort to accomplish what is undertaken." While we know that apart from Jesus we can do nothing (John 15:5), and that those who are in the flesh cannot please God (Romans 8:8), we do have a part in our spiritual growth. If I am "constant and earnest" in praying and reading my Bible, my soul will be made rich. If I daily oversleep and allow my time with the Lord to be cut short, my soul will desire, yet have nothing. I will be spiritually starved.

We recently planted a garden and then became too busy to tend it. After a month, the weeds between the plants were growing as profusely as the plants. I had not been diligent. It took a lot of effort to pull those thick, strong weeds. If I had diligently pulled them when they first appeared, it would have saved much time and labor.

Diligence means that I keep at it; I don't give up. I remember that *something is better than nothing.* Are you overwhelmed thinking about all that you need to do today? Remember that the Lord's yoke is easy and His load is light, and pray for diligence. He wants to enrich you!

Diligence is a man's precious possession.
Proverbs 12:27

Ginger Kosobucki
Horizon Christian Fellowship-Central
Indianapolis, Indiana

November 26

Serving Like the Master

"The Son of Man did not come to be served, but to serve . . ."
Matthew 20:28

Recently, while studying the beginning of Jesus' ministry, an important principle struck me from the model of servanthood He displayed. In Mark 1:21–27, Jesus entered the city of Capernaum and *immediately* went into the synagogue and taught. After the people were astonished at the authority with which He taught, Jesus freed a man from an unclean spirit.

What I noticed was the order in which Jesus displayed His servitude. Prioritizing their needs, He taught them *before* He served them. As I pondered this, I wondered how many times I have served people hoping that my actions alone would somehow proclaim the gospel. If I were characterized in the Bible, my name would be Martha. I enjoy serving—therefore the act of service without proclaiming the Word of God is little effort for me.

When I am following my Master's lead, however, I am challenged to be bold about the Word, so there is no mistaking who inspires my service. The time I have with a person may be shorter than I realize, and I need to prioritize their needs appropriately. I want them to see Jesus in what I am doing, and nothing better declares Him than His own Word.

Lord, make me more bold as I serve those around me, that my service would support and not replace Your Word. Amen.

Suzanne Holyde
Shoreline Calvary Chapel
Morro Bay, California

November 27

Our Freedom Was Not Free

He is so rich in kindness that he purchased our freedom through the
blood of his Son, and our sins are forgiven.
Ephesians 1:7 NLT

One day as I walked my son to school, I noticed a bumper sticker on a car. Its background was an American flag and it said, "Our Freedom Was Not Free."

The same thing is true in our lives as Christians. Even though salvation was a free gift to me, it was extremely costly for the Father and His Son.

As we cherish our freedom as Americans, how much more should we cherish our freedom in Christ? Has anyone ever received such a gift—not only one that cost so much, but one that was worth so much?

"The Spirit is God's guarantee that he will give us everything he promised and that he has purchased us to be his own people" (Ephesians 1:14 NLT). Wow! Not only an awesome gift, but what a guarantee! If it sounds too good to be true, it usually is. But God gave His Son, gave us freedom in Him, gave us an inheritance in His kingdom, and gave the Holy Spirit to guarantee it. As Paul says, "This is just one more reason for us to praise our glorious God" (Ephesians 1:14 NLT).

Take time today to make a list of the ways your freedom in Christ blesses you. Then give thanks to God the Father and the Son for these specific blessings.

Wendi Fraley
Wildwood Calvary Chapel
Yucaipa, California

November 28

Got Faith?

Now faith is the assurance of things hoped for, the conviction of
things not seen.
Hebrews 11:1 NASB

As a little girl, I believed that the "boogie man" was under my bed. I
would run and jump into my bed as fast as I could so that he wouldn't
grab my feet. That fear faded with childhood, but my belief was so strong
that I sometimes catch myself even now jumping quickly into bed!

The Bible teaches us to believe in God. But as adults, we place our
faith in other things: our looks, our careers, our relationships. That's like
putting your car in the wrong gear. If you put your faith in the wrong
place, you will stop moving in your relationship with God.

When I first came to know the Lord, my faith in God was so strong.
Keeping a faith journal has shown me how faith builds on faith, but it
also reveals how often I have lacked faith. Perhaps that's why Jesus asked,
"When the Son of Man comes, will He find faith on the earth?" (Luke
18:8 NASB). When was the last time that you walked completely by faith,
trusting God as your only resource?

Thankfully, God has provided us with the perfect way to recover
childlike faith that trusts completely in Him. All we have to do is to pick
up the Bible and get into God's Word.

So faith comes by hearing, and hearing by the word of Christ.
Romans 10:17 NASB

Cheryl R. Plourde
Calvary Chapel Jupiter
Jupiter, Florida

November 29

Covered by His Feathers

He will cover you with his feathers, and under his wings you will
find refuge.
Psalm 91:4 NIV

It came out of nowhere: the car, the sudden impact, the wreck. Our 1998 Jeep flipped two-and-a-half times before coming to rest upside down. I looked over at my husband and screamed his name—I thought he was dead! He looked up, and we climbed out of that completely demolished car: no blood, no broken bones, no major injuries.

Later I said to him, "It was like God had wrapped His wings around us and His feathers softened the impact!"

I know Christians can be injured and bad things do happen. But, that summer afternoon God was with us. Good things also happen, and God does protect and watch over His children. A few months after the accident I discovered this verse in the Psalms, and realized that I had lived this promise:

He will cover you with his feathers . . .

Lynn Spencer
Calvary Chapel Gulf Breeze
Gulf Breeze, Florida

November 30

When Fear Comes In

He will not be afraid of evil tidings; his heart is steadfast, trusting in
the LORD.
Psalm 112:7

When I was first diagnosed with melanoma, what a shock it was! My
mind was flooded with so many questions and so many fears. I knew I had
a choice to make—to trust the Lord no matter what or to be overcome
with fear. "Whenever I am afraid, I will trust in You" (Psalm 56:3).

What is it that has come into your life and caused you to be fearful?
Perhaps it's financial distress, a prodigal child, problems in the church, or
even a life-threatening illness. Whatever it is, remember the faithfulness
of our loving God. He is right there with you to bring you through the
fiery trial.

In this you greatly rejoice, though now for a little while, if need be, you
have been grieved by various trials, that the genuineness of your faith,
being much more precious than gold that perishes, though it is tested
by fire, may be found to praise, honor, and glory at the revelation of
Jesus Christ.
1 Peter 1:6–7

Trust the Lord to use this situation in your life to make you more like
Him. Choose faith—not fear.

In my distress I called upon the LORD, and cried out to my God; He
heard my voice.
Psalm 18:6

Cheryl Cahill
Calvary Chapel Boston
Rockland, Massachusetts

December 1

He Is My Great Reward

They defeated him by the blood of the Lamb and by their testimony;
for they did not love their lives but laid them down for him.
Revelation 12:11 TLB

The saints loved Him. They would not, could not, deny Him . . .

It was by faith that Moses, when he grew up, refused to be treated as
the grandson of the king, but chose to share ill-treatment with God's
people instead of enjoying the fleeting pleasures of sin. He thought
that it was better to suffer for the promised Christ than to own all the
treasures of Egypt, for he was looking forward to *the great reward* that
God *would give him.*
Hebrews 11:24–26 TLB, emphasis added

We overcome the flesh, Satan, and the world because we know Him
and love Him supremely. There is no other way. In the choices I make
when no one else sees, or knows, He does. He knows by my everyday
choices whether or not I love Him most. It's simply between Him and me,
in the quiet, unseen places of my everyday life.

Lord grant me a clear vision of You today, so I can make the choices
that please You most.

Where there is no vision [revelation of Him], the people perish [cast
off restraint].
Proverbs 29:18 KJV

You are my great reward!

Charlotte Giardine
Calvary Chapel Johnson County
Olathe, Kansas

December 2

A Gift of God

～∞～

Every good gift and every perfect gift is from above . . .
James 1:17

A few months ago my eight-month-old son, Matthew, became ill with viral encephalitis. We rushed him to the hospital on a Thursday night. On the following Sunday morning the Lord took him home.

During those long hours, the Lord met me mightily through His Word. He reminded me how precious our children are in His sight. The name Matthew means, "gift of God," and was especially chosen because he was our only son, born late in our lives. As I sat beside Matthew's bed praying, I began reading the book of Matthew. I got to the Sermon on the Mount where Jesus asks a rhetorical question:

"If you then, being evil, know how to give good gifts to your children,
how much more will your Father who is in heaven give good things to
those who ask Him!"
Matthew 7:11

Matthew was a precious gift that God gave us for eight months. I know some days may seem ever so difficult when it comes to motherhood, but rejoice in your gifts and cherish every day as though it were the last.

What gifts has your heavenly Father given you? How can you show your appreciation to Him today?

Donna Brock
Calvary Chapel Dixon
Dixon, California

December 3

Your Song

❧

. . . And with my song will I praise Him.
Psalm 28:7

As I was sitting before the Lord, the stillness was broken by a beautiful birdsong. Just as I began to take notice of the lovely sound it suddenly changed to a deep, throaty "squawk." Then it changed again, this time to a soft peeping. As the song kept changing, I realized I was listening to a mockingbird.

Mockingbirds imitate the calls of other birds; they have even been known to imitate dogs and cats! They are the most famous mimics of the bird world.

I felt distracted from my devotions. As I tried to remember what I had been thinking, the Lord spoke to my heart. He said: "There are times when *you* imitate the songs of other believers."

I had to admit that I sometimes look to those around me for cues as to how to worship the Lord. I don't always trust the "song" He has put in my own heart.

We are each uniquely special. God has created a wonderful variety of people. If He had wanted all of us to be the same, He could easily have created us that way. He didn't, so why should we try to imitate anyone else?

Learn from others, but don't mimic them. God created only one of you for a reason—to bring Him pleasure as He hearkens to your voice lifted up in praise.

Pam Pensiero
Calvary Chapel Hanford
Hanford, California

December 4

No Greater Treasure

I love those who love me, and those who seek diligently will find me.
Proverbs 8:17

My husband and I were blessed to visit Europe for the first time this year. It was such an awesome experience, such wonders to behold! However, to observe all the beautiful artwork, spectacular buildings, and landscape was not without effort. "Seeking them out" usually meant much walking, climbing, or air/land travel. We often grew weary, but it was worth it!

Seeking out a closer relationship with our Lord is not always effortless either. This can be accomplished through prayer, Bible reading, and fellowship. Though we can become weary through everyday life, we must continue to seek Him out. This is a mandated and attainable goal and there is no greater treasure to be found.

*But from there you will seek the L*ORD *your God, and you will find*
Him if you seek Him with all your heart and with all your soul.
Deuteronomy 4:29

Donna Watson
Liberty Christian Fellowship
Hemet, California

December 5

What Is Your Weight?

Let us lay aside every weight, and the sin which so easily ensnares us,
and let us run with endurance the race that is set before us, looking
unto Jesus, the author and finisher of our faith, who for the joy that
was set before Him endured the cross, despising the shame.
Hebrews 12:1–2

Every day my "weight," or circumstances change. If I don't choose to lay
these "weights" aside, they will become sin and I will be crushed.

No runner can finish the race unless she is focused on the finish line.
It's the same with Christians. Our focus must be on Jesus; anything else is
a "weight" that will keep us from the goal.

Think of what Jesus went through. He was able to endure the cross
because of the joy set before Him. What was that joy? Jesus knew there
was no other way for us to have fellowship with God apart from the cross.
His joy is to spend time with His children!

I challenge you today to lay aside your "weight" for the joy of being
able to spend time with Jesus. Seek Him while He may be found!

Seek the LORD while He may be found, call upon Him while He is
near.
Isaiah 55:6

Sally Van Wick
Calvary Chapel Bible Fellowship
Temecula, California

December 6

Treasure Chest

I rejoice at Your Word as one who finds great treasure.
Psalm 119:162

I love antiques! I enjoy going into antique stores, especially the stores that are so cluttered with paraphernalia that I have to dig through it all to find something I can truly treasure. It is thrilling to uncover something of great value that was hidden among the junk!

While I was at the Calvary Chapel Pastors' Wives retreat in Murrieta, California, I went into many antique stores. I was on a search to find a Chintz teapot, and I wasn't going to be satisfied until I found one. After searching through umpteen stores, I finally found one, and boy, did I rejoice! In fact, the entire store was aware of my joy.

Have you ever thought of God's Word as a "treasure chest" full of rare finds just waiting to be discovered? God's Word is more precious than any antique you could find. When you go to His Word, take time to allow Him to speak to you. He has treasures to reveal to you for each and every day. What can you do when you find a treasure? Turn that gem into a prayer. Praying God's Word is a wonderful way to memorize Scripture and to pray according to His will. So what are you waiting for? Your heavenly Father has treasures galore in His Word waiting for you to discover!

Karen Stangel
North Shore Christian Fellowship
Haleiwa, Hawaii

December 7

Wait for the Lord

Wait for the LORD and keep his way. He will exalt you to inherit the
land; when the wicked are cut off, you will see it.
Psalm 37:34 NIV

Wait for the Lord and keep to His pathway. That is not always an easy
thing to do.

How many times have we gotten into our cars to go on a long trip and
in fifteen minutes our little ones ask if we are almost there? We can be just
like that in our walks with God—impatient to reach the destination or
the outcome of a situation in our lives.

Webster's Dictionary defines *destination* as "an act of appointing or pre-
determining; a place which is set for the end of a journey." What is in your
life today that you are struggling with because you have predetermined
the outcome and things are not turning out that way? Perhaps it is a struggling relationship, financial problems, health problems, a rebellious child,
a struggling marriage, or the illness or death of a loved one. It is easy for
us to doubt when things don't work out the way we thought they should,
when God requires us to wait and trust.

Are you feeling impatient? The Lord promises that if you will wait
for Him, and keep to His way, you will inherit the land. You will find
victory!

Lynda Kelly
Calvary Chapel Bullhead City
Bullhead City, Arizona

December 8

He Owns It All

⤳

For every beast of the forest is Mine, the cattle on a thousand hills.
Psalm 50:10 NASB

When I started walking with the Lord, I worked as a plainclothes security officer for a large department store. My hunger for the Bible was insatiable. I would read before leaving for work and again when I got home—and the hours in between stretched endlessly. I read whenever I took a break. Sometimes, sitting in my office in the back of the store, I'd get so caught up in a passage that my fifteen-minute break would stretch to half-an-hour.

A small feeling of guilt would gnaw at me, but I always reasoned it away. Didn't I frequently come in early? Didn't I sometimes work through lunch? I didn't feel truly convicted until one day when I came upon Colossians 3:23, "Whatever you do, do your work heartily, as for the Lord rather than for men" (NASB).

I saw in an instant that I'd been hurting the Lord by cheating my employer. I realized that regardless of the name on the front door, God was the true owner of that store. Knowing that my ultimate "boss" was Jesus gave me the motivation I needed to work faithfully from that day on.

No matter what work you're doing, it's much easier to work joyfully when you adore the One you work for.

Shannon Woodward
Calvary Chapel Marysville
Marysville, Washington

December 9

Snow Seen

"Come now, and let us reason together," says the LORD, "Though your
sins are like scarlet, they shall be as white as snow."
Isaiah 1:18

It always brings tremendous insight from the Lord when we research the illustrations God uses in His Word. The image of deep scarlet representing sin transformed into picturesque white snow is an illustration with rich applications.

Snow is a rare phenomenon. It only occurs in a very small percentage of the world's regions. Although snowflakes each conform to a consistent six-spoked pattern, they are unique—no two are exactly alike. When exposed to sunlight, snow has a remarkable, reflective property. Snow's greatest power is released as seasonal changes melt it, producing raging rivers flowing to reservoirs with power plants that serve to light otherwise darkened communities.

Those who accept the Lord's cleansing are rare in today's world of scarlet sinfulness. Although Christ gave His life for all, few have acknowledged Him personally. Each individual's account of redemption is unique though the Redeemer's work was accomplished with the same formula. Our goal, as redeemed women, should be to consistently reflect the Light of the Lord. The Spirit's power is released within the believer when trials melt us and mold us into the image of Christ. May we be the snow seen reflecting the Redeemer's radiance to our dark world!

Isel Vázquez
Calvary Chapel Miami
Miami, Florida

December 10

Nothing Wavering

But let him ask in faith, nothing wavering. For he that wavereth is
like a wave of the sea driven with the wind and tossed.
James 1:6 KJV

God is pleased when we ask, believing that He hears us and will answer
us. He's waiting for us to speak out our needs and concerns to Him. Help
is right here with us; we need only to call out. But we need to exercise
unwavering faith in Him and unwavering trust in His ways of answering
our prayers.

James 1:5–8 says that a double-minded man [or woman] is unstable
in all his ways and will receive nothing of the Lord. God's answer can be
right in front of our noses, and we won't receive it. Wavering faith hinders discernment. We don't see God working, or we don't understand His
answers.

We need to make it a personal pursuit to really know the character of
God through His Word and spend time in intimate communication with
Him. Then we will more likely risk trusting Him unconditionally—even
when He doesn't seem to be getting things done in the way or the time
frame that makes sense to us. We need to pray, expecting God to respond.
Let God be God—if His plan doesn't match ours, He's right and we're
wrong.

And if we know that he hear us, whatsoever we ask, we know that we
have the petitions that we desired of Him.
1 John 5:15 KJV

Jeanie Matranga
Calvary Chapel Downey
Downey, California

December 11

The Silence of God

❧

Go to the great city of Nineveh . . .
Jonah 1:2 NIV

I picture Jonah standing on the beach, seaweed strewn in his hair, spitting sand out of his mouth after the "fish belly" ordeal. He hasn't heard a word from God since the last dreadful command he ran from. Now, he stands on shaky legs bleached from fish digestive juices.

"Whew, I'm glad *that's* over," he muses as he plucks plankton from between his teeth. "Now, which way is home?" He's scanning the horizon when God's voice resounds within him once again. "Go to the great city of Nineveh . . ." (Jonah 3:2 NIV).

Is it disbelief? Shock? Jonah is astounded. Is God still requiring the same thing of him? Hasn't he shown himself too weak for the task? Too un-spiritual? "Awwww, God . . ." Jonah kicks a seashell across the beach. But the silence of God is now louder than God's words.

In our Christian lives we will often reach plateaus where God asks us to take a new step of faith. Maybe it's giving up something we cling to: our reputation or free time. There is a strange silence from the heavens until we let go of the object and entrust ourselves to God. Otherwise, we wander.

Jonah could have ignored the call and wandered about. Maybe even found another fish belly! Thankfully for Nineveh, Jonah understood he could only go on with God when he heeded the call.

Joni Woolley
Calvary Chapel Alpha
Alpha, Michigan

December 12

A Flickering Candle

You, O Lord, keep my lamp burning.
Psalm 18:28 NIV

One of the great statements about the character of Christ was written by the prophet Isaiah. Isaiah 42:3 states, "A bruised reed He will not break, and smoking flax He will not quench." During the time of Isaiah, reeds were commonly used by shepherds to play music. They would make small holes in the reed and play it like a flute. When it got old, it would begin to bend so they would simply snap it and throw it away. Flax was another very common commodity. Typically a piece of flax in an oil lamp was lit to illuminate a room. When the flax burned to its end, instead of lighting the room, it would just smolder and make smoke. So again, the flax would be thrown away and replaced with a new piece.

The prophet says of Christ, "He will not break the bruised reed and He will not extinguish the smoking flax." In other words, when a person is bruised because of sin, when their candle is low, making only smoke instead of light, Jesus Christ doesn't throw them away!

Maybe today you feel like that bruised reed or that smoldering flax. Perhaps there are things in your life you regret, circumstances you would have handled differently if given the opportunity. Then, beloved, the Lord has something to say to you: You are not going to be thrown away! He still wants to use you and restore you. All you need to do is recognize your need, turn to Him, and with a heart ready to obey, accept His love and care for you. You can start a new day with the assurance that He has a great plan that only you can fulfill!

Kym Hindt
Calvary Chapel Houston
Friendswood, Texas

December 13

Holiday Perfection

❧

Whatever He says to you, do it.
John 2:5

Why is it that as soon as I flip the calendar page to December, I start acting strangely? My pace quickens and I easily become tense. I experience all these things in spite of prayer, reading my Bible, and being in fellowship. Just as the rich young ruler would ask Jesus, I, too, ask, "All these things I have kept. . . . What do I still lack?" (Matthew 19:20).

As God speaks to me through the Scriptures, I realize that, once again, I'm in the world's trap. The Lord is not directing my life. I'm not sensing His peace; instead, all I feel is pressure! So much expectation is put on women during this time of year. Baking holiday cookies, giving handmade gifts, and beginning *new* family traditions, yet *still* keeping all the old ones. It's so easy to lose our perspective of what's really important.

When folks began stressing at the wedding in Cana because the wine ran out, what was Mary's advice to them regarding Her Son? "Whatever He says . . ." This holiday season, with all the little extras calling out to us, let's ask ourselves if Jesus is directing us. May the Holy Spirit guide us in our celebration of Christmas. With God, all things are possible! Let's choose to do as He says and we'll see God transform a time often characterized by stress into a wonderful blessing.

Susie Tuttle
Calvary Chapel Savannah
Savannah, Georgia

Had the Winter Not Come

Consider it all joy my brethren, when you encounter various trials.
James 1:2

I grew up in one of the mildest climates on the face of the earth, the San Francisco Bay area. The Lord called us to the St. Louis area thirteen years ago and our first Midwest winter was quite a shock! We had a storm that brought a minus-sixty degree wind chill factor and deposited a thick layer of ice across the landscape. The locals told us it was the most severe winter in years; we haven't had one like it since. After three days, we could finally get out of our country home. The beauty was breathtaking! It was like we had been magically transported into a crystal kingdom. Every blade of grass, every tree, everything as far as the eye could see was covered in sparkling ice, which glimmered in the sun with beauty I had never imagined. Immediately the Lord spoke to my heart, "Had the winter not come, you would never have known such beauty."

And so it is in our lives, the fruits of a beautiful, godly character will never come without the trials and difficulties. Don't resist the hand of our loving Lord who seeks to refine you and mold you after His image. If you look to Him, in trusting surrender, He will bring forth beauty you never imagined possible.

Cherisse Denham
Calvary Chapel Troy
Troy, Missouri

December 15

Hidden Treasure

*. . . that they may know the mystery of God, namely, Christ, in whom
are hidden all the treasures of wisdom and knowledge.*
Colossians 2:2–3 NIV

I love to read a good mystery! And a novel that includes finding a hidden
treasure is always intriguing. Even when I'm tired, I find myself tempted
to stay up and continue reading until the villain is captured, the mystery
is solved, and the treasure has been returned to its rightful owner.

In Colossians 2 the apostle Paul describes another type of valuable
treasure, and he assures the believers in Colosse that they can understand
the greatest mystery of all time: the mystery of God, which is in Christ.
We can know Him by reading the story of His life, meditating on and
memorizing His Word, and experiencing the life-changing power of His
Spirit in our hearts and minds.

All the treasures of wisdom and knowledge are hidden in Christ.
When we know Him and grow in our relationship with Him, we tap into
the greatest source of wisdom and knowledge available anywhere. Now
that's a treasure to get excited about!

*[Turn] your ear to wisdom . . . look for it as for silver and search for it
as for hidden treasure, then you will understand the fear of the LORD
and find the knowledge of God.*
Proverbs 2:2, 4–5 NIV

Carrie Turansky
Calvary Chapel Mercer County
Mercer County, New Jersey

December 16

Why That Face, Mommy?

❦

"For if you forgive men when they sin against you, your heavenly
Father will also forgive you."
Matthew 6:14 NIV

One day my daughter said something that really saddened my heart. She said she was sorry. I told her that, yes, I would forgive her. Later she came and saw my face hadn't changed much. Even though I had forgiven her, my heart was still sad. She said, "Mommy, why that face? Are you still mad at me?" I told her, "No sweetie, I'm not mad, I'm still just sad." "It isn't fair," she said, "Jesus has forgiven me, why can't you?" Oh, the words that can pierce our hearts.

Have you not forgiven someone for something they have said or done to you? Are you harboring feelings of bitterness or resentment against them? In Colossians 3:13 Paul says, "even as Christ forgave you, so you also must do."

May the Lord give us the capacity to forgive others and truly show His compassion and mercy towards them, and may those characteristics be seen even on our faces. "The LORD make His face shine upon you . . ." (Numbers 6:25).

Hallie Martinez
Calvary Chapel Golden Springs
Diamond Bar, California

December 17

Clean and Cozy[23]

For whenever you eat the bread and drink this cup, you proclaim the
Lord's death until he comes.
1 Corinthians 11:26 NIV

I will never forget the day I brought my five-year-old grandson home after
a hot and dusty day at school. As he walked in the door, he began to take
off his shirt and head for the bathroom. "Where are you going?" I asked.
"To take a bath, Mimi; you always give me a bath and then you feed me."
He was right! Every time my grandson came for a visit, I would clean
him up, give him fresh clean clothes, and a plate of food. One cold night
he sat on the couch wrapped in a warm blanket drinking hot chocolate.
He looked at me and said, "You always make me feel so clean and cozy!"
What a way to be remembered!

Our Lord Jesus asked us to remember Him in the cup and the bread
of the Lord's Supper. "Do this in remembrance of me," He explained. I
love to take Communion! I love to remember how His shed blood cleanses
me from my sins. I love to remember how His body was broken for me.
I always feel so clean and full after Communion. I am going to live forever with Jesus. I don't have to worry about the future. He meets all my
needs.

I am clean and cozy.

Karyn Johnson
Calvary Chapel Downey
Downey, California

Imitators of Jesus

But the fruit of the Spirit is love, joy, peace, longsuffering, kindness, goodness, faithfulness, gentleness, self-control. Against such there is no law.
Galatians 5:22–23

We live in a society of imitators. Many times, we find ourselves imitating movie stars, singing stars, clothing gurus, political figures, and other personalities of popular society. However, after a careful study of those whom we aspire to be like, as well as much of our time, money, and hard work, we still end up not knowing who we really are. The people we imitate quickly pass from fame to obscurity, from being stylish to being outmoded, from being popular to being forgotten and unknown. Imitating the world is unfulfilling and fruitless. We must be imitators of Christ.

If we do not become imitators of Christ, our Christian character becomes compromised, we end up frustrated and angry, and our lives show no evidence of self-control. As Christians, we must set our "affections on things above, not on things on the earth" (Colossians 3:2 KJV). By setting our affections on Christ, He will show us who we really are, producing Christ-like qualities, and a godly character full of the fruit of the Spirit. Let's make this worship song our theme:

To be like Jesus
To be—to be like Him.
All through life's journey
From earth to glory,
All I ask—to be like Him.[24]

Shirley Craver
Calvary Chapel Golden Springs
Diamond Bar, California

God's "To Do" List

Search me, O God, and know my heart; test me and know my anxious
thoughts. See if there is any offensive way in me, and lead me in the
way everlasting.
Psalm 139:23–24 NIV

I awoke beneath an avalanche of anxious thoughts. So I closed my eyes,
hoping the Lord would take them away. Then He opened my heart to
see that He had searched me and knew every anxious thought that would
threaten, torment, or distract me that day. And He had deliberately allowed them to come all at once, not so I would fear, become overwhelmed,
or depressed, and not so I would run from them. No, He allowed them so
that I would write them all down, one by one, and give them to Him as
His "To Do" list. He wanted to take care of each and every one of them
for me!

You know my heart, O Lord. You search me, O God, even while I
sleep! You have revealed my anxious thoughts to me so I will surrender
and commit them to You, that I might represent You with freedom and
joy for Your honor and glory! Show me any selfish, offensive, or sinful
ways that have taken hold of me because of my anxieties, fears, and unbelief. Forgive me. Put me back on the path of right thinking, which is Your
eternal perspective!

Denise Nelson
Morning Star Community Church
Salem, Oregon

December 20

Intimate Christmas

Thanks be to God for His indescribable gift!
2 Corinthians 9:15

The Christmas season is upon us. Don't you love opening gifts? Can you imagine receiving a huge, beautifully wrapped gift from someone and then just letting it sit there and not opening it? I don't think you would do that because you want to see what's inside!

Do you find it challenging to remain intimate with your Lord at this time of year? This verse has a key to help us—it's the word *indescribable*. Have you ever tried to describe God's indescribable gift? Why not put into words how thankful you are for the gift of His Son. Take each letter from A–Z and find a word beginning with that letter that best describes what His wonderful gift means to you. For example, **A**wesome, **B**eautiful, **C**ounselor, **D**elightful, and so forth. You can then use this list during your prayer time as a way of spurring on more thanksgiving and intimacy with God. Soon you'll be echoing Paul the apostle, saying, "Thanks be to God for His indescribable gift!"

Happy unwrapping, and may God bless you with the gift of His presence this Christmas season.

Karen Stangel
North Shore Christian Fellowship
Haleiwa, Hawaii

December 21

Receiving with Gladness

A woman came to Him having an alabaster flask of very costly
fragrant oil, and she poured it on His head as He sat at the table.
Matthew 26:7

I love making my favorite recipes and preparing a fine feast—everything homemade, even the bread. It's a blessing, pampering folks in this way. When I invite them for a meal, I get responses like, "Oh, I'd love to!" or, "That sounds wonderful!" I remember times when I've responded to similar invitations with, "You don't have to do all that; that's not necessary."

God convicted me about my ungracious attitude, reminding me of Jesus' reaction to His disciple's complaint about the "wastefulness" of pouring fragrant, costly oil upon His head. He told everyone what a good work she had done for Him—a gift given in love, and graciously received.

When you're complimented, given a gift, or invited somewhere, accept joyfully. Think how you would feel if those you offered love gifts to responded with, "Oh, don't go to so much trouble . . ." Wouldn't you feel robbed of the joy of blessing them?

Jesus said it is more blessed to give than to receive (Acts 20:35). Remember that when someone else has the opportunity to give. A friend once said, "If you have difficulty receiving, try picturing every gift as if it were a fragrant rose." At the end of our days we can offer back to the Lord a beautiful bouquet of the blessings He led others to bless us with.

Lori Jahn
Calvary Chapel Lakeland
Lakeland, Florida

December 22

God's Work

❧

Create in me a clean heart, O God . . .
Psalm 51:10

If we look at David's prayer carefully, we glean two applications for our lives. First, it is a prayer of repentance. David acknowledged that his heart was not clean, and that troubled him. Sin in our hearts should trouble us as well and make us quick to pray the prayer of repentance.

Once there is repentance, we can make the second application. David asks God to "create" in him a clean heart. The word "create" is the same as Genesis 1:1 when God created the heavens and the earth out of nothing. It speaks of God's work, not ours. The way we live each day is determined by the condition of our hearts, so it is vital that our hearts be cleaned on a continual basis. The prayer of confession and need is always accepted because we have a compassionate High Priest, Jesus, who invites us to come with confidence to His throne of grace. There we can receive mercy and help in time of need.

Like David, simply ask the Lord to "create" in you a clean heart, and renew a steadfast spirit within you. Don't depend upon yourself to do this impossible work, but depend on Him who is able.

Renew a steadfast spirit within me.
Psalm 51:10

Traci Renner
Calvary Chapel Oak Harbor
Oak Harbor, Washington

December 23

Adorned in His Righteousness

I am overwhelmed with joy in the LORD my God! For he has dressed
me with the clothing of salvation and draped me in a robe of
righteousness. I am like a bridegroom in his wedding suit or a bride
with her jewels.
Isaiah 61:10 NLT

My twenty-year-old niece, Iris, died from an overdose of heroin. At a vulnerable stage in her life, drugs had made their way into her hands. While Iris was still in a coma, my sister chose to bring her home to breathe her last breath. She wanted to hold and care for her daughter one more time. Iris' mother desired to clean her up and make her a new dress. On day one, her new dress was completed. My sister bathed Iris and washed her long black hair and put her new dress on. Iris died a short time later.

This beautiful act of love from a mother was a clear picture to me of what Christ has done for us. When we were dirty with sin, He came to us to offer salvation. He took us as we were, cleansed us with His blood, and clothed us with His robe of righteousness.

How our hearts burst with joy because of such love! Won't you take a few minutes today to meditate on all that Christ has done for you, that you may share this joy with another?

Janice Orate
Calvary Chapel Rancho Cucamonga
Rancho Cucamonga, California

December 24

Does Anybody Need a Savior?

I know that nothing good lives in me, that is, in my sinful nature. For
I have the desire to do what is good, but I cannot carry it out.
Romans 7:18 NIV

Some people say that we are all victims of the circumstances of our lives
and that we can't help ourselves or change ourselves. Others say that each
person is responsible for his or her own sin and will be held accountable
for what he or she has done.

Well, the biblical view sounds even worse. The Bible says that we are
victims of a sinful world and we are powerless to change ourselves, and *we*
will be held responsible and judged for our sin.

Does anybody need a Savior?

For unto you is born this day in the city of David a *Saviour*, which
is *Christ the Lord*.
Luke 2:11 KJV, emphasis added

I sure do need a Savior! My prayer is that you will be filled with that
same awareness of the desperate need you have for our Lord and Savior
Jesus Christ! Thanks be to God for His indescribable gift!

Peggy Kravig
Calvary Chapel Downey
Downey, California

December 25

His Christmas Presence

In Your presence is fullness of joy; at Your right hand are pleasures
forevermore.
Psalm 16:11

Divorce shattered my family when I was eight. The first Christmas without my father watching us open brightly wrapped packages seemed empty. Our stockings were hung on the mantle with care. But, on the night before Christmas, the only creature I longed to hear stirring was Dad, not a mouse.

The next day we went to my uncle's for a Christmas feast, dressed in our Sunday best. Dinner was interrupted by a knock on the door and in walked the skinniest Santa I'd ever seen. He beckoned, "Sit on my lap and tell me what you want." I thought, "What I really want is my father's presence, not a shiny present." Just then Santa's eyes twinkled as he pulled off his white beard. Underneath the disguise I discovered the loving face of my dad!

It's been over thirty years since that holiday surprise. Over time, Dad has given me lots of great gifts from purses to pearls. But my father's Christmas presence was the best gift ever. Our heavenly Father did something similar. Realizing how lonely we were, He wrapped up His only Son in flesh and bones and sent Him to the earth, filling our lives with His Christmas presence. God wasn't satisfied with giving us things that don't fit or that need to be exchanged. He gave us the greatest gift possible—Himself!

Lenya Heitzig
Ocean Hills Community Church
San Juan Capistrano, California

December 26

Seasons of Blessings

I will make them and the places all around My hill a blessing; and
I will cause showers to come down in their season; there shall be
showers of blessing.
Ezekiel 34:26

Have you ever felt like God has forgotten you, His presence and blessings
seeming so far away? You think back for a moment and recall that you've
been faithful, you've prayed, you've wept, and you've been in church whenever the doors were open—and yet those around you are experiencing the
very things your heart has been longing for while you're not.

In times like those, continue to hold on and rejoice! Keep being faithful to our Lord and Savior. Your season of blessing is on its way! Continue
to seek Him with all your heart. Take your focus off what you see happening in others, which can produce envy, covetousness, and strife. Fix your
eyes on Jesus and wait for your seasons of His blessings to come.

Psalm 27:13–14 says:

I would have lost heart, unless I had believed that I would see the
goodness of the LORD in the land of the living. Wait on the LORD; be
of good courage, and He shall strengthen your heart; wait, I say, on
the LORD!

Norma Pittman
Calvary Worship Center
Colorado Springs, Colorado

December 27

God Does Strengthen Us!

I can do all things through Him who strengthens me.
Philippians 4:13 NASB

This verse has taken on new meaning in my life as well as my family's life.

My husband was in a crash landing in a Cessna 172 while flying with a friend. They both survived; my husband with broken bones and a severe hand injury that affected the nerves in his hand. A week later, our four-year-old granddaughter was put in our custody because my stepdaughter was unable to care for her. The next week my mother found out she had cancer. Soon the only son I gave birth to will be married.

Now most of this seems like bad news. These events could break the faith of some. Thanks to God's faithfulness, the faithful prayers of our church, and our strong love for the Lord, we are able to rely on His strength. The Lord has helped us see good in all these circumstances.

Philippians 4:11 tells us to be content in whatever circumstances we are in. My husband is glad to be alive and is being healed daily. The Lord has shown us clearly that with His strength we are able to raise our granddaughter in the admonition of the Lord. My mom is a believer, and handling her cancer with grace. My son has chosen a beautiful young lady who loves the Lord. God has strengthened us all.

Marleen Smith
Calvary Chapel McMinnville
McMinnville, Oregon

December 28

Courage

The trees of the LORD are full of sap.
Psalm 104:16

Blessed is the man who trusts in the LORD, and whose hope is the LORD. For he shall be like a tree planted by the waters, which spreads out its roots by the river, and will not fear when heat comes; but its leaf will be green, and will not be anxious in the year of drought, nor will cease from yielding fruit.
Jeremiah 17:7–8

As I mulled this passage over in my mind, my thoughts wandered to all the disappointments in ministry here in Utah, and it occurred to me how much like the disciples I am. Jesus said, "Let us cross over to the other side" (Mark 4:35). They all got into the boat and then a raging storm came. They thought they were going to die, like I have thought so many times since we moved here. Jesus rebuked the storm but said, "Why are ye fearful, O ye of little faith?" (Matthew 8:26 KJV). What did Jesus mean by that? Did He simply want them to endure the storm and know they would make it? Definitely it was an experience for them to learn from and remember.

So when the Lord says to me, "O ye of little faith," He is saying, "Everything I have promised I will bring to pass; but don't let the storm—discouragements, disappointments, impossible finances, or other circumstances—keep you from believing what I have said." He doesn't guarantee a problem-free ride on the way there. I am to totally depend on Him to accomplish His purpose. So maybe in that storm the disciples should have just joined Jesus in the hull for a nap! I wonder if He would have laughed with delight.

Lord, help me today to choose faith in You over my circumstances.

Karen Ellis
Calvary Chapel Park City
Park City, Utah

December 29

Me . . . an Atheist?

"Therefore I say to you, do not worry . . ."
Matthew 6:25

All worry is atheism, because it is a want of trust in God.
Fulton J. Sheen[25]

I came across this quote in my devotional time several months ago and it has forever changed the way I view the sin of worry.

I do believe we, as women, can be prone to worry. This is probably because we are such caregivers and so relationship oriented. Although I must confess there have been times in my life when certain situations, which were initially motivated by genuine concern, advanced to worry in my mind.

Worry is birthed when we take upon ourselves responsibility God never intended for us to have. The Lord tells us not to worry and gives us countless reasons for not being anxious. He is so very personal with each of us and continually proves His faithfulness towards us, reminding us that He is in control.

Our heavenly Father even instructs us what to do if we feel anxiousness pressing against our hearts, pushing us towards worry.

Be anxious for nothing, but in everything by prayer and supplication, with thanksgiving, let your requests be made known to God, and the peace of God, which surpasses all understanding, will guard your hearts and minds through Christ Jesus.
Philippians 4:6–7

Hide in your heart verses for today:

♥ Psalm 42:5 ♥ Psalm 55:22 ♥ Isaiah 41:13 ♥ Matthew 11:28 ♥ 1 Peter 5:7

Carla Lawson
Calvary Chapel of the Sandhills
Aberdeen, North Carolina

December 30

Passing Through

Blessed are those . . . who have set their hearts upon pilgrimage.
Psalm 84:5 NIV

It had been years since I prayed with reckless abandon, "Lord, wherever You lead me, I will go. I'll follow You anywhere." When God finally called me to leave all that I call home—my church, my family, and my friends—I began to rescind my offer. I began to grope at every possible excuse why I should stay put. I was planted, settled, and comfortable in my familiar world.

Jesus said, "Foxes have holes and birds of the air have nests, but the Son of Man has no place to lay his head" (Luke 9:58 NIV). Certainly Jesus had family and friends to offer this hospitality. So why would He say such a thing? He knew He was here on business and He knew He would not be here long. Jesus kept this eternal perspective in all He said and did.

God does not desire us to be "planted" in the wilderness of this world, but rather with each step of obedience, to be led closer to the Promised Land. He may or may not be calling you to pack up and head out. He is however calling each of us who has put our lives in His care to set our hearts upon pilgrimage and hold lightly to the things of this world. We are of a heavenly dwelling, just passing through.

Lynnette Ridgeley
Calvary Chapel Orange County
Goshen, New York

December 31

Our One Passion

꧁꧂

That I may know him . . .
Philippians 3:10 KJV

Paul had one passion and that was to know Jesus. All of his life revolved around this one objective. He didn't want to know *about* Jesus, he wanted to know Him personally. He wanted Jesus to be his closest friend. One of the ways he came to know Jesus better was during his times of thorough suffering. He could have resented that Jesus allowed him to suffer, but instead he accepted it. He accepted it because he understood God's great love for him. He knew that if it weren't necessary, then his loving heavenly Father just wouldn't allow it. But since the Lord had allowed it, then it must be for a greater purpose. And it was. Not only did the suffering refine Paul's character, but it allowed him to know His Jesus in a far deeper way.

What is your passion in life? Do you have a burning desire to know Jesus? Spend time reading God's Word. Read until He speaks to your heart. Write down what He says in your journal so you won't forget what He's teaching you. Then take time to pray. Pray about what you just wrote down. Don't forget to sit quietly and still your heart and listen for God to speak. Whatever He says to you, trust Him. He means what He says and He is able to perform all that He promises.

Gail Mays
Calvary Chapel South Bay
Gardena, California

Notes

[1] Adapted from "Jesus People Reunion" program, April 24, 1999.

[2] Maciel, Johnson. *Women's Thirty-One-Day Devotional.* Downey, CA: Calvary Chapel of Downey, 1999, p. i.

[3] Herbert, George. "Teach Me, My God and King." The Cyber Hymnal. http://www. cyberhymnal.org/htm/g/i/gisthyf.htm, 1633. (Accessed October 25, 2004.)

[4] Source unknown.

[5] Source unknown.

[6] Source unknown.

[7] Source unknown.

[8] Adapted from *The Renewed Mind* by Larry Christenson. Minneapolis, MN: Bethany House Publishers, 1974, pgs. 104–105.

[9] Maciel, Johnson. *Women's Thirty-One-Day Devotional,* p. 3.

[10] Maciel, Johnson. *Women's Thirty-One-Day Devotional,* p. 5.

[11] Graham, Billy. "Christianity 101 Sermon Series." August 1, 1999. University Baptist Church. www.ubcbakersfield.org/sermons/ubc.101.8.1.99.htm. (Accessed October 13, 2004.)

[12] Who Shall Deliver Me? by Christina Georgina Rossetti (1830–1894).

[13] Havergal, Frances. "Take My Life and Let It Be." The Cyber Hymnal. http://www. cyberhymnal.org/htm/g/i/gisthyf.htm, 1874. (Accessed October 25, 2004.)

[14] Maciel, Johnson. *Women's Thirty-One-Day Devotional,* p. 17.

[15] This quote was obtained personally from Mr. Willis, who lived with Vi and her husband during the last ten years of his life. Mr. Willis was saved in 1905, year two of the Welsh Revival.

[16] Chisholm, Thomas O. "Great is Thy Faithfulness." The Cyber Hymnal. http://www. cyberhymnal.org/htm/g/i/gisthyf.htm, 1923. (Accessed October 20, 2004.)

[17] Ibid.

[18] Murray, Andrew. *The Secret of Fellowship.* Fort Washington, PA: CLC Publications, 2003, p. 15.

[19] Maciel, Johnson. *Women's Thirty-One-Day Devotional,* p. 29.

[20] Maciel, Johnson. *Women's Thirty-One-Day Devotional*, p. 41.

[21] Robinson, Robert. "Come, Thou Fount of Every Blessing." The Cyber Hymnal. http://www.cyberhymnal.org/htm/g/i/gisthyf.htm, 1758. (Accessed October 20, 2004.)

[22] Warner, Anna B. "Jesus Loves Me." The Cyber Hymnal. http://www.cyberhymnal.org/htm/g/i/gisthyf.htm, 1860. (Accessed October 20, 2004.)

[23] Maciel, Johnson. *Women's Thirty-One-Day Devotional*, p. 61.

[24] Source unknown.

[25] "Discovering Our Real Needs." In Touch Ministries. Posted June 4, 2001. http://www.intouch.org/intouch/site.show_page?p_id=76096&p_devotional_date=06%2F04%2F2001. (Accessed October 26, 2004.)